MW00781866

TO ABYSSINIA
THROUGH AN UNKNOWN LAND

TO

MY MOTHER

TO WHOSE HELP AND ENCOURAGEMENT

I OWE MUCH

PREFACE

BETWEEN the highlands of British East Africa and the mountainous region of Southern Abyssinia is a broad tract of desolate and unexplored country. Great natural obstacles have to be surmounted in crossing this belt. It is waterless, and affords no food for man, and sometimes no grazing for animals.

A great part of the country is a mass of volcanic débris, utterly uninhabited, and no guides are obtainable.

It required a certain amount of persuasion and encouragement to hearten up my men to the enterprise of crossing this unknown land, especially at that period when we were without guides.

At times they were mutinous, fearing that they would die of thirst, and we were perhaps only saved from that fate by the happy discovery of a water-hole. At other times they straggled, and appeared too worn out to care what happened, or to make any effort to reach the next water-hole. Nevertheless a great measure of praise is due to my men for the manner in which they accomplished the journey.

On an occasion of this sort it is easy enough to lead,

but a very much harder matter to follow blindly and obediently, and so they deserve the highest tribute.

With the exception of the two headmen and my boy, they were all highlanders—men absolutely unsuited to the conditions of life in the low country. Dependent in their villages almost entirely on grain, and used to the cool air of the East African Highlands, and no lack of running streams, they suffered terribly from the heat and thirst of the lava desert and the reduced rations of cereal food. After passing through this waterless strip, and reaching the southern borders of Abyssinia, one comes to a country profuse in little tribes, all differing from one another to a greater or lesser degree in customs and language.

Putting aside those tribes a little off my route, of whom I met only one or two individuals, there were over twenty different tribes through whose country my journey took me. The study of these peoples and their varied characteristics was to me a most interesting part of the journey. Many of these are but uncivilized barbarians, but others, such as the Wallamu, undoubtedly show traces of having sprung from an old civilization, perhaps emanating from ancient Egypt.

Another interesting feature was to see the way in which the Abyssinians administrate their southern borders and the numerous subject-tribes therein. Although their methods leave much to be desired, they undoubtedly manage to rule their territories with an organization and a rough justice which, all things considered, are surprising.

All my photographs have been developed and printed
by my aunt, Mrs. Edgar Clark. My most grateful thanks
are due to her for the great skill and patience with which
she has produced the results here shown.

My thanks are also due to Major C. W. Gwynn, C.M.G.,
D.S.O., R.E., for placing at my disposal materials from
which the sketch of the route from the Omo River to
Addis Ababa is compiled.

My route sketches and observations which appear in
the map of the Rudolf district were based on points fixed
by Captain P. Maud, C.M.G., R.E.

I must not omit to mention Abdi Hassan, my headman, to whose faithful services the successful issue of
the trip was mainly attributable.

C. H. STIGAND.

LONDON,
January, 1910.

CONTENTS

LIST OF ILLUSTRATIONS

LIST OF ILLUSTRATIONS

xiii

*

A BRIEF SUMMARY OF THE CHIEF FORMER EXPLORATIONS OF THE RUDOLF DISTRICT

1. The discovery of Lakes Rudolf and Stefanie by Count Teleki in 1888.

This expedition, as described by his companion, Lieutenant von Höhnel, passed up through East Africa, via Lake Baringo, then almost unknown, and from there struck northwards to the south end of Lake Rudolf. They followed up the east shore till they arrived at the north end of the lake, and crossed from there to Stefanie.

They returned by the same route to the south end of Rudolf, whence they made a détour westwards into the Turkana country, and thence back to Baringo.

2. The Italian, Captain Bottego, in 1895-1897 started up the Juba River, and then cut across the Borana country westwards, and discovered Lake Margherita. From this lake he proceeded westwards, crossed the Omo River, visited the north-west end of Rudolf, and then went through the Kaffa country. From there he crossed to Addis Ababa, and on his way from that place to the coast met with his death.

3. Dr. Donaldson Smith came down through the Somali country, crossed the Borana, and arrived at the Omo River. On his return he passed what he refers to as Mount Koroli, 1897.

4. About the same time the late A. H. Neumann, starting from British East Africa, made a hunting trip up the east shore of Lake Rudolf to the Reshiat, and then a few days up the Omo River. He was there badly mauled by an elephant, and after a long illness became well enough to return by the same route.

He has given a description of this trip in his book, "Elephan Hunting in East Equatorial Africa," but he did not take any observations or make any maps.

5. In 1898 Captain Welby made a trip from Addis Ababa, passing down the chain of Lakes Zwai, Margherita, Stefanie, and thence to the north of Lake Rudolf. He travelled down the east shore to the south end, and thence struck north-west to the Sobat.

6. In 1900-1901 Carlo Freiherr v. Erlanger passed down this same chain of lakes as far as Lake Margherita, and from there he struck across to the Juba River.

7. In 1903 the Butter survey thoroughly explored the proposed southern boundary of Abyssinia, through the Borana country, and thence westwards past Lake Stefanie to Rudolf. They then followed the east shore to the south end of the lake, and from there struck for Lake Baringo.

It will be seen from the above that all the travellers who have visited these parts have followed much the same route, either in whole or part—viz., Baringo, east shore of Rudolf, Stefanie, Margherita, Zwai, Addis Ababa.

It was my ambition to avoid this route as much as possible, and find a new route east of Lake Rudolf, then to strike the Omo River, follow it up a short distance, and thence proceed north-east to Addis Ababa, avoiding the Margherita route.

TO ABYSSINIA
THROUGH AN UNKNOWN LAND

CHAPTER I

PREPARATIONS FOR THE JOURNEY

MANY unknown little patches and corners still exist in the dark continent for the would-be explorer who wishes to break new ground. It has long been one of my favourite recreations to sit with the map of Africa before me and plan out exploring and hunting expeditions traversing such unfrequented spots. There can be few unexplored patches of the continent still remaining which I have not, in imagination at least, traversed and re-traversed.

When I leave my land of dreams to come face to face with stern reality, two ridiculous little matters have ever been present to frustrate my plans. These, whose names are " time " and " money," have served to restrict my wanderings, with a few small exceptions, to the immediate neighbourhood of my duties.

However, I have always been ready to seize the opportunity of taking a more extended journey whenever it occurred. In anticipation of such a chance, it was necessary to select a general route for a trip. The unknown tract north of the administrated portions of British East Africa and Uganda and south of Abyssinia seemed most suited to my purpose. The reasons for which I chose this country were chiefly : that it was near the scene of my official duties, and so time and expense in arriving at the point of departure were obviated ; that it was nearly the only large tract of unknown country in British territory on the eastern side of Africa ; that my knowledge of the country and natives on this side of Africa would permit of preparations being made more expeditiously and with less expense than in a totally strange country ; that an extension of the journey would take me through Abyssinia, a country I had often wished to visit and whose language I had long wished to study.

This trip I had had in view for several years before there was a chance of executing it. At last, in April, 1908, I found myself at Nairobi, British East Africa, with a year's leave before me, but, unfortunately, the money I had been so laboriously saving was not quite sufficient for so long and expensive a journey. Something had to be done to raise the extra funds, or I must forego my chance, perhaps for ever. This being the case, I set out with my brother-officer, Captain R. S. Hart, for an elephant-hunting trip in Uganda and the Congo. This proved a most interesting expedition, and was so successful that towards the end of the same year we found ourselves on the way back to Nairobi with a balance substantial enough to put through the Abyssinian trip on a modest scale. The time, however, now at our disposal was barely sufficient for such a journey.

I sent on word to my friend R. G. Stone in Nairobi, asking him to enrol thirty picked porters and a headman for me, if possible obtaining men who had been with me on former trips. My idea was then to start off immediately on my return, remaining in Nairobi only long enough to make the necessary purchases of trade goods and other requisites for the journey.

Both of us were rather run down, the result of fevers, want of provisions, and other causes in the Congo, and on arrival at Nairobi we had to take to our beds. Unfortunately, Hart, who had intended to accompany me on this second trip, was ordered home by the doctor, and I had to suffer a delay of three weeks before I could start.

Stone had been unable to find any of my old porters in Nairobi, this being a busy season for them, but he had carefully selected a very promising-looking crew of stalwart Wanyamwezi ruffians. I did not, however, take to the headman, a tall, thin Comoro-Swahili with a Hebraic nose, called Omari. A native friend advised me to change him, but as there appeared to be no one else forthcoming, and, moreover, as he had been waiting for me some time, and seemed anxious to please, I retained him.

In Uganda and the Congo we had used local porters, and the only members of my staff who returned with me were my cook and Tengeneza, my gun-bearer. As they both drew the large sum due to them at the end of the journey, I did not expect to see either of them again, although they both promised to accompany me on the next trip. However, Tengeneza spent all his back pay in a few days, and then appeared and asked for an advance. While regretting the recklessness of the African savage, I could not help being pleased to hear of this, as I now knew that he was certain of coming with me. He was a man of a somewhat surly and cantankerous disposition, but he had proved his pluck and nerve on many occasions with dangerous game.

With regard to provisions and stores for the journey, I had had all I wanted sent out from home, with the exception of a few odds and ends such as porters' tents and cooking-pots, axes, etc., which I obtained locally.

However, the most important item for the traveller in uncivilized parts is a comprehensive and useful collection of trade goods, and these had yet to be purchased.

Goods for this purpose must be most carefully chosen to suit the requirements of the countries and tribes to be visited. Some people seem to have an idea that a naked savage ought to be glad to receive anything from a European, but this is not the case. If you do not take him exactly what he wants, you will be unable to purchase food or anything else, although you may have hundreds of pounds' worth of goods.

Teleki mentions how he was unable to purchase a single sheep amongst the Reshiat, although he had bales of the most beautiful Maskat stuffs. If he had had a few yards of coarse *amerikani* (calico), he would have experienced no difficulty.

In one part of the Lado enclave the most valuable goods for barter are empty, plain glass bottles, such as gin or Worcester sauce bottles. Out of these the natives chip lip ornaments. For an empty Worcester sauce bottle one could often get several chickens, whilst many of our trade goods, such as frock-coats, mouth-organs, and looking-glasses, they would not have at all.

While I was still pondering over the subject of trade goods and making out lists, I ran up against a Somali called Ibrahim, whom I had known before in Somaliland. This man had travelled extensively in Africa, and when he heard of my present trip he at once volunteered to get my trade goods for me.

With his help I made out a list of my requirements, and he then effected the purchases for me from Indian traders at two-thirds the price I should have had to pay myself. He had them done up in sixty-pound loads for donkeys, all ready for the start. The *amerikani*, however, I obtained from Mombasa, as there was no saving to be made on this by local purchase.

One of the great advantages of obtaining Ibrahim's advice was that he knew at once the cheapest form of each article required which would serve my purpose. Of some things he chose an inferior kind for use on the first part of the journey, and a superior kind ready to meet the more critical gaze of the Abyssinian when I should arrive in his country.

During my journey I had often cause to congratulate myself on having obtained this expert advice in the selection of my goods, for if it had not been for Ibrahim I should have started without some of the things which proved most useful. I append here a list of the trade goods I took with me :

6 loads coarse thick *amerikani* (calico),
4 ,, *maradufu* (white twill),
3 ,, *sengenge* (iron wire),
1 ,, *kisango* (brass wire),
2 ,, blue Masai beads,
1 ,, white, yellow, and other beads,
2 ,, native tobacco,
3 dozen large clasp-knives,
2 ,, small clasp-knives,
60 yards *doria* (coloured muslins),
Sewing-needles,
Packing-needles,
Small looking-glasses, snuff-boxes, brass chains, and a variety of odds and ends.

In all, I had twenty-two loads of trade goods.

I obtained one hundred brand-new Marie-Thérèse dollars, the coin used in Abyssinia, in case I should want them. More than these would have been heavy to carry, and I did not expect to use them much in Southern Abyssinia. I also took a letter of credit on the Abyssinian Bank at Addis Ababa.

I bought twenty donkeys with which to perform the first part of the journey, and had saddles and saddle-bags sewn for them of sacking, the former being stuffed with straw. I enlisted a few more porters who had been accustomed to work with donkeys, and now a headman for the transport was required.

Ibrahim said that he knew of a Somali who would suit me, and brought along a little man called Abdi Hassan. Abdi had been in the Masai company of the 3rd Battalion King's African Rifles. He could speak Swahili fairly well, and gave me to understand that he had been a Masai, but that when a child he had been captured by a raiding expedition of Somalis and taken to Kismayu, and that there he had become a naturalized Somali.

I was surprised at the time, as I had never heard of any conflict between Somalis and Masai. It afterwards transpired that Abdi was really a Rendile. However, he now considered himself quite a Somali.

I was favourably impressed with Abdi from the first. I do not care for Somalis as a rule, though I must confess to a sneaking admiration for them. Abdi possessed all the good qualities of a Somali, and none of his vices. He was quick and intelligent, a rare hand at driving a bargain ; moreover, he knew the Somali and Galla languages, and had great confidence in himself, and knew how to keep the other men in their place. He was careful and considerate with the animals, and had not the overweening self-conceit or the grasping nature of the ordinary Somali. In fact, Abdi proved of untold value, and the success of the expedition was mainly attributable to him.

Now the caravan was practically ready to start, but I had not as yet a cook or a boy. Sadi, a Malindi boy who had served a brother-officer, had turned up and offered his services, and I had refused him, as I thought that he did not look strong enough for such a journey. Fortunately he insisted on coming in spite of my refusal, and as it turned out, he stood the heat and thirst of the low country as well as anybody, only excepting Abdi, who was, of course, quite at home in a waterless country.

My old cook came almost every day to tell me that he would accompany me, so I guessed that he did not really intend coming at all. This proved to be correct, as a day or two before I started he called off. In the nick of time a Manyema called Bakari, who had been cook's boy on a former trip, turned up. He said that now he was a full-fledged cook, and cooked my dinner the same night to prove it.

I thus had two old followers with me, Tengeneza and Bakari, but all the rest were new to my ways and methods.

The armament of the caravan consisted of ten Martini-Henris and a box of ammunition, besides my own sporting rifles and ammunition. As many of the men had been in the police or King's African Rifles, I had little difficulty in choosing from amongst the porters ten men sufficiently qualified to carry a rifle.

I was not yet quite fit to move, so I decided to send on the porters and donkeys to Gilgil Station by road, and to meet them there by train. This gave me a few more days' rest before starting. So I called all the porters up, and explained to them, as much as was desirable, the scope of the journey in some such words as these :

"We are now all ready to start. The journey before us is long, and in the way we shall meet hunger and thirst, adversities and trials, difficulties and dangers. We shall journey for many days through a bad country without food or water, and finally we shall come to the country of the Wahabashi (Abyssinians). We shall cross that country, and reach the sea. There I will put you in ships, and send you back to Mombasa. Now, this is not an ordinary shooting-trip, but a big journey, so I want only men. Further, I want men hard of heart. A man whose heart turns to water is of no use to me. So if any one of you is afraid in his heart, let him say so now and turn back, for I want only men to accompany me. You have all had your advance of pay. Let him who is afraid take this, and go his way. My loss thus will be but little, whereas if such an one comes with us men it may be great. What say you?" Omari, the headman, replied : "Master, you have spoken true words, words worthy of being followed." Then, turning to the men, he said : "Do you hear what the master says? Speak up, anyone who has fear in his heart."

The porters all disclaimed the possession of any such feeling, so I continued :

"Now I wish to make an agreement with you all. I have told you that we are passing through a country where there is but little food. We will carry with us as much food as we are able, but the difficulties of feeding you will be great ; therefore I want to make an agreement with you. Where there is food, you shall have it. Where there is no food, I shall, if necessary, give you only half a *kibaba* of food a day ; but when I do this I shall also give you meat, so that you may eat, and not feel the pain of hunger in your stomachs. When I am unable to shoot

meat for you, then will I give you your full *kibaba* of
flour or grain. Further, if I find it necessary to do this,
when we reach a country with much food, then will I give
you to eat till you can eat no more. Do you agree?"

This statement was received with cheers of approval
from all the porters. One would have imagined that I
had offered them double pay instead of reduced rations.
Typical happy-go-lucky African natives, they only dwelt
on the possibilities of overeating themselves in the time of
plenty, while the possibility of hunger was forgotten as
soon as mentioned.

Abdi, Sadi, and Bakari remained behind to help me
with the last preparations, while the porters and donkeys
set off for Gilgil. Here were about thirty men whom I
had never clapped eyes on before, starting out alone, with
twenty donkeys and a lot of my effects, to go to a place
six days distant. After they had departed I wondered
how many men and donkeys and loads this haphazard
crew would lose on the way, and how many, if any, of
them would turn up at Gilgil at the appointed time.

However, it does not do for the African traveller to
worry over anything that might happen; what actually
does happen is as a rule trying and difficult enough to
deal with.

A few days later I bade good-bye to my friends in
Nairobi, and got on the Kisumu train. I had with me
Abdi, Sadi, Bakari, a mule, a Masai sais called Juma,
and Narok, a retriever bitch.

The mule was always known as "*the* mule" (*nyumbu*)
till we reached Abyssinia. When we had other mules
in our caravan a new name had to be found for it. The
men then always called it "our mule" (*nyumbu yetu*),
but the sais and I called it "Nairobi." We took up with

us also the donkey-saddles, some of the trade goods, and a few other things. The calico and *maradufu* was to meet us at Gilgil, whither it had been despatched by train from Mombasa.

The journey from Nairobi to Gilgil is perhaps the most picturesque on the whole length of the Uganda Railway. The line slowly winds up through cultivated Kikuyu-land, and then through the forests which crown the escarpment. Suddenly a most magnificent view of the Rift Valley is seen over a sheer descent of several thousand feet. Lakes and extinct craters dot the floor of the valley, while at the opposite side is the forested wall of the Mau escarpment.

One winds down the steep escarpment through forests and across ravines, till at last one reaches the bottom, and arrives at the station of Naivasha. Here I asked a native policeman on the platform if he had seen my caravan, as they were to pass through this place. He denied all knowledge of them. Presently a police-officer came up, and cheered me up with the intelligence that they certainly had not passed. It was impossible that they could have passed without his knowledge, as he had police out on all the roads, who reported everything. A big caravan with donkeys could not possibly have passed without being at once reported to him.

I could not help feeling rather anxious as the train continued on its way lest my trip should be still further delayed by the non-appearance of my men. I was not afraid that they would bolt with my things, but the African native is capable of making such wonderful and unexpected mistakes that I revolved in my mind all the things that they could possibly have done.

The road I had explained carefully, I had impressed

THE MULE, THE SAIS, AND NAROK

on them where to camp each day, and a variety of other things. Perhaps the donkeys had run away, perhaps the men had got drunk or fallen out with the headman, perhaps anything.

As we neared Gilgil Station just before sunset I put my head out of the window, and, to my intense satisfaction, saw my tent pitched beside the line on the short veldt, then the donkeys tethered in a row ; I counted them, and there were twenty, and everything in order.

A howling mob of porters rushed down to meet the train, and hung on to the foot-boards before it stopped. "How are you, master ?" "Good-evening, master." "Have you arrived safely ?" "What is the news of Nairobi ?"

I was delighted to see them in such good spirits on the eve of departure, and so I said : " I have arrived safely, and, moreover, I have brought a bag of rice to eat to-night, so that we may start with our stomachs full."

They seized on the loads, and, throwing them up to their shoulders, ran off with them to the camp. They were a strong and sturdy lot.

I asked the headman Omari which way they had come, and told him that they were said not to have passed Naivasha. " Why," said he, " we camped alongside the station there !" Everything had gone well so far, and things seemed doubly satisfactory after the fears I had entertained lest my men should not have arrived.

After three weeks laid up in bed in a house in Nairobi, the fresh air, the camp, the short grass—everything seemed glorious. Above all was the fascination of the unknown in front, and the feeling that I was absolutely free to go where I pleased and do as I liked. As I stepped into my tent, a place already associated with many happy memories, I felt as if all the fetters of civilization and its abominations slipped from me.

There was a time when I felt strange and lonely in the bush, a want of confidence in my ability to find my way about, and a feeling of insecurity if I should get out of sight of native guides. Now, even when utterly alone, I feel a strange exultant confidence in myself. Whether the country is known or unknown to me, it all seems familiar. The bush now wears a friendly aspect, and welcomes me to its bosom. It is only when I meet with roads and houses that the feeling of insecurity returns.

I was fortunate in finding Collyer, the District Commissioner of Rumuruti, camped at Gilgil. He gave me dinner that night, and many useful tips about the country I was to visit. He had sent for guides to meet me at Rumuruti ; he placed his house, stores, drinks, and boys at my disposal, helped me to fit my donkey-saddles, and altogether rendered me invaluable assistance. For all his kindnesses I here offer him my most grateful thanks

Next morning everyone was up early, and we commenced fitting donkey-saddles, adjusting loads, and performing the hundred and one little operations which crop up at the last moment.

At last, at 2 p.m., all was ready. The great point about the first day is to get somewhere, if it is only a mile or two, as it then insures a satisfactory start for the next day, as everything has shaken down into its place. If the start is deferred to the next morning, a further distribution and arrangement of loads is generally required, and nothing gets ship-shape.

So, as I knew there was a stream about five miles ahead on the Laikipia road, I arranged to camp there, and with

THE START FROM GILGIL.

On the left is the mule and the Masai Sais. Tengeneza, my gunbearer, is seen on the right. In the centre is a policeman, who escorted us as far as Kumuruti. The donkeys are peacefully grazing with their packs on, waiting to be driven off.

final adjustments and arranging of loads and donkeys, the caravan eventually straggled off.

The numerical strength was as follows :

19 porters for loads,
6 men for donkeys,
1 headman of porters,
1 headman of transport,
2 men to carry theodolite and instruments in use,
1 gun-bearer,
1 sais for mule,
2 servants,
1 dog,

making thirty-four mouths to be fed, besides which there were twenty donkeys and one mule.

The tribes represented by this band were very varied. They chiefly consisted of Wanyamwezi porters, but there were also one Manyema, one Swahili, one Comoro, one Masai, one Kikuyu, one Somali, and one Mganda.

As they were all old hands on trek, the common language amongst them was Swahili, although some of the Wanyamwezi used occasionally to speak to each other in their own tongue.

The gun-bearer, Tengeneza, had been with me for the best part of two years, but I had never inquired to which tribe he belonged. It was only now, when I heard him speaking Kinyamwezi to the porters, that I discovered that he was a Mnyamwezi.

Excellent porters are the Wanyamwezi, but in bush-craft they are painfully weak. Tengeneza is the only Mnyamwezi I have ever met who has any idea of tracking and bush-craft.

Of food for the porters we took sufficient to last us to Rumuruti, and also some loads of rice to be given out at intervals during the trek as a change from ordinary food. I had ascertained that plenty of food was to be had from a native trader at Rumuruti. I hoped also to obtain more donkeys there to carry the food.

Now, although I had settled on my general route some years ago—viz., that I should start from Nairobi and finish up at Djibouti—I had never made any very definite plans with regard to the journey. My intention was to avoid Teleki's route along Rudolf, and pass somewhere eastwards, thus striking new country, and also to visit the Omo River, and the country immediately north-east of it, which was almost unknown.

Up to the day before my departure I had not decided whether I should leave the administrated part of British East Africa by Baringo or by Rumuruti. I finally decided in favour of Rumuruti, because that would enable me to strike new country sooner.

However, the country north of the Laikipia plateau was reported as waterless, and several men whom I consulted thought that I should be unable to find a route northwards from there, and should eventually be compelled to take the known Baringo route.

Thus, even now that I was on my way to Rumuruti, I did not know that I might not be forced to travel westwards from there, and start from Baringo, instead of proceeding directly northwards.

CHAPTER II

TREK TO LAIKIPIA

THE distance from Gilgil to Rumuruti is about sixty-five miles. We had covered but a few miles the first day, and now there were sixty more to traverse. This I intended to accomplish in four days.

We started to load the donkeys at sunrise on the second day, but as the men were new to the work, they were not ready until about an hour later.

Our way led along the bottom of the Rift Valley, through woods of juniper-trees and a stunted camphor-tree called by the Masai *ol-leleshwa*. The scented leaves of this tree are used to spread on the raised hurdles or couches on which they sleep. These two are the commonest of the Rift Valley trees, and both of them are noticeable in that they are so often dead and dry.

Sometimes acres of these dead trees are found together, whilst amongst the camphor-trees almost all those which are alive, except the merest shoots, are springing from the side of a dead tree.

On our right, as we trekked northwards, could be seen the pointed peak of Kinangop, and the flat top of the Aberdare range, called Simbara by the Kikuyus, a massive hill thirteen thousand feet high. North of this the Aberdares tail away in a long ridge, sloping down to the Laikipia plains.

31

After marching twelve miles we came to a stream joining the Morendat River, just on the edge of the open plains which stretch away from the foot of the Aberdares. Not wishing to tire the men and donkeys at the beginning of the journey, I camped here. The water was good, and there was plentiful firewood from the camphor-trees. Had we gone on, we should have been obliged to cross the open plain, a distance of five or six miles, before finding a suitable site for a camp.

On starting on trek with a new set of men I am always very fastidious about the arrangement of camp, the duties of the different porters, and other little items, for the first few days, until everyone has got into my ways. By taking a little trouble at the start an infinity of bother is afterwards saved, and the men start with the idea that no small detail will be overlooked or slipshod ways condoned.

New porters with a new white man are exactly like schoolboys with a new master. The new schoolmaster, if he is not very careful during the first few days, may give the boys the impression that they can make a fool of him —an impression which he will probably never outlive as long as he remains at the school. If, however, he wins the boys' respect and confidence at the start, it will matter little what he does later, or how lax he is with them.

So during these first few days I used to pry round camp, and insist on having everything in its place—loads neatly stacked under the waterproof sheet, donkey-saddles ready to hand for the early morning start, porters' tents and fires down wind of my camp, and a variety of other little matters. I used to see that the donkeys were properly grazed, that the loads were not tampered with, that the food was measured out correctly, and that every-

thing was as it should be. Later on I was able to re-
linquish such daily and personal supervision, only
examining things from time to time to see that everything
was done according to my orders.

Porters are good enough fellows on the whole, but
however good they are at their ordinary work, they always
worry one with a lot of minor delinquencies, such as petty
thefts, quarrels amongst each other and with the headman,
or with the natives of the country, also periods of carelessness and forgetfulness. Such smaller matters are often
difficult to deal with or to bring home to the right offender.

However, there is one thing which they never seem to
realize, and that is that they talk so loudly that even in
one's tent one cannot, as a rule, help hearing what they
say. Often when sitting at night working in my tent I
have heard some guilty secret being discussed in loud and
shouting whispers.

If the matter was of minor importance I would forget
that I had heard it, but if it seemed advisable to take
notice of it I would perhaps wait a day or two, and then
appear to find it out suddenly. Perhaps I might ask
Abdi, and if he knew anything about it, he would generally
tell me frankly all he knew. Omari, on the other hand,
would make frantic efforts to keep in with both me and
the porters. Sometimes he would expose, with embellish-
ments, the most trivial offence, and at others try to shield
the men by feigning ignorance, with the result that he
won respect neither from myself nor the men.

To return from this digression to our camp. After
seeing everything put ship-shape, I strolled out with my
rifle and secured a steinbok for the table. Next day we
got the donkeys off by sunrise, and proceeded north-east
across the plain. We crossed the Morendat River at the

site of one of my old camps, and proceeded past the southern end of the Olbolossat swamp to the foot of the Aberdares, and then turned off northwards along the bottom of the range.

Here were plenty of streams coming from the hills and flowing into the swamp. After a sixteen-miles trek we camped above the swamp in some thick grass. Just below camp I saw something moving in the grass. I went down to investigate, and found that it was a reedbuck, which I shot for the men.

After dinner I moved out to the camp-fire, as it was cold at night, the altitude being about seven thousand feet. Here I found the men sitting round the fire, talking and telling stories. Listening to these stories always interests and amuses me, as some of them are distinctly humorous, while at all times they give one a very good insight into native ideas and ways of thinking.

The conversation turned on blind men. In the eyes of the Arab and Swahili a blind man represents a person possessed of such evil cunning that the Almighty has purposely deprived him of sight so as to protect his fellow-men. The Arabs say that there is no thief to equal a blind man, so what would he be if he had sight like other folk ?

Omari, the headman, began : " Once upon a time a blind man and a friend were walking together down a road ; the latter was carrying a bag of money. The blind man said to his fellow : 'What is that you are carrying ?' The other replied: ' A bag of money.'

" Presently the blind man said : ' Let us sit down a while and talk.' After sitting a while the blind man groped about till he felt the bag. This he took and hid under his clothes. Presently he got up, and said he must be going. Finding his bag gone, the other knew that the blind man must have taken it. So he followed him, and discovered him hiding the stolen money. He drew near and said : ' That is my money.' ' That is untrue,' replied the blind man ; ' it is mine.' ' Where did you obtain it ?' ' Oh, I prayed to Allah, and he sent it me.' So he withdrew a short distance, and, picking up stones, began pelting the blind man. The blind man said : ' What are you throwing stones at a poor distressed blind man for ?' ' I am not throwing stones at you,' said the other. ' I prayed to Allah that he would punish you, and he is throwing stones at you.' At this the blind man fled, leaving the money to the rightful owner."

Sadi, my Malindi boy, then said that blind men could perceive almost anything that a man with sight could see. " Once upon a time, at Malindi, there was an Arab who had a blind man in his house. One day he came with a sweet potato in his hand, and said to the blind man : ' Here, take this mango.' The blind man said : ' No ; it is a sweet potato.' The next day he brought a mango, and said : ' Take this sweet potato.' ' No,' said the blind man ; ' it is a mango.' Then the Arab said : ' Get out of my house ; you are only half blind.' "

" Oh," continued Sadi, " blind men are very bad men, and Arabs never give them alms. Is not that true, master ?" he said, turning to me.

" Yes," I replied. " Have you not heard the story of Musa [Moses] and the blind man ? It is written that once Musa was bathing in a big river, and he lifted up his eyes and saw a blind man slowly making his way along the bank. Then Musa had compassion on his affliction, and prayed to Allah : ' Oh, how hast thou afflicted one of these thy creatures without cause ! Here is this poor man con-

demned to walk in darkness through no fault of his own.
Take compassion on him, and give him his sight.'

" Allah answered Musa's prayer, and gave the man
sight. The blind man started and looked round, and his
eyes fell on Musa's garments lying on the bank. These
he hastily picked up, and then hurried off.

" Musa shouted : ' Stop ! those are my clothes.' ' Not
so,' said the blind man. ' These are mine which I have
but this moment put down here.'

" Then was Musa greatly angered, and prayed to Allah
to afflict this man with blindness once more. Allah
heard his prayer, and afflicted the man with blindness
again. Then he spake to Musa, and said : ' How little
is thy faith, O Musa, in that thou sayest that I have
afflicted one of my creatures without cause.' "

While sitting thus with the men I had an opportunity
of noticing the good discipline which existed amongst
them. For as they were chatting and talking with me, in
a manner which in the Indian native would savour of
disrespect or familiarity, I had occasion to speak to the
man sitting next me on a matter of duty connected with
the night watch. He immediately sprang to attention
to receive my orders, ran off and informed the sentry of
my wishes, and returned to report that he had executed
my order, and then rejoined his comrades.

Next day our road led up to the top of the down-like
northern end of the Aberdares, and then gradually down
along the ridge through patches of junipers till, at the
foot of the slope, we camped at the edge of the great open
plains of Laikipia. Here we met with the first kraals of
the El-burrgu Masai.

The old Masai inhabitants of Laikipia were the Loikop,
or people inhabiting the country called Laikipia. The

country of Laikipia then reached practically from Gilgil to the Borana. This word is now only used to denote the open plains south-west of the Lorogai Mountains and north of the Aberdares. The old Loikop died out—some say because their cattle died of rinderpest, others that they were scourged with smallpox, and others, again, that they were exterminated in battle by the southern Masai. The Laikipia plains were then left uninhabited except for a few hunters.

Lately the El-burrgu Masai have been given this country, and moved up here on condition that they gave up all claims on the Rift Valley, and left it open to white settlers. The grazing is exceptionally good, but water is scarce enough to make the country unsuitable for white settlers.

Abdi, who posed as a Masai as long as he remained in Masai country, went off to call on the neighbouring *manyata* (kraal). I put off my dinner for some time, hoping that he would bring me some milk to drink with my tea. Finally I commenced it, and while at dinner heard plover calling. This I guessed was Abdi returning, which proved to be the case, for shortly afterwards he turned up with a gourd of milk for me. These plover sleep on the ground, and if they are heard calling at night it generally means that someone is walking about and has disturbed them.

Abdi reported that the goats in the kraal were suffering from a very malignant foot and mouth disease, and that many were dying.

Directly one leaves the shelter of the Aberdares a strong east wind is felt. It blew all day, but died down at night. This wind remained with us till we reached the north of Lake Rudolf, and we used to hate it intensely, especially in the low country, where it was more powerful, and laden with dust and sand.

The next day we marched just over sixteen miles in to Rumuruti, the last station at which we should touch. The Guas Ñgiro (or Red River) runs in a broad dip through the level of the plains, and in this dip, close to the station on either bank, were planted crops of millet and maize to serve as food for the hands employed here. This was the last cultivation we were to see for many months, and from here enough food-supplies for the men must be carried to last till we reached Abyssinia.

The Masai live entirely on meat, blood, and milk, and so there is no cultivation in their country.

Close to the station on the bare wall of the valley were some camels grazing, and I asked the Indian clerk in charge to whom they belonged. He told me that a white man had just arrived, and these were his baggage camels. This was Mr. G. Fenwick, whom I met later in the day. He had just trekked through from Dôlo in Jubaland, and was now on his way to Nairobi.

Collyer's house was thrown open for me, and his boys made me most comfortable, and plied me with all kinds of luxuries from the District Commissioner's stores.

Here I met Fathili, the late A. H. Neumann's headman, and from him I was able to gain a good deal of information concerning the country I intended to visit. He was most interested in my intended trip, as he had been up to the Omo River with Neumann. He told me that if I visited the Reshiat I must ask for some loads that Neumann left there in charge of the chief and never had an opportunity of reclaiming.

A Suk guide turned up who said that he knew the country ahead, and so I engaged him. Neither this guide nor Fathili seemed to know whether I should be able to make my way northwards from here. I could get to the Lorogai Mountains easily enough, they said, and from there to Barasoloi (not the place of this name visited by Teleki), but whether I could proceed from there they were uncertain.

It was finally decided that I should visit a Wandorobo kraal several days to the north-east, and there obtain the services of some Wandorobo, who were said to know the country. To take me to this place, which was called Kisima, two Masai were furnished by the local chief Beua.

Donkeys were unobtainable at Rumuruti, so I enrolled twenty Kikuyu porters to carry as many loads of food as far as Barasoloi, at which place I hoped to get a few donkeys from the Samburr.

I reduced some of my own loads, and exchanged some of my provisions with a local trader for loads of food for the men. Finally, I managed to take with me, all told, some fifty loads of men's food, some being carried by porters, some on donkeys, and some on each man as reserve rations.

A Kikuyu called Masharia offered his services as a guide, and was taken on. It turned out that he only knew the country for a few days from Rumuruti, but he proved himself most useful in other ways, and came right through with me to the end of the journey. He turned out to be the only reliable Kikuyu I have ever met.

The Kikuyu, as a rule, can seldom be induced to go far from their homes. Porters from this tribe are subject to panics if they get it into their heads that they are going to be taken to a distant place. They will then often run away, for they appear to have little confidence in the white man.

Masharia announced his intention of coming as far as I would take him, and later, when I expected him to go back with the remainder of the Kikuyu, he stoutly refused, and said he wanted to go on.

With regard to the other twenty Kikuyu porters, knowing well the eccentricities of this race, I made every man say that he agreed to the wages I offered in the presence of witnesses, and also made them each say that they understood to what place they were to go. I was glad later that I had taken this precaution, for a day or two after we left Rumuruti they said that they had reached their destination, and wanted their pay, that they might return. I then had no compunction in forcing them to fulfil their agreement.

Fenwick's Somalis looked on my porters with great contempt, and would not at first believe that we intended to tackle the waterless Rendile and Borana countries. They said that we should never reach anywhere, and should all die on the way, telling Fenwick : " You had better say good-bye to your friend ; you will never see him again."

Fenwick made me some most valuable and useful presents—viz., two water-casks and some *gras* ammunition. The latter was of service when we reached Abyssinia, and the former indispensable on the way.

Porters, guides, and food being all arranged for, Fenwick and I dined together, and went over his accomplished journey and my prospective trip till a late hour.

Early next morning we started loading up our respective animals, he to return to civilization and I to leave it. I said good-bye to Fathili, and then shook hands with Fenwick, the last white man I was to see for half a year ; his camels filed out of the station southwards and my donkeys jostled out eastwards.

CHAPTER III

THE LAIKIPIA PLAINS

It was with a feeling of relief that I left Rumuruti behind me, as now my journey had begun in earnest. I had been haunted by a fear that something unexpected might turn up to spoil my trip. Now that we had left the last outposts of civilization, it only depended on myself as to whether the trip would be successfully accomplished or not.

As loads had been redistributed and the donkeys were all now laden, the first day out from Rumuruti much resembled the first day's trek. We only travelled six or seven miles, so that everything might shake down into its proper place. We camped on a little permanent stream called Haiyam. Close to our camp were some Masai kraals, and it was the path to these kraals that we had followed on the march. Some Masai elders came to visit me, and brought a gourd of milk.

These Masai gourds are decorated with cowries, which are sewn on in rows with the tail hairs of zebra or giraffe. Little holes are bored in the sides of the gourd, through which these hairs pass and repass. As the mouth of the gourd is often too small to admit the hand, it is a puzzle how a hair, after being pushed through a hole, is made to turn round inside and come out at the next hole.

The solution of the problem is that a doubled hair is

pushed through a hole. This, on reaching the inside of the gourd, opens into a loop. A straight hair is then pushed down the neck of the gourd, till it passes through this loop, and the loop is then drawn out again, bringing the end of the second hair with it.

I gave the old men some strings of blue Masai beads in return for the milk. It was at once apparent how much more satisfactory are trade goods with natives than payments in money. Had I given them a rupee, one of the old men would have looked at it, tied it up in a corner of his robe, and walked off, feeling somehow that he had received a thing of little value.

On receipt of a few strings of beads, worth an anna or two, they all sat down on the ground and talked over them, broke the strings, and kept on letting the beads slip off; carefully picked them up, restrung them, and divided them up again; dropped and picked them up again, and altogether had a lot of fun with them, finally going off delighted.

The El-burrgu Masai now occupy the Laikipia plateau, extending to the north-east as far as the Lorogai Mountains. Their chief is Beua, whom we saw at Rumuruti. The chief of all the Masai is Ol-lunana, who lives at Ngong Mountain, near Nairobi.

The greater Masai chiefs are supposed to be seers and medicine-men. Amongst other miraculous powers of which they are supposed to be possessed is that of being able to transfer themselves to distant places at will. Beua told us : " Ol-lunana comes here almost every night to talk with me, and if he does not come here, I go down to Ngong to see him."

With reference to this thought-transference, believed in by the Masai, I was at another time informed that,

THE SAIS WITH MASAI SULSUL

The sulsul is made of ostrich feathers, and affixed to the point of a spear as an emblem of peace.

whilst Ol-lunana was at war with his brother Sindeyo, they visited one another in spirit, and patched up their dispute.

There does not appear to be ever a very heavy rainfall on this Laikipia plateau, and, as the country is dry, whatever rain there is sinks quickly into the soil, and so does not cut up the surface into deep ravines and watercourses. It is only just below the rocky ground and steep descents such as the Aberdares and Lorogai Mountains that these are found.

The greater part of the plains consists of very gently undulating downs of short grass and good grazing, but with little water. Occasionally, however, there are patches of rocky soil, and just below these are found watercourses, and water often accumulates in pools in ravines such as these.

In a few places water wells up to the surface and forms little pools surrounded by rushes and black, saltish earth. These places are called *sokota* by the Masai. The water is often brackish and very foul, as flocks are brought from far to drink, and paw up and eat the saltish earth round the margin.

As camp had to be arranged to suit water-holes, and the two Masai guides were as vague about distances as African guides generally are, it was rather hard always to insure a good day's march. When he arrives at a water-hole after a short march, the traveller generally does not wish to waste time by camping after such a short journey, but to go on to the next water-hole, if it is within reasonable distance. On the other hand, he does not wish to let his men in for a long waterless march during the heat of the day and on top of the march already made.

He then has recourse to his guides, and wastes perhaps

an hour trying to ascertain the distance to the next water, without being able to arrive at any conclusion. After this he does what he might have done at the beginning— he either camps or goes forward on the chance that it is only a short distance.

My two Masai guides knew the country quite well, and were frequently present when there was any difficulty about finding the way. However, they were as annoying as most guides about distances, for they had two stock times for the distance to the next water. If I asked them how far the next water was on arrival at a water-hole, it was always six hours distant. If I camped there and asked them the distance the next morning to the same place, it was always four hours.

The first distance, six hours or eighteen miles, was a bit too much for men and donkeys after even a short march of a couple of hours. If, however, the next morning's distance of four hours had been given, it would often have been worth while going on.

We left the path at Haiyam, and trekked fifteen miles across country to some pools in a rocky bed called Margwe. There was no track till we came within a mile or two of the pools, when we struck an old path leading past some disused kraals. From this track game paths led down to the pools. These pools are said to dry up occasionally, and in any case they are insufficient for watering stock except during rain.

When we got into camp it was found that the headman and two porters were lost. This was due to my carelessness in not ascertaining that everyone was present every time we halted to close up. The men have an annoying way of always saying " Yes " when one asks if all are present.

We fired off rifles, and after waiting a little, I sent out two parties in different directions, and myself took a third way. I thought that perhaps they had got on the old path, and followed it without turning off on the game tracks. However, I found no tracks on this path, so made a circular tour, and then returned to camp, seeing one rhino, one cock ostrich, and one greater bustard, as well as a certain amount of other game, on the way.

As I got near the camp, I saw Omari and the two missing porters being brought in from the other side, and a line of porters in extended order advancing up the ridge towards me. When I met them I asked what they were doing, and they said that they thought that perhaps I was lost now, and that they had come to look for me.

Next day we marched northward from Margwe for five or six miles, and then struck a broad cattle-road, which led us to a *sokota*, where thousands of sheep and goats were being watered.

The heat haze distorts objects so much on these great open plains that at a thousand yards' distance it would often be impossible to distinguish between a flock of sheep and a herd of cattle or game if it were not for the herdsmen. In this case we saw waves of moving animals, and every here and there a narrow black object rising to a higher level, so we knew them to be sheep and goats.

A strong east wind was blowing as usual, and the air to their leeward side was dense with the dust they disturbed. Passing round the south of the *sokota*, we travelled up a nullah, in which were a few pools, and there crossed a stony rise, from which we obtained our first view of the Lorogai Mountains, and also saw below us the Sokota Naibor (the White Swamp), where we were to camp. The day's trek was just over sixteen miles.

Soon after arrival in camp the mule uprooted the bush to which he was tied. When he moved and saw the bush following him on the end of his halter, he galloped off in wild alarm, dragging the bush after him. We followed and tracked him back to the stony hill we had descended, and there we saw that he had taken the track by which we had come down. I never thought to see him again, feeling certain that he would go straight back to Rumuruti or Nairobi. I sent the sais to look for him with one of the guides, arranging that he should catch us up at Kisima while we were arranging for new guides.

We moved on about twelve miles to Sokota Almarr-marr, and here they caught us up again, bringing the mule and two Torobo hunters.

It appeared that the mule went straight back to our last camp at Margwe, and having arrived there, took up his position under the tree to which he had been tethered, and waited for food and water to be brought him. The two Torobo had found him there, and catching him, had been bringing him along when the sais met them.

The Torobo are a race of hunters of much the same origin as the Masai, and speaking a language something like the Nandi. They call themselves Ogieg, but the Masai call them Torobo, and the Swahili Wandorobo.

Many natives would have been afraid to handle a strange beast like a mule, whilst others, again, would have left it alone lest they should be accused of theft. The Torobo are, however, a very intelligent and very independent people, and I was much impressed by the sensible way in which these men had brought the mule along without even waiting for someone to come and claim it.

Being overjoyed at getting him back, I naturally wished to reward them adequately, but they did not seem to care about anything I offered them. Being simple hunters who wore no clothes, it was rather a problem to find something to give them. At last, in despair, I told the sais, who spoke their language, to ask them what they wanted, and if it was anything I could give them, they should have it. After conferring together, they said that they would like some meat, so I had then and there to go out and procure them some.

The same night we heard lions roaring, and I felt very thankful that they had not got my mule.

Next day we passed over some stony rises, and then came to a plain, at the other side of which rose up the Lorogai Range, or, as it is called here, Ol-grisiăn. In the midst of this plain is a watercourse, in which there were pools of water. On the banks were the usual thorn-trees, such as are found along the course of the Athi River on the plains of that name. We camped here near a Masai kraal.

This watercourse was called Engare Narok (the Blackwater), and a few miles to the east was the watercourse called Kisima, to which we had intended to go.

We learnt here that the Torobo guide recommended by Fathili, for whom we were searching, had moved his kraal southwards. I sent the guides and one porter to fetch him, whilst I remained to take observations. The Masai here said that they killed a lion a few days back. Oryx appeared to be fairly plentiful near here, especially towards Ol-grisiăn.

Whilst taking an azimuth of the sun at this place, I got the rays directly on my forehead, which gave me a slight sunstroke, and I had to spend the night with towels soaked in cold water round my head. Although I continued to take observations, my head was so affected that they were of no use, for when I came to look at them later, I found that I had written down all sorts of wrong figures.

The party sent to look for the Torobo returned with him, but as he appeared to know nothing of the country in front, I left him. The Masai here also know nothing of the country at the other side of the Lorogai, and seemed never to have visited the Samburr country.

They said, however, that there was a Torobo kraal northwards where there were men who knew the Samburr country. We therefore trekked on to their kraal, which was at a place called Sukota Luporr.

One of the donkeys died of tsetse-bite at Engare Narok. This made me anxious to push on quickly to the Samburr country, where I hoped to be able to buy more donkeys, as I feared that many more might suddenly die, for if one had tsetse, others were certain to have it likewise.

The Kikuyu porters had been complaining bitterly for several days that they had never agreed to come so far, and they threatened to run away. I have come to the conclusion that Kikuyu are really not such fools as they pretend to be. They always feign so innocently not to have understood the arrangements that one is half bluffed into thinking that they really believe they are being treated unfairly.

On this occasion I had given out so many days' rations to each man, and it was carefully explained to them for how many days they had drawn food. A day before this should have been finished they came to ask for more. They swore that I had said one day less than I had, and also counted the day to which their last issue of rations extended as the first of the new issue. This they did so well that I was really bluffed into thinking that they had not understood. Rather than that they should think themselves defrauded, I gave out an extra ration, as I was afraid that they might carry out their threat and run away otherwise.

When the headman giving out rations came to Masharia (the Kikuyu who wanted to accompany us the whole way), he said that he had, as a matter of fact, finished his rations because he had eaten too much, but that he knew perfectly well that he was not entitled to another ration till the morrow. I then realized that I had been taken in by the others, as they must have understood as well as Masharia. The only difference was that they were anxious to get back, and lost nothing by making trouble, whereas their fellow, who wanted permanent work with us, thought it inadvisable to play the fool.

So when they told me that they were going to run away, and had not understood that they were coming so far, I merely ordered my other porters to put a guard over them at night, and to tie up anyone who tried to run away. We found two Torobo who knew the path across the Lorogai to the Samburr country, and they agreed to take us as far as the first Samburr kraal, but no farther. There was no water to be had on the way we were taking across the mountains, and so preparations had to be made to carry it. The tanks and barrels up to now had been carried empty, one man taking two.

As some of the loads of food had been eaten, we had some spare men, so were able to fill the tanks, giving one to each man. These tanks had been specially made for me so as to be a one-man load when filled. A donkey would take two and a camel four.

There was a little hill just above our camp called

Ladero (The Rat). In front of us, to the north-east, we could see that there was a pass in the Lorogai Range. The natives here only call the part of the range north-west of this pass Lorogai, and also Losirgon. That part of the chain to the south-east they call Ol-grisian, and also Bawa.

Our guides said that it was one march to the top of the pass, where there was no water, and another long march from there to water on the other side of the range.

For this reason we decided to start about midday, instead of in the morning. Where there is a stretch of two days between water this is a convenient arrangement, for the men can cook their food in the morning and eat it just before starting, and the animals can be watered at the same time. They then trek for the rest of that day, and, if there is a moon, part of the night, sleep, and start early next morning, arriving at water the following noon. If a morning start is made, more time is occupied in travelling between the two watering places, and this means that a longer time is spent without the men being able to cook.

We did not, however, get away from camp at noon as intended, for my sketching and observations took longer than I had thought, and I did not get back to camp until 1.30. I found the donkeys ready to start, so I sent them off, and after a hurried breakfast, followed with the men. Our way led up and over a low spur from Ol-grisian called Ol doinyo Motio (Cooking-Pot Hill), and then by a gradual and easy ascent to the top of the pass. Here we arrived at dark, and camped in a place called Ol-laredanari-lo'olmesi, not a bad rival in names to the Llanfair pwllgwyngyll, etc., of North Wales.

There were plenty of fallen junipers lying about, so we

made up big fires, as the night was chilly, the altitude being about eight thousand feet.

During the march there had been abundant evidences that elephant and rhino visited these mountains during the rains, but there were no recent traces, probably owing to the lack of water at this time of the year. It seemed extraordinary that there should be no water at such an altitude, and every moment we expected to come across a stream or find a spring oozing out of the side of a hill. I hardly believed the guides till I had inspected the valleys and hollows myself. They were quite right, however, though they said that there was water in other parts of the range.

Another proof was the presence of uninhabited Masai kraals here and there. They, like the elephant and rhino, only visited this spot during the rains.

Ol-laredanarilo'olmesi was our first waterless camp, and it proved to be the first in a very long series of waterless halts and long forced marches between water-holes. Although I did not then know how many months it would be before we reached a well-watered country again, I thought fit to improve the minds of the men on the subject of being careful of water.

Each of the men and the guides had the regulation water-bottle, and in addition to that I made them carry gourds, either a small one each or a large one between two or three. The Kikuyu porters had, of course, no water-bottles or gourds, as they had been enlisted only for the journey to Barasoloi, so I distributed first of all sufficient water for them, and then, putting aside a small reserve in case we should not reach water as early as anticipated, divided the remainder amongst the others.

Then, as they were sitting round their fires, talking

loudly, I called for silence, and said : "Now hear my words. To-day I have given you water over and above that in your water-bottles out of my kindness. For I know the hearts of you men, and that you are fools. For on leaving water you will say, 'What need is there of filling our bottles ? We shall find water presently'; or on the way you will say, 'Our water-bottles are heavy; let us pour away the water'; and later you will say, 'Master, we are dying of thirst ; give us water.' Such is the custom of black men. Now listen well. The country we are going to is bad ; there will be no water to drink, far less will there be *ku ogea* (to bathe in), *ku nawa* (to wash the hands and face), *ku tawaza* (to wash the feet before praying), *ku tamba* (to make ceremonial ablution). (Laughter.)

"Therefore, every drop of water you got you must guard carefully. Not a drop must be wasted, for that drop may be your life.

"Now, on the first night in a waterless place you will never get water from the tanks ; that in your bottles and gourds must suffice. Only on the second day will you got water from the tanks.

"Moreover, that you may not think I am troubling you without cause, I will make this agreement with you. Whatever water is given out will be divided equally, to every man his share, and my share will be the same as yours. Therefore you will not be able to come to me and say, 'Master, we suffer from thirst,' for you will know that we shall all suffer equally. Moreover, the heat of the sun is greater to me, a white man ; therefore you will know that the water which suffices for me will suffice also for you."

To this the porters replied, "Right ho !" (*E walla*), and immediately dismissed the matter from their minds.

FIRST VIEW OF THE SAMBURR COUNTRY

This photograph was taken from the spot at which I first saw the Samburr kraals from the Lorogai mountains
The watering place of the Samburr cattle is at the head of the valley

As it was dark on our arrival in camp we did not get a view of the country at the other side of the pass. Next morning, when the mists cleared away, we found that the country was more mountainous and the descent much steeper and much greater. For the Lorogai Mountains mark a change in the level of the country. On the one side is the higher Laikipia plateau, and on the other side a low thorn desert country, probably two thousand feet below the level of the plains. Owing to the hilly nature of the country, the day proved a long and tiring one for the donkeys. Moreover, the guides at one place lost the track, and we had to cut a way through bush up a steep hillside into the open again, so as to allow the donkeys to pass. When we emerged from the undergrowth, it was apparent that there was a more level and open way we might have taken. So we halted here, and I sent back men, who were just in time to meet the tail-end of the caravan and bring them up by this track.

We then proceeded, and after crossing a shoulder, suddenly obtained a view to the front. Just at our feet, some thousand feet below us, was a valley running far up into the hills. I could see through my glasses kraals here and there, and cattle grazing on the floor of the valley, and I knew that these must be the Samburr, a people who are outside the range of our administration.

Following the valley down, I could see that it led out into an arid thorn plain bounded to the north-east by a great range of mountains, which must be the General Matthews Range.

It was to me a wonderfully interesting sight, this bird's-eye view of the kraals of a strange people and country so suddenly opened out below me. I learnt from the guides that no white man had ever traversed this pass before.

I watched the herds being driven up the valley to water, the herdsmen as yet unconscious of our presence. I wondered what these people would think of my sudden advent amongst them.

Would they be friendly, surly, or merely frightened ? Anyhow, I thought that our sudden appearance in their midst would cause them considerable astonishment.

At last I put away my glasses, and we commenced the long and steep descent, speculating the while as to what reception we should meet with at the hands of the Sambnrr.

CHAPTER IV

THE SAMBURR COUNTRY

If I had thought that the Samburr would be alarmed or even astonished at my sudden appearance, I was to be disappointed. After a long and tedious descent, which was especially severe on the donkeys, we arrived on the floor of the valley, and here struck a cattle road leading up and down.

As we were resting beside this road we heard the sound of wooden cattle-bells coming towards us, and presently a herd of cattle appeared on the road. They looked up and saw me sitting beside the way, and suddenly stood stock-still, staring. After staring awhile they decided that I was dangerous, and turned round and bolted. They had evidently never seen an object dressed in hat and coat before.

If this was what the Samburr cattle thought of me, I wondered how the Samburr themselves would behave, and waited for the appearance of the herdsman with some interest. Presently the cattle began to return, evidently being driven by someone behind, but this time they made a détour to avoid me and my porters, who were sitting behind me. Finally the herdsman appeared, cast a casual glance in my direction, and unconcernedly walked on, as if a white man sitting beside the road was the most

ordinary object in the world. I was astonished and somewhat piqued at his want of interest in me.

I called to Abdi to bring him to me, and interrogated
him about the Samburr kraals and the nearest water.
The Samburr youth told us that their kraal was farther
down the valley, and that the only water here was higher
up in the direction in which he was driving the cattle.

The language of the Samburr is practically the same
as that of the Masai, although many of their manners and
customs are different. There was thus no difficulty in
communicating with them through Abdi, while I understood enough to follow the drift of the conversation.

It was now past noon, so we continued on our way
down the valley, first of all distributing the water which
remained and sending men with the tanks to follow the
Samburr herdsman and refill them.

A mile or two down the valley we came in sight of a
large kraal, and passing close to this, selected a camp
under some thorn-trees just beyond. The people in the
kraal took a faint interest in us as we passed, and then
returned to their duties, which chiefly consisted of sitting
and doing nothing. No one came out to stare at us or
showed themselves in the least inquisitive.

One might have imagined that they were going to ignore
us completely if it had not been that, directly the donkeys
were unloaded, a youth stepped forward, and herding them
together, without saying a word, drove them off to water
three miles back. He grazed them during the rest of the
day, and brought them back in the evening. This, I
think, was the most hospitable and considerate act I have
ever seen a native perform, as the men were tired and the
donkeys thirsty after a long day.

Camp was pitched, and then, having given us time to

SAMBURR

One of the Samburr old men is standing with the spear in the foreground. By the head of the mule is Masharia the Kikuyu, while the three figures to the right are some of my porters.

settle down and get some food, a deputation of old men arrived. They stopped a little way off, and sent word to say that they were coming to see me. They came in, and after each shaking hands and greeting me with *seriăn*, they sat round my tent. They brought with them a sheep, a goat, and multitudinous gourds of milk of all ages and states of decomposition, from fresh milk to curdled milk a few weeks old. Most natives appreciate old and curdled milk, and would not thank you for fresh.

These were, I think, the most delightful old men I have ever seen amongst natives. They were extraordinarily intelligent, and talked about things and countries one would have imagined quite outside their ken.

Especially were they interesting to me in that they knew all the politics and current events of the Rendile and Borana countries—countries I knew nothing about, and which were practically unknown to any of the natives of the countries I had left. The Samburr used at one time to have scattered kraals extending up to Rudolf, although now they do not live northwards of General Matthews Range and Ol doinyo Ñgiro.

They were able to give me a very good general idea of the country I was to visit. They told me where one could go and where not for want of water. Information can only, as a rule, be had from natives by questioning, and as I did not know what questions to ask, it was somewhat difficult to elicit all they knew. However, I plied them with questions on this and two subsequent days, and gained a wonderful lot of information from them. These long conversations were not at all boring, as they were such interesting old men, and most hospitable and friendly.

Information from natives is generally of such a vague description that after it has been obtained with much difficulty it is hardly worth having. Here, however, I took down pages of notes in my pocket-book of names of places with water, different routes, and the distances between places, history, customs, and distribution of various tribes, much of which was of the greatest value afterwards.

I thought, however, that if the Samburr knew all this about a distant country, how much more the Rendile would be able to tell me when I reached them. In this I was quite wrong, as the information I got about the Rendile country from the Samburr was much more intelligible and accurate than the Rendile themselves afterwards gave me of their own country.

The place at which we were camped was called Obiroi, and the *Legwanan* (chief) here was named Londoiyen. It appeared that from here there were three routes north-ward—viz., one north-east to Marsabit, one north to the Rendile country, and one north-west to Embarta steppe. However, at our first meeting the old men only stopped a short time, for they said that I must be tired after my journey, and that they would leave me.

Later in the evening the *Legwanan* arrived by himself, sat down by my tent, and said : "Now I have come to hear all the news." I replied that the news was that the white men were going to open a station at Marsabit. Had they heard that ? Yes, they had heard a rumour, but they wanted to know more about it.

Then I said that I had heard there was a very bad cattle disease (rinderpest) in the north of the Borana. Yes, they had heard that. I warned them to keep clear of all cattle coming from there, not to buy or exchange any cattle that might have come from that part, or mix them with their herds.

As Barasoloi, the place to which the Kikuyu porters had agreed to go, was now only a day's march farther, I let them go home from here, hoping to be able to buy a few donkeys from the Samburr, as they appeared to have plenty.

Next day I went out early, and shot two Grevy's zebra, as I wanted the meat for the men and the skins to make into new donkey saddle-bags. One zebra I distributed, and the other I made into biltong and put by. Some of my old men friends went out with me to show me where the game was likely to be found. This was the first time we met with Grevy's zebra, as it is not found south of the Lorogai.

The Masai do not eat game meat at all. The Samburr eat certain kinds of game, such as rhino, oryx, and gazelle, but not zebra. They said that women eat the klipspringer and small buck ; the men do not.

On return to camp, after having some food, a conclave of the old men was assembled, and we broached the subject of buying donkeys. We talked for hours on the subject without coming to any satisfactory conclusion. For some reason or other they appeared unwilling to sell, although they had plenty. Then we suggested that we should hire donkeys as far as the Rendile country, and more time was spent in discussing this idea.

Abdi was splendid at this sort of thing, and argued away for hours without ever losing his temper or patience, but was always good-tempered and resourceful. At last he nudged the *Legwanan*, and said to him chaffingly : "Look here, you had better fix up some arrangement quickly, or else the white man will run all you old men

in, and make you carry his loads for him." The *Legwanan*
looked at my tent, and held up his hands, saying : " Who
could be found to carry a house like this ?"

Finally the old men withdrew a short distance, and,
sitting round in a circle, consulted with each other, a
procedure which always takes place, even if only one ox
is to be sold from a kraal. Presently the *Legwanan* returned, and asked whether it would please me best to buy
donkeys or hire them. I replied that I would like to buy
them best, but that if I could not buy them I would hire
them.

The *Legwanan* returned to the conference, and after a
further discussion they came back to my tent, and the
Legwanan said : " Our news is good : you shall have the
donkeys, but we do not know yet if we will sell them to
you or only lend them. You must wait here two days
while we get in some donkeys and consult with the
neighbouring kraals. While you stop here you can shoot
game, and we will come and see you, for we would not
like you to go away at once, but want you to stop for a
long time."

I was very glad to hear this, as, now the Kikuyu porters
had returned, I was practically dependent on getting
donkeys in order to proceed, unless I throw away trade
goods. I did not like the delay, but as the Samburr were
so pleasant, I was glad to fall in with their wishes as much
as possible. They did their best to entertain me whilst
I stopped with them, and one or other of the old men was
always at my camp, or accompanied me if I went abroad.
They certainly used to ask for small presents occasionally
—I have scarcely ever met with natives who do not—
but they were not so offensively clamorous as most
natives.

SAMBURR ELDERS

Holding a consultation as to whether they will let me buy donkeys from them. In the background is a group of my porters.

The old man shown in the photo with the spear was very anxious to know what my name was, for, he said, if any other white man passed he would be able to say, " I knew such a one." I told him, and after practising it several times, he went off. After that they used to bob in and out at all times of the day, calling out " Sirrgon," which was the nearest they could get to it.

The Samburr are referred to by Von Hohnel and Teleki as the Burkeneji. This word, or, to be more accurate, Lo'eborkeneji, meaning " the (people) of the white goats," is the Masai name for the Samburr.

Their dress is much the same as the Masai, consisting of roughly tanned goat-skins. The men generally wear a patch of skin hanging from the shoulder, being otherwise naked, while the women are carefully dressed all over in skins, drawn in at the waist by a cord, and the lower part worn in the " directoire " style.

Their ornaments are much the same as the Masai, but their weapons are different. The spear is long-hafted, with a short, fat blade. Over this blade a neat little leather sheath is often worn. This is also found with the Turkana, Suk, and Reshiat, but not with the tribes to the south.

The shield differs from that of the Masai, being quite small. Youths are sometimes seen with long, thin, basket-work shields, as are found also amongst the Reshiat.

The tribe appears to be divided into several clans, eight different names being given me. Of these, the kraals at Obiroi and those north of that place were of the Elmasulla clan. The other clans appeared to be mixed together, and, as is usual with natives, they were unable to tell me anything intelligible about their distribution and origin.

Two of the clans are Lorogishu and Elbisigishu, these

words being corruptions of *lo' orok ngishu* and *lo'el bus ngishu*, meaning " of the black cow " and " of the spotted cow." They said that the founders of these clans possessed nothing until they got one cow each, one a black and the other a spotted cow. These multiplied till they had a large herd, and started clans of their own.

One of my old men friends had bad eyes, and asked if I could do something for them. I made him up a lotion for them, and he went off happy. My fame as a medicine-man spread, and half the people in the kraal, some of them stone-blind, came down to have their eyes doctored.

In these cattle kraals flies always swarm, and the natives are so used to them that they do not attempt to brush them away, but allow them to cluster in crowds about their eyes. It is quite evident that these flies convey disease from one to the other, as the number of people suffering from cataract and bad eyes in this kraal was enormous, whereas in some others few, if any, were affected.

The Samburr women are very fond of giraffe-hair necklaces, and I was asked to go out and shoot a giraffe for this purpose. By the spoor there appeared to be plenty in the neighbourhood, but I always think that it is rather a shame to kill such an interesting and useless beast unless one really wants a whole skin for a museum, so I refused.

I asked my old men what was the origin of the name of Embarta steppe, for *embarta* means " a horse." They replied : " Oh, that is just its name." I then asked if there were never any horses there, to which they replied that once the Borana came on horses and fought there. Whether this is an historical fact, or was just said to please me, I do not know. They also told me that formerly the Samburr had horses, although now they have none.

One must always be so careful with natives not to suggest an answer when asking a question, or they jump to the conclusion that a certain answer is required. One can make a native say almost anything one likes by putting questions to him in certain forms. I have often heard white men settle some discussion amongst themselves by asking their boys some such questions as these :

" Did Mr. Jones come here this afternoon ?"

" I don't know, master."

" Didn't any white man come here ?"

" Oh yes, master."

" A tall man ?"

" Yes, master, very tall."

" With a black beard ?"

" Yes, master."

Turning round to his friend triumphantly : " There, you see it was Jones who came."

I have sometimes continued the interlocution on these lines :

" A very old man ?"

" Yes, master."

" With grey hair ?"

" Yes, master."

" And a white beard ?"

" Yes, master."

" As short as you, or a little shorter ?"

" Yes, master."

" Funny sort of fellow, your friend Jones."

For this reason one has to be most careful when eliciting information from natives, and sometimes it takes hours to find out some quite small matter.

I was sitting in my tent at Obiroi one night writing while there was a very inharmonious concert proceeding in the kraal. This had continued for some hours, and was rather worrying me, when it was brought to an abrupt conclusion. There was suddenly a rush of thousands of feet and tinkling of cattle-bells as all the cattle in the zariba, perhaps several thousand, stampeded to one side. The concert ceased, donkeys brayed, dogs barked, cattle lowed, and men called out. When peace reigned again I saw burning faggots being thrown about, and a voice said : " You think it is a hyena, or some small animal ? Not so."

Next morning I learnt that a lion had jumped the wall of the zariba, fallen on some sheep and goats, killing four or five, and then, jumping on the roof of a hut, had cleared out again, frightened by the noise, and leaving its victims behind.

The *Legwanan* came to me, and said that they had lost many cattle owing to this lion, who visited them regularly, and that I would be doing them a great kindness if I killed it for them. I said that I would do my best, so I went up and examined the spot at which it had jumped over, and told them to make a hole in the side of the zariba through which to fire, and to have a goat tied up outside that night.

The rest of the day was spent in further palavers about the donkeys, and it was finally agreed that six donkeys should be lent me on the following day to take me as far as some Samburr kraals under the General Matthews Range. If I could not obtain donkeys there, they were to come as far as the Rendile country. Two guides were also to be produced.

This being settled, I took some observations, and obtained some last tips from the *Legwanan* about the country in front. He told me that the other side of the

General Matthews Range, which the Samburr call Dôto at the north-west end, and Lengiyo at the south-east, I should meet with a Rendile chief called Leshaulil. Curiously enough, this was the first Rendile whom I met. The Samburr are on very friendly terms with the Rendile, and have been so for a long time, although both these tribes have exchanged hostilities with most of the other tribes of the neighbourhood.

It appeared that the Samburr had a few baggage-camels. I had not seen them, as they had been away, but this evening they came back to the kraal. After dinner I went up to the kraal with Abdi and Tengeneza to sit up for the lion.

The kraal was a very big one, being perhaps three hundred yards across. There was an inside zariba in which the cattle were herded, and outside this was another wall. Between these two walls were the huts, separated into little groups, each group divided off from the next by a low wall of branches. In these partitions were kept the camels, donkeys, sheep, and goats belonging to the owners of the huts. At either end of the zariba was an opening, blocked at night, leading straight into the inner cattle zariba.

We entered at the lower entrance, which was nearest our camp, and passed up between the two walls and the huts. The huts were made of gipsy poles, on which were strung sheep and goat skins. As rain is scarce here, and the climate warm, these afford sufficient protection. The huts were circular, and quite different to the long, many-compartmented, cowdung-plastered huts of the Masai.

On arrival at the top end of the zariba, I found that the Samburr had very large ideas as to the opening through which I was to fire. Instead of the nice little loophole I

5

had anticipated in the zariba, I found that a whole section of wall about six yards wide had been removed.

This did not please me a bit, as it meant that I should have to lie practically in the open, visible to an animal like a lion, which can see fairly well at night. Moreover,

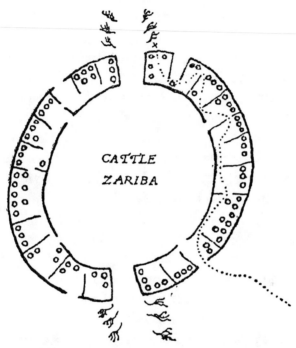

PLAN OF A SAMBURR KRAAL, OR "MANYATA."

The low partition-walls by the huts form enclosures for camels, donkeys, and sheep. The branches by the two main entrances are to close them at night. The dotted line shows our route from the camp. At the upper end of it is the place where the lion leaped over.

seeing me in such a position, a wary lion would not advance straight on the kraal, but would creep round the edge, and might suddenly appear round the corner on either side of me. Like anyone who has had much to do with lions, I have a great respect for them, especially at night, and this arrangement did not make me feel at all comfortable.

However, it was too late to call off now, so the goat was tied up, and I lay down in the gap in the fence, while Tengeneza lay behind me, and Abdi remained inside. I had brought the latter so as to be able to use him as an interpreter.

The night was very dark, and the white goat, only a few yards away, was just discernible as a shadowy form. The ground sloped up a little behind the goat, and the top of the little rise showed against the sky-line. It was for this reason that I had chosen this spot.

A long and tedious wait of several hours ensued, and then suddenly something moved on the sky-line. I felt almost certain it must be the lion, when it moved again, and from the movement I saw that it was a hyena. Tengeneza nudged me from behind, so he evidently had seen it, and thought that it was the lion.

Directly it moved down towards the zariba it was invisible, but shortly afterwards I suddenly made out its form by the goat ; in fact, I thought that it had collared it. I immediately shouted out, and Tengeneza moved up, very much excited, digging the muzzle of my spare rifle into my side, while his fingers were playing about somewhere near the trigger. I moved the muzzle away from my person, and he said : "What is the matter ?" I said : "It is a hyena. Get a faggot from the fire, and throw it out."

Abdi, who had heard me call out, got a piece of burning wood, and threw it out towards the goat, and we saw that it was all right. The hyena had, of course, moved off when I called out. We then waited again till near midnight, when I gave it up, as we were starting early next morning.

If a lion does not come before ten or eleven o'clock on an occasion like this, it is pretty certain that he is not coming at all.

The Samburr had been talking very grandly about how they were going to keep guard all night. They said: "There is no sleep for anybody in the kraal to-night; we will all be awake, and watching for the lion." About eight o'clock their talking had died away, and only loud snores were heard.

It now took all our combined efforts to wake a man up to take in the goat. At last he roused himself, fetched the goat in, put it in its compartment, and immediately went to sleep again without troubling about the aperture in the zariba.

We made our way back to the other end, and were about to let ourselves out by pulling away the branches, when it struck us that we should not be able to close it again from the outside.

Abdi went to the nearest hut, and tapped and called out for some time, saying that we wanted someone to close up the zariba. At last a sleepy man's voice ordered out a woman, and she crawled out.

Every hut had one or more spears stuck upright in the ground on the left-hand side of the doorway, and from these can be told how many warriors are in each hut. The object of putting the spear on the left-hand side is that in case of alarm the warrior can, as he comes out, snatch it up with his right hand. Maŝai warriors as they enter a hut throw the spear into the left hand, and plunge the butt into the ground with a sort of military precision and smartness.

We pulled away the branches at the opening of the zariba, and the woman who had come out to close it asked us to wait outside until she had replaced them and got back into her hut. This we did, and when we saw her flying back to her hut we returned to camp.

SAMBURR KRAAL

This was the aspect of the Samburr kraal from our camp. Its size can be estimated from the little figures of the men on the ant-hill to the left of the leaning tree.

SWIVAN

The water-holes here are in the trees to the left. There was not a blade of grass to be found anywhere in the vicinity. Our donkeys, seen in the centre of the picture, had to occupy themselves with rolling in the sand of the river-bed instead of grazing.

Next morning the six donkeys and the two guides turned up correctly. The guides wanted to know what I was going to give them for the journey, and after I had agreed upon the amount of calico and wire, which was not exorbitant, they asked me to give it to them now, that they might leave it in their home. I do not like paying natives in advance, but as they had treated me so well here I complied.

Then the *Legwanan* said : " Here are the six donkeys I promised to lend you. Take them to Dôto, and if you do not get other donkeys there, take them to the Rendile country, and take these guides also. When you have done with the donkeys these men will bring them back, and you can give them what you think a fit reward for their owners. If a donkey dies on the way, we shall know that it is the hand of God, for men do not eat donkeys."

Now, I always like to try to understand the native point of view and ways of thinking, and this puzzled me. The two guides who were going to accompany me wanted their pay in advance, while the owners of the donkeys, who were not going with me, were to have theirs sent them. I could not think of any solution which would explain this, and so I asked Abdi. He said that he did not know, so finally I had to ask the *Legwanan*. "I have paid these guides in advance : would it not have been more fitting if I had paid the owners of the donkeys in advance, and the guides who come with me at the end of the journey ?"

The *Legwanan* laughed, and offered the explanation. If the guides returned with their present of brass wire or calico in their hands, they might be robbed in the way by anyone they met ; meaning that another Samburr might say, " Oh, you might give me half ; you can't want it all," and make him go shares. Then the next man they met would do likewise, till by the time they reached home they would have nothing left. If, however, they were bearing presents for someone else, no one would touch them.

The Samburr put a withy through the nostrils of their donkeys and catch them by this, or hold them whilst they are being loaded. While we were loading a man came up and said that he wanted to sell a donkey. We asked how much, and he named his price in brass wire and calico. It was a very reasonable price, and so I told Abdi to buy it.

The trade goods had already been loaded up, but they undid two loads, and gave him what he asked for. He then said he wanted more, so, after arguing a bit, I said, " Give him ten rounds more of brass wire." The man then insisted on twenty-five rounds more, and took his donkey away again.

Abdi said that several of them had been bargaining with him like that, and he did not understand it. " They start at a lower price than they want, and when you agree they raise it, and when you agree again they raise it again. How can you do business with people like that ? "

At last we got all our loads on to our donkeys, and after making final presents to the *Legwanan*, who had treated us so well, and his delightful old men, we made our adieux.

I shook hands with the *Legwanan*, and he said : " *Seriăn, Seriăn*, good-bye, and may God preserve you and give you a safe journey ! "

CHAPTER V

THE BARTA STEPPE

UNDER the Lorogai Mountains, at the head of the valley in which we camped, was a spring, and to this we had sent daily for water. Once the mountains were left, however, water was only to be had in wells dug in the dry river-beds until we should arrive at the General Matthews Range, under which there were said to be springs.

The country between these two ranges is an arid desert of stony ground, dotted with thorn-bushes and aloes, with occasional rocky ravines. The thorn-bush of this country is a leafless, low-spreading bush with cruelly hooked thorns. These thorns tore the donkeys' saddle-bags and our clothes and flesh. So bad are they that the thick-skinned giraffe give them a wide birth. I had occasion to notice this once when, in a thick patch of bush, a giraffe pushed into and broke the branches of an acacia to avoid brushing against the ends of the branches of one of these thorn-bushes next to it.

At night these thorns were especially bad, as one could not see how far their low branches stretched, and so would run against them. Sometimes they grew singly and sometimes in patches impossible to push through. It was not until we reached the mountains of Abyssinia that we finally lost sight of these diabolical thorns.

Grass grew in patches here and there, and the grazing

was fairly good in places, especially close to the mountains and in the valleys. The rest of the vegetation was that of the rocky, waterless type of country—stunted trees on the sides of the ravines, aloes, and cacti.

The animals also differed from those of the country we had left, for here were found only such animals as required little water—giraffe, oryx, the northern form of Grant's gazelle, and Grevy's zebra.

On the Laikipia plains, also a poorly-watered district, we had indeed seen a few oryx and this form of Grant's gazelle, but there had been eland, Thomson's gazelle, Chapman's zebra, and hartebeest.

About sixteen miles through such country northwards brought us to a dry, sandy watercourse, in which were dug a few wells. This was Barasoloi. There were Samburr near here, and sheep were being watered at the wells. The water was passed up in wooden vessels by hand and poured into troughs made of mud and stone.

We followed down the watercourse for a mile or so, and there camped near some wells. The grazing here was poor for the donkeys, used to the luxuriant grass of the upland prairies. However, they seemed to have stood the long march very well. Abdi proved himself splendid as donkey headman, being one of the few natives I have met who have been really kind to animals.

These donkeys, used by the tribes of these parts for baggage, are the quietest and most tractable animals imaginable. If their load slips down, they just wait for it to be put right again, or start grazing, but do not career about and kick it off as do mules. The loading of the donkeys in the morning was always a lengthy business, and the porters used to handle them rather roughly. If a donkey would not immediately come to where his loads were waiting for him, they used to haul at his ears and push and shove, which of course made him more obstinate.

Abdi used often to say, "You men do not understand donkeys ; you behave as fools towards them. Leave him alone." Then he used to go quietly up to the animal, pat him on the neck, and, taking him by the nose, lead him gently up.

New donkeys were sometimes rather difficult to load before they had got used to the porters, and the men would increase their natural alarm by rushing two or three at a time for one donkey, perhaps waving a saddlebag in its face and shouting loudly. One of the donkey-men called Tumbo (Stomach), a rather portly person, was quieter than the others and fairly trustworthy, and so I made him second-in-command of the transport, while I made a porter called Kitabu (Book) second-in-command of the porters. Both these men did exceedingly well.

One of the great secrets of trekking with donkeys is to have the loads on either side of an animal equally balanced. Sometimes only the matter of a few ounces on one side or the other will make the loads ride badly, and hence give the animal a sore back, besides giving the men the constant trouble of readjusting them.

As trade goods were given out constantly from one package or another, it was impossible to keep them absolutely balanced, and so we used sometimes to pick up a stone and put it on one side or the other to restore the balance. Over this sometimes the men used to display real African intelligence, for they might pick up a large boulder and put it in the saddle-bag on one side, and when that proved too heavy they would put another stone on the other side. These might be added to from time to time, till the donkey might be found carrying the superfluous load of half a dozen stones on either side besides its proper load.

On the morning after camping at Barasoloi, as I had not yet finished my observations, I sent the men and donkeys on ahead to Swiyan, following later with one of the guides. As we approached this place the country became most desolate, being merely a succession of stony hills and ravines without any vegetation.

I arrived at Swiyan, a water-hole in a river-bed, after midday, and found the men and donkeys here. The surrounding country was nothing but rock, and there was not a blade of grass anywhere in the vicinity for the donkeys to eat. Our guides told us that the first day to Barasoloi was the longest we should do, and that from there only two short marches remained to Lesirikän, the place under General Matthews Range to which we were going. The country between Swiyan and Lesirikän was absolutely uninhabited, being nothing but a rocky descent intersected by ravines.

We left Swiyan almost immediately after I arrived, so as to push on and sleep at some place where the donkeys might get a little food. After going for about five miles we met with some grass, and the guides wanted to halt here, saying that we could reach Lesirikän next morning after a short march.

Very fortunately I insisted on going farther, as I suspected, from the position of the range ahead, that the next day's march would not be as short as they said. We went on till dark, and camped in a ravine. I was only able to fill two tanks at Swiyan, as there were not enough men and animals without loads to carry all of them full.

Of these two tanks I kept one as a reserve, as I had lost faith in the guides.

During the night one of the men stole the water out of one of the guides' gourds, and the day before someone had helped himself out of my water-bottle. It was on both occasions impossible to tell who had done it, but in view of the waterless country we were about to tackle, I resolved to watch carefully, and to punish severely the next offence of a similar nature.

The first part of the next day's march was up and down rocky ridges very trying to the donkeys. The guides seemed rather at sea, and changed directions several times, and whenever I asked where Lesirikăn was, they pointed to a different part of the range ahead. I then asked when they had last been to Lesirikăn, and one of them said he had never been there, and the other, a very old man, said that he had been there when he was a warrior—viz., a young man.

This is a peculiarity of African guides. It is never necessary that they should know the way, and I have often had guides specially selected for me by a friendly chief who have never been to the place they are supposed to lead me to. When one reproaches them for taking one miles out of the way, they are generally quite indignant at the injustice of the rebuke, and say : " How could we do any better ? We have never been there before." If one asks why they came, they say, " Oh, we were told to," or, " We were frightened of you," or something equally intelligent.

On this occasion we had a very long and trying day, till at last, at about four o'clock, I found myself still five or six miles from the range, and the donkeys a long way behind, but between me and the mountain was a short grass prairie. When we reached the hill it was not certain that we should hit on water, as there might be water in some valleys and not in others. I could not see any signs of kraals under the mountain, so there was nothing to steer for except a likely-looking valley.

I resolved for the present to leave the donkeys and press on with the men with me, and try to reach the mountains to locate water before dark, and then we could make a fire to guide those behind.

While crossing this prairie I saw something on the ground two or three hundred yards to my left. I thought that it might be a small buck lying down, but brought out my glasses to make certain. There did not appear cover enough to conceal a hare, but as I watched the figure got up, and proved to be a lion, while five others sprang up from the same spot, one a fine black-maned lion. They turned, and started trotting away over the plain, having seen us.

They were too far off to risk a shot, so the only thing to do was to race after them in the hopes that they would stand and wheel round. After running the best part of a mile without gaining on them I was done, but couldn't resist even then taking a long pot-shot at the black-maned one. In my pumped condition I of course missed him, and there was nothing to do but to return to the porters.

As we reached the hill and came to a valley, we saw a rocky shelf at its base, and along this, to our joy, a herd of cattle was being driven. After ascending the rocky wall, we arrived on this shelf, and saw a couple of kraals.

As it was now after sunset, we paid no attention to them, but cut into the cattle-track, and followed this up the valley to water. Telling the rest to light a big fire there, I took two or three men, and returned to look for the donkeys. After five miles back across the plain we heard the voices of the donkey-men urging them on, and we presently located them in the dark. I gave out the water of the reserve tank to the men, who had not had water all day.

We got into camp just before midnight, and very glad were both men and donkeys to reach the end of the day's journey.

Next morning the local natives turned up with presents of milk and sheep. The milk brought in was divided up amongst the men. Soon afterwards Omari complained that while he was about his duties his portion had been stolen. Of course, the offender could not be found, but the gourd of milk had been left under a tree where four men were sitting, and either they must have taken it, or known who had done so.

I noticed that Omari had little hold over the men, and wanted to establish his authority. Moreover, I intended to stop these petty thefts. I therefore had all the men up, and explained the case to them, and said : " You may think that the theft of milk or water is a small matter, but it is not so. The taking of a man's water in a water-less country may be the taking of his life " (making a play on a Swahili word meaning " life," and also the condition of extreme thirst). " These men here, if they did not take this milk, know who took it. They must tell me, or all of them will be beaten."

I gave them a few minutes to make up their minds, and at the end of that time asked them again who had taken the milk. They said that they did not know, so I had them all put down and beaten.

This may sound cruel and unjust, but I dared not face the waterless country in front with men who thought that thefts of water or liquid would be overlooked. Under the provocation of extreme thirst men might bore holes in the water-tanks or barrels, and so endanger the lives of all, if discipline amongst them was not perfect.

The sheep of this country are of the fat-tailed variety, a circumstance which enables them to withstand short periods of drought and poor grazing, for the fat in the tail acts as a sort of reservoir, from which nutriment for the body may be drawn. One of the sheep they brought me was so enormously fat, and had such a huge.tail, that he was hardly able to move, and certainly could not have marched with us.

The people at Lesirikăn told me that they were formerly Torobo hunters, which statement I should like to have inquired into. Now they went in for breeding stock, and had become Samburr. They said that they had no donkeys to dispose of.

These Ogieg are a very widely though thinly distributed tribe, and although they call themselves by one name, Ogieg, and say that they are of one tribe, they differ much in customs and appearance, and somewhat in language, in each locality. For instance, the Ogieg on the Kikuyu escarpment have many differences in vocabulary from those on the Mau escarpment. Those we had met with on the Laikipia plains had a different appearance, but I had no opportunity of comparing their dialect with that of the former.

These at Lesirikăn appeared slightly different again, and spoke the same language as the Samburr. Probably some of them were originally Ogieg, and these had mixed with Samburr.

I heard that a day's march to the west there were both Turkana and Samburr, at a place called Baragoi, and two days northwards the Rendile country commenced. The Turkana and Samburr at Baragoi, it appeared, had fallen out over grazing grounds, and war between them was imminent.

I should like to have stopped here and tried for lion, as they told me that there were plenty, but I could not afford the time, so, after remaining that day to graze the donkeys and talk to the Samburr, we trekked to Baragoi.

Baragoi was a little *elañgata*—*i.e.*, dry river-bed in the plains which led to nothing, and emptied itself into nothing. Two watercourses flowing from opposite directions meet in a little dip, and in pools here enough water collects to last through the dry season. One large tree marks the spot.

On the plains west of this watercourse were situated the Turkana kraals, while the Samburr lived to the east, and both watered their flocks at the same holes. As I passed the Samburr kraals on my way to Baragoi some old men turned out, and escorted me down to the water, where I pitched camp. They poured out their troubles to me. It appeared from their accounts that the Turkana wished to oust them from their grazing ground, and from the well-grassed plains of Em Barta, threatening to fight them if they did not go. They said that they were not strong enough to fight with the Turkana, and they could not move, for they had nowhere else to go.

They naïvely told me that a few days back the Turkana had delivered an ultimatum, and were going to fight them, but that the news had come that I was on the way up. So they said to the Turkana : " You cannot fight with us, as we belong to the white men, and the white men will be very angry with you if you fight us, and our own white man is even now on the way up to help us."

Later in the evening the Turkana chief, an intelligent-looking little man, called Lôngellich, came in with some warriors. They were fine-looking fellows, but not so big as former accounts of the Turkana would have led one to imagine. One could hardly call them "a race of giants." I only saw one tall, thin youth who was my own height ; but the wonderful head-dresses, and the contrast between them and the usual small native of five foot six or so, makes them look perhaps taller than they really are.

The head-dresses are most curious and varied, consisting of the hair of their dead ancestors matted together with red earth, and plaited on to their own hair. The most popular style is that of the old-fashioned chignon, only rather exaggerated, as it sometimes reaches down the back almost to the waist. In this are poked a few ostrich-feathers, while at the end is often a long bit of wire, which curls backwards and upwards over the head. Some of these can be seen in the photograph.

The Turkana said that they had some donkeys, and would consider the question of selling to me. In the evening I secured some meat for the men.

The Baragoi plains resemble those of Laikipia, and are quite unlike the barren country through which we had passed. Grazing is good and game plentiful, consisting of lion, rhino, buffalo, oryx, eland, giraffe, and ostrich. The natives said that a lion had just killed an ostrich there, and after that two sheep. This is the only time I have heard of an ostrich being killed by a lion.

The Samburr brought in some sheep as a present, while the Turkana brought a bull. As the latter ran back to the kraal every time his attendant went away, I had finally to return it to them.

TURKANA WARRIORS

These are Turkana who came into my camp at Baragoi. Abdi is seen in a peaked cap on the right talking to Longellich, the Turkana chief. The right-hand figure of all is Masharia, the Kikuyu. In the foreground are the horns of a Grant's gazelle.

Next day they brought in three donkeys, which I bought for iron wire, calico, tobacco, and beads. This enabled me to send my Samburr donkeys back, so, giving the guides presents for the donkeys' owners, and messages for the *Legwanan*, I sent them off.

I was then asked to settle the dispute between the Turkana and the Samburr. The chief, Legarbes, of the Samburr, with his old men, sat on one side, and Lôngellich and his old men on the other, while Abdi interpreted, and I sat at the door of my tent. I said : " You have asked me to settle this dispute of yours, and if you wish I will do so, but first I must tell you that I am only a traveller who has come to see your country ; I am not the man at Nairobi (the Governor), or even the man at Laikipia (the nearest District Commissioner). If you want my judgment as a white man who favours neither the Turkana on the one side, nor the Samburr on the other, then I will give it you."

" Now I have come to this country, and wish to be friends with you both, and my judgment will be clearer than yours, for you are just as children or animals to me. To me it is just as it might be to you to settle the dispute between one and another sheep of your flocks. However, before I trouble myself with your affairs, you must promise to abide by my decision, or my work will be in vain."

To this they agreed.

Then I listened patiently to long dissertations on grazing grounds, ancient rights, etc., first from one side and then from the other. After each side had exhausted itself I sat awhile in silence to impress them, and also wrote a little in my pocket-book. Then I gave judgment, and said : " Listen to my words. War is a bad thing, and there is no need for war over this matter. There is much grass

6

in this place, and the water suffices for both. God gives grass that the cattle of man may feed and grow fat, and no man may say, 'This is my grass, and not yours.'

"Yet if two peoples live in one place, there will always be war and strife. Now, if there is strife here, the white men will not recognize that one party is the aggressor; they will look on you as both bad. If you see two dogs fighting, do you say, 'This one is right, and that wrong?' No; you beat them both, and they leave off fighting. If there is strife here, then may the white men come and say, 'These are bad people; let us beat them both.' So desist from strife between yourselves.

"Now, if one man has two wives in the same house there is always dissension in that house, so if two tribes have cattle on one grazing ground, and kraals in one place, so will there always be dissension in that place. It may arise over a big matter, or it may be over a small. It may be that two children quarrel over a small thing, and war is brought about between two tribes. Therefore I say to you, O Turkana, you must not cross this stream and build your kraals on the same side as the Samburr, and I charge you, O Samburr, that you do not move your kraals likewise to the west side of the stream.

"Now, this is my decision: You, the Samburr, graze your cattle on the east side of Baragoi, and when you come to water, approach from the east, and water your cattle from that side, and do not let even one lamb cross over to drink from the other side. You, the Turkana, graze your cattle on the west side, and likewise water from that side, and not one man or animal must cross to this side.

"Now as to grazing grounds, take this stream as your boundary, and after the stream take this big tree of Baragoi and the rocky peak of Ol doinyo Ñgiro you all see before you, and let this line be a boundary to you that neither tribe may cross to the other side.

" And during the time of the rains, when you move back from Baragoi, let the chief of the Turkana bid goodbye to the chief of the Samburr, and when you return again after the rains you must greet each other again, and renew the friendship and agreement you will make this day. What say you to my words—are they good or bad ?"

The two chiefs both agreed that they were good, and shook hands, and swore eternal friendship in my presence.

Having settled this dispute, the rival chiefs both said that they had heard about the Abyssinians, and feared aggression on their part. What were they to do ? 1 replied that the Abyssinians were old friends of the English, and that we should be seriously annoyed if they embroiled themselves with these people. However, there was no fear of this, as we were about to open a station at Marsabit, and so any complaints they had to make against the Abyssinians they could take there, and they would be settled.

I then said good-bye to the Turkana and Samburr, and made for the east side of Ol doinyo Ñgiro, which rose up to our front as a great, square, flat-topped mountain, about ten thousand feet high.

I was in front of the caravan as usual with Tengeneza, while my two boys were close behind, when we met an old rhino strolling towards us. We had seen a good few that day. I beckoned to the men with me to stop, and I went on alone towards him till I got within a hundred yards. As he was still advancing, I awaited him here with my camera. When he got to within fifty yards, I took the portrait here reproduced.

My men behind me, astonished that I did not shoot,
and seeing the rhino still advancing, could not contain
their excitement, and let loose a few stage-whispers.
The rhino heard, cocked up his ears, and made off to one
side. He then passed about a mile off the tail-end of
the caravan, who were straggling in the rear.

When they got into camp that day they were full of
the rhino, and tried to make out that it had nearly charged
them, and passed quite close. Tengeneza received these
remarks with a certain amount of scepticism, till at last
they said : " Of course, you people in front did not see
him." " See him ?" said Tengeneza. " Why, we took
his picture, and are sending it to Europe."

Two days' march brought us to a small brackish *sokota*
called Naisichu, under a spur of Ol doinyo Ngiro called
El-lebusi.

We camped here in a sandy hollow, which we reached
after a long stony descent. Near this place were some
Samburr kraals, the last we were to see.

Before we bid good-bye to these people and the Turkana
I must say a few words about their customs. Amongst
the Samburr their dead are sometimes buried, sometimes
not, but laid out in the bush for hyenas to eat, as is the
custom among the Masai. Big chiefs are always buried.
The Turkana and Rendile bury their dead, and probably
it is intercourse with these people which makes the
Samburr occasionally follow this custom.

The Samburr are usually referred to as "Samburu " by
those who do not know them, this word being a Swahili
corruption of their name, which is unpronounceable to the
Bantu.

A certain number of Samburr have intermarried with
the Rendile, and these can immediately be recognized

RHINOCEROS

He came advancing towards us all unsuspecting till one of my men made a noise which he heard. He then galloped off. The black rhinoceros, wandering about in the open as it does in British East Africa, falls a ridiculously easy victim to the rifle of the sportsman. This photograph was taken on the plains north of Baragoi.

from the fact that they have two front teeth, the two lower incisors, knocked out. This custom they hold in common with the Masai, but it is not practised by the Rendile.

The wooden cattle-bells of the Samburr are identical with the camel-bells of the Rendile and Somali, whereas the Masai generally have metal bells.

They are circumcised in the Masai manner, whereas the Turkana do not practise this rite, and the Rendile follow the Muhammadan custom in this matter.

The payment for a bride is three cows paid to the father. The Rendile payment is three female camels which have not yet given birth, one young female camel, and two eating camels, making six in all. Of these the latter two are the perquisites of the family, while the father has the remainder. On marriage the father sends two baggage-camels with his daughter to take her belongings to the husband's kraal. Later he visits them, and gives them two milk-camels, and takes back the two baggage-camels.

The Borana said that with them only two camels, one male and one female, are given for a girl. The Somalis sometimes give an enormous number of camels, as many as sixty or eighty.

The Samburr and many other natives I met struck me as being extraordinarily unobservant over matters strange to them. It often happened that they would come in to talk to me at night, and sit in the light of my lamp for perhaps half an hour or more without noticing it. Then suddenly one of them would see it, and point it out to the others, and they would exhibit great astonishment, and want to touch it. They used to ask whether it was really fire they saw inside it.

The Turkana, and many of the tribes to the north subsequently met with, carried about little wooden semi-circular stools or pillows. These would be used during the daytime as a very inadequate seat, and at night to keep their wonderful chignons off the ground.

They are credited with being a very treacherous people, and both Abdi and Omari used to rebuke me severely for letting them troop into my camp with their spears. They said that it was customary to make the Turkana leave their spears at a distance, and come in unarmed to a strange camp. I replied : "That would indeed be a silly thing to make them do, as they would at once think that we are afraid of them, which is not the case, is it ?" Abdi and Omari answered : "Oh, they are a very bad people."

They certainly must be very fine warriors, as this sentiment was reiterated by every tribe we passed through. The Reshiat said : "The war of the Turkana is a very bad war, for they follow a defeated people for days. When you go to look for them they are not there, and then they suddenly appear. They also fight at night; oh, their war is very bad." All the tribes seemed to think that this making of war at night was a very low-down game.

I was sorry that I was not able to see more of these people, as I took a great liking to them, and think that in the future some very fine material for troops may be forthcoming from amongst their numbers.

A curious weapon worn by them is a circular knife strapped round the wrist, and protected by a leather sheath. I asked to be shown how it was used, and I was again rebuked by Abdi, as he said that it was used only in treachery on a man standing talking to them, as I had been doing. Certainly the exposition of its use given me

TURKANA WARRIORS

The "chignon" of the third man from the front can be well seen, with an ostrich feather stuck in it. The Turkana men, like the Masai and Samburr, if they wear anything at all, wear a patch of skin suspended from the shoulders.

CAMP AT NAISICHU

On the right is my tent. In the foreground is the dusty track followed by herds coming in to water, who announce their approach by raising clouds of dust.

did not impress me with much idea of its value as a legitimate weapon of war, for the only possible method of using it is by giving a very cumbrous back-hander.

The shield is a small shield like that of the Samburr. It is made of ox or buffalo hide, the latter being preferred. The ears are not distorted and stretched as with the Masai ; they are only pierced to receive a small brass ring or pendant.

To return to our camp, Ol doinyo Ñgiro, a magnificent mountain, about ten thousand feet high, steep-sided and flat-topped, towered above us. There is said to be a settlement of Samburr on or near the top. The climate there must be excellent, for it must be cool, but not damp, as there is little or no rain in this country. Teleki passed the western side of this mountain on his journey to Rudolf.

CHAPTER VI

THE RENDILE COUNTRY

I ARRIVED at Naisichu late in the day, as I had stopped on the way to do some mapping. I found camp already pitched near the *sokota*, and everything buried in clouds of dust. Abdi said that some of the Rendile had been in to water their sheep here ; they waited some time to see me, but had now returned home.

The heat during the day had been great, especially when taking observations from the top of a rock. The daily east wind was more scorching here than we had hitherto experienced, as it blew off the sun-baked rocks, and the clouds of dust added to one's discomfort. The water from the *sokota* was brackish and most unpalatable.

Very glad were we to see the sun set, and at the same time the sirocco-like wind ceased, as was always the case. The night seemed so peaceful and cool after the tearing wind, dust, and heat of the day that it was a pleasure to sit out under the stars, and think over the events of the trek, and the possibilities of the future.

I had been hard at work all day ; the night before we had had an uncomfortable bivouac in a waterless camp, and the night before that I had been up nearly all night taking observations. Now I felt that I wanted a little relaxation before setting to work on my calculations and other work in hand.   So I called Sadi, my boy, and Abdi, and asked for a story.

Abdi told a Somali story about a jackal, which Sadi rudely said had neither point nor sweetness.   He himself then told some stories concerning Ibn Nuas, an Arab sage buried at Makka, only he put them into an East African setting.   These are Sadi's stories as far as I can remember them :

" Once upon a time there was a Sultan who disliked Ibn Nuas, and wanted to break up his house. To frustrate him Nuas burnt down his own house. When nothing but ashes remained, he gathered them up, and put them in sacks, and in the mouth of each sack he put a little coffee. He then loaded his sacks on donkeys, and left the town.

" Presently he met with a caravan of people who were coming to buy coffee. They asked him what he was carrying, and he said, ' Coffee.' Then they tried to persuade him to sell, but he said that he was going on a journey, and wanted it.

" At last they offered him a sack of gold for each sack of coffee, and he sold them his sacks after this manner. Ibn Nuas then returned to the city with sacks of gold, and people marvelled exceedingly.

" The Sultan called him, and asked whence he had obtained the money. He replied : ' There are people encamped outside the city who buy ashes for gold.'

" On hearing this news, the Sultan immediately burnt down his house, and packing up the ashes, sent forth his slaves to sell them. They met the caravan, and said : ' We have brought these ashes to sell for sacks of gold.' The strangers, who had already discovered how they had been deceived by Ibn Nuas, took these slaves and bound them.

" When the Sultan heard that his slaves had been taken and bound, and his house burnt down for no purpose, he was exceeding wroth, and took Ibn Nuas, and, sewing him up in a sack, left him anchored on the shore to be drowned by the incoming tide.

" Shortly afterwards a man passing heard a voice complaining from inside the sack : ' To be sewn up like this, just because I refused to marry the Sultan's daughter— truly this is tyranny !'

" Hearing this, the man unfastened the sack, and himself got inside, thinking that he would thereby obtain the Sultan's daughter. Ibn Nuas sewed him up, and went home, and sat for seven days forging letters in the handwriting of the deceased parents of the Sultan and the Wazir.

" The following Friday he bound the letters to his head, plunged into the sea, and then appeared, all dripping, before the Sultan in the congregational mosque. He unfastened them from his head, and gave them to the Sultan and the Wazir.

" They read the letters, and found that they were invitations from their deceased relations to visit them in the next world. The Sultan and Wazir requested Nuas to lead them to their parents, so all set out in a boat.

" Ibn Nuas then said : ' You remain here while I go down first to open the gate.' He plunged into the sea, and hid under the stern of the boat for an hour, and then reappeared, and invited them to follow him. Whereupon they plunged in, while Ibn Nuas clambered into the boat, and left them there to drown.

" When he arrived on shore, he said that they had found the next world so pleasant that they had decided to remain there, and so had sent him back to become Sultan."

" It is also said concerning Ibn Nuas that once upon a time a man was condemned by the Sultan to death. Ibn Nuas asked that he should be spared, and the Sultan said : ' Yes, he shall be spared if you will do two things for me.'

" Ibn Nuas replied : ' And what is the first ?'

" ' The first is to make me a bag of stone.'

" Ibn Nuas then told the Sultan to prepare the materials, so a heap of stones was collected. He then said : ' This is good, but where is the thread ? How can I sew a bag without thread ? Bring some stone thread, and I will sew your bag for you.'

" The Sultan said : ' You have defeated me, O Ibn Nuas, but you will not do the next thing, which is to build me a house in the air.'

" Ibn Nuas then secretly made large kites, with a framework of bamboo, and to these he fixed dummy figures and bells, and then floated them over the palace at night. The Sultan heard the bells at night, and in the morning wanted to know the meaning.

" Ibn Nuas said : ' My workmen have been up all night, measuring the trenches and digging the foundations, and they are now ready for the coral,* mortar, and water. Will you please send it up to them, that they may continue the work.'

" The Sultan said : ' Your wisdom is great, O Ibn Nuas, and so I will pardon this man.' "

Omari, who had joined us, then said :

" Once upon a time there was a Sultan who had a thousand goats. Then all the Sultan's goats died, except one female.

" At this time a stranger arrived in the city who had

* Coral rag is the general building material on this coast.

one male goat. The Sultan borrowed the goat, and bred from it till three kids were born.

" The stranger then asked for his goat to be returned, but the Sultan said : ' Wait till I get ten kids, and then I will divide them.' When ten had been born, the Sultan said : ' You must first plant my field for me before you have the goats.'

" The stranger did this, and by the time he had finished there were twenty young goats.

" He then asked for his share of the goats, but the Sultan refused to give him either his male goat back or any of the kids, saying : ' The kids belong to the female, and are therefore mine, and the male goat is a tax you must pay me.'

" The stranger then complained to Ibn Nuas, who replied : ' Do as I bid you, and you shall have your goats.'

" He then went to the Sultan, and said : ' It were fitting that you had a new audience - chamber built. Therefore you must send the crier round, to order every person in the town—man and woman, great and small— to repair to the palace to-morrow, and set to work on this building.'

" The Sultan agreed, and the crier was sent round. Everyone in the town went to work at the new building, except the stranger, who had been told by Ibn Nuas what to do. As they were at work, he passed, carrying a water-pot on his head.

" The Sultan had him called, and asked why he was not working. He replied : ' My father has given birth to a child, and so I have to look after him.'

" The Sultan said : ' Who has ever heard of a man giving birth to a child ?'

"Ibn Nuas, who was sitting with him, said : ' Have you never heard of a man giving birth ?'

"The Sultan said : ' No, never.'

"Then said Ibn Nuas : "If a husband comes from afar and lives with a woman, to whom do the children belong, and whom do they work for ?'

"The Sultan replied : ' The husband.'

"' And if the husband goes away again, who takes the children ?'

"The Sultan replied : ' The husband takes as many as he pleases.' " (This is according to the Sheria and Muhammadan law.)

"Then said Ibn Nuas : ' Why did a male goat come and give birth to children here, and when he wanted to go away again, you said that the children were not his ?' "

The Samburr at Naisichu informed me that there was fresh water under Ol doinyo Mara, rather nearer the Rendile kraals, but that the Rendile brought their camels here, as the brackish water was better for them. The clouds of dust disturbed by the herds of camels coming in to water could be seen from afar, so the Samburr always knew when they were coming.

In most of the low country, in places where there was both salt and fresh water, the camels are taken to the salt water in preference by both the Borana and Rendile.

Four Rendile old men came in to see me the morning after I arrived at Naisichu. One of these was a chief, called Leshaulil, the man I had heard of at Obiroi from my old friends there.

The first thing I noticed about the Rendile was their hoarse voices, which at once reminded me of Somalis.

They also made use of the Somali stomatic gutturals, which I have never heard amongst any other people. This fact alone leaves little doubt in my mind that they were, as they themselves say, once Somalis, but have been driven out of Somaliland.

They are supposed to be descended from the Garre Somali, and were formerly Muhammadan, but have now lost this religion. This contention that they were once Muhammadan seems true, as they invoke Allah, "Illahu," as do the Somalis ; and sometimes a man may be heard droning, as if reading the Koran, but no distinct words are uttered. As Abdi said, "It would take but little to make them embrace Islam."

We can thus assume that they were driven out of Somaliland some time subsequent to the advent of Islam in that country, but probably before it had got much hold. Their present religion is a most primitive belief in God, and is rather like that of the Masai.

It is probable that after they left Somaliland their incipient Muhammadism was forgotten, and they reverted to their ancient belief in a Supreme Being and spirits. Their present religion probably represents the ancient worship of the Somalis before the advent of the Muhammadan era.

After greeting me with "Nabai'da," which some of them pronounce "Nabiai'da," they sat down, and by much questioning I elicited a fair amount of news from them, though it took me over five hours' solid talking to do so. It appeared that there was a large kraal a few hours eastward, and that probably some camels could be purchased there.

They informed me that the current rate of exchange was thirteen sheep and goats for a baggage-camel, trained

RENDILE STOCK

The Rendile are very rich in stock, especially in camels. It is usual for boys and women to herd the goats close by the kraal, whilst the men take the camels out to graze, perhaps several miles away. Different herds of camels can be seen in all directions being driven back to the kraal, which can be seen in the distance rather to the left.

to carry loads, and twelve for an untrained one. However, I was told that they would not be likely to sell them for sheep and goats only. They would probably want—

2 *dotis* of *maradufu,*
2 *dotis* of *amerikani,*
2 rounds of brass wire,
2 rounds of iron wire,
2 male sheep or goats,
2 female sheep or goats.

This sounded cheap enough, but to be prepared to meet the demand, I thought it wise to increase my stock of sheep and goats. As the Samburr at this place had been offering some for sale, I instructed Omari to buy all that came in. We obtained forty in this way, which were subsequently used to feed the men, as the Rendile did not want them.

It appeared that there are three routes from Naisichu outwards—viz. :

1. Round south of Ñgiro, and then northwards to Rudolf and Mount Kulal. On this route they reported water at every day's camp. This would, when it reached the west of Ñgiro, be the same as that taken by Teleki.

2. Round east of Ñgiro, and between that mountain and Ol doinyo Mara to Kulal. This had water at the end of every day. From Kulal the route up Rudolf could then be taken, or a waterless route inland.

3. A route to Koroli, crossing a waterless desert called the Elges.

I immediately decided in favour of the last, if I could obtain camels, as it would cross quite unknown country. However, it would have been hopeless to try it with donkeys, and so my first consideration was to obtain camels. I did not attempt to obtain any more information from Leshaulil at present, except the names of camps, a few notes about customs, and a little local news.

It may seem, to anyone unversed in native methods, that an unnecessarily long time was spent in eliciting such information, but it was not, as at the end of that time I felt practically certain that all the notes I had made were as accurate as it was possible to have them from native sources.

The patience required to get accurate information from natives is infinite. One first of all goes through a series of questions, and jots down the pith of the replies. Sometimes an answer will be a long dissertation on nothing in particular, which must be patiently listened to till it has exhausted itself, and then the original question must be asked again in a slightly modified form. Having been through one's list once, it is then necessary to go through the whole thing again, only this time so wording each question that it is not recognizable as the same as that asked before, and so does not suggest to the native mind the answer just given.

For instance, supposing a question in the first list was, "What is the name of the first camp on the way to Koroli ?" the similar question in the second series might be, "What is the nearest water in that direction ?" or, "Where do the camels of such a place water ?" Having gone through your second series, you find that practically none of the answers tally—some, no doubt, because your own questions are at fault, and the others because the answers are wrong.

You then go through a third time, trying, if possible, to reconcile the two answers by asking, perhaps : "Why do not the camels water at Arsim ?" (the first camp given).

Then you either hear that there is no water there, when you were told before that there was plenty, or you get a reasonable answer, such as that it is too fresh for them, or that it is drawn up from a well.

According as the answers are favourable or unfavourable, I mentally mark up the names or distances given with good or bad marks, and when one place gets a preponderance of good marks, it is allowed to stand in my notes, perhaps with a query mark after it, till I can find an opportunity of checking it with someone else.

I gave the Rendile each a length of *maradufu*, and over this present there was a discussion as to the measurement of a *doti*. A *doti* is a length of two yards of calico or other stuff. As natives have no fixed measures, they generally use the length of the forearm from the elbow-point to the tips of the fingers as a measure. Four of these are supposed to go to a *doti*, but with a long-armed man it would probably measure rather over two yards.

The Rendile stoutly maintained that six arms'-lengths went to a *doti*, and that four lengths were too short to wear. As I wished to make a favourable impression, I waived this point, and allowed them each to measure out one of their own *dotis* of six lengths. However, apparently they thought that this was too short, and after each measurement of an arm's-length they ran their hands six inches or a foot along the cloth before the next measurement. Abdi good-humouredly stopped them, and then explained that this was a present, and perhaps it did not matter, but when it came to business and buying camels, they would have to measure fairly.

In all my subsequent dealings with the Rendile I

noticed this Somali trait of trying to make a bit coming
out, as they would always insist on taking the measures
themselves, and always attempted to cheat in so doing.
Abdi was very down on them at first, and used to make
them measure over and over again, sometimes pretending
to drop the end of the calico by accident if he thought
that they had made too much, and at others turning
round sharply, as if to speak to someone, and pulling it
out of their hands.

However, I often gave Abdi the tip to overlook these
little perquisites later, as I found that it gave them such
intense satisfaction to think that they had been sharp
enough to cheat us out of a yard or two that they would
often come to easier terms. The sight of one man
cheating a little at each measure while Abdi and I pretended not to see would perhaps encourage another man,
who had no intention of selling, to part with a camel.

After receiving the price agreed upon, further presents
were always demanded before the camel was handed over.
These would generally take the form of a knife, some
beads, cotton, needles, tobacco, and a few odds and ends.
Then perhaps the seller would insist on another length
of calico in addition, or the deal was off.

We would then say that we wanted to measure the
stuff he had already had, to see if it was all right. The
man would be so frightened at losing the few inches
he had made with great difficulty on each measurement
that he would at once waive his claim to another length.

On parting with Leshaulil, he told me that they expected to see me at their kraal next day, but that they
could not attend to the selling of camels for two days,
as there was a yearly festival to pray for rain, in which
all took part.

RENDILE COUNTRY

This is the forbidding-looking land of flat desert, covered with dust and stones, which we entered after descending from the Samburr country. Arid and devoid of vegetation as it looks, however, the numerous Rendile camels are able to find plenty of grazing amongst the stones.

Finally, they carried off Abdi to their kraal that night, saying that then I should be sure to turn up next morning. Abdi went off, delighted at the prospect of filling himself with camel-milk, a luxury he had not tasted for some time.

In the morning we descended by a stony path to the Rendile country, which is situated at a still lower level than the country we had left. On the way down we suddenly came round a corner, and met some Samburr sheep being driven by a woman and a man. Directly they saw me they dropped down and clutched up handfuls of grass, and then advanced slowly and pressed them into my hands, as a sign of peace.

If the low thorn country under the Lorogai had seemed an inhospitable desert to us, it was only because we had not seen the Rendile country. To anyone coming the other way it must appear like Paradise. A bare, desolate waste, covered with rocks and dust, and dotted with little stony hills, was the country we struck at the foot of the descent. The only vegetation apparent was the bare thorn-bush we already hated so cordially, and a dry, leafless plant which affords grazing for the camel.

In the distance we could see the little huts of the Rendile kraal, blurred by heat and dust. Close to this, near a dry river-bed, were a few isolated clumps of bush, and for these we steered.

As we approached, Abdi and some old men appeared, and conducted us to one of these clumps, which was quite thick and offered fair shade inside. Two old men busied themselves cutting a space in this retreat for my tent, while women brought twenty *hans* of water, which they had fetched for us that morning from the nearest water-hole, several hours distant.

7—2

The *han* is a water-vessel made out of closely-plaited grass, with a tight-fitting lid. It is generally kept in a little crate of sticks, which prevents it being staved in, especially when being carried on a camel. It is identical in both name and make to that in use in Somaliland.

It appeared that Leshaulil was only an under chief, and the chief of the kraal, a stoutish party, came over presently to see me. My retriever Narok had felt the heat and dust of this low country intensely, and was now lying panting in the shade of the clump. The Rendile chief was very interested in her, and drew my attention to the *hans* of water, saying that the dog was thirsty. I was very struck with this, as natives are generally so callous of the sufferings of animals. I had refrained from giving Narok a drink out of a *han* for fear it should be as offensive to the Rendile as it is to the Somali to see a dog touch any of their belongings, and therefore I was awaiting the advent of the loads and Narok's plate.

The two old men, who, having cleared a space for the tent, were now making a little zariba, I learnt were Tumals. These are a race of blacksmiths who live amongst the Somalis, but who do not share their religion. They are looked down on, and not allowed to intermarry with the Somali. They are, by some, supposed to be, with the Midgans or hunters, the original inhabitants of the country.

It was interesting to find these people also existed among the Rendile. They were now busy at work with an implement I had not seen for a long time. This was a *hangol*—a stick with a fork at one end and a hook at the other, used for hooking out or shoving in the thorn branches of a zariba.

When my loads arrived, I gave out a string of beads to

RENDILE MAN AND WOMAN

The lady is very coy about having her photograph taken, and is clutching the man's hand to give her confidence. The Rendile do not, as a rule, wear so much brass and iron wire as the Masai. This lady has a certain amount, and it can be seen even in the picture how tight it is round the arms. Leaves are sometimes stuffed in underneath the coils to relieve the friction on the skin. In the thick clump to the left a place was prepared by the Tumals for my tent.

each of the ladies who had brought in water. Many of them wore their hair in a peculiar fashion, resembling a cock's comb, on the top of their head. This was made by drawing the hair up, tightly plaiting it on the top of the head, and plastering it with red earth. Others wore their hair in ringlets, like the Somalis. Their hair was longer and straighter, and their features more regular, than the women of the tribes. I had just left—the Masai and Samburr.

In spite of the harsh gutturals, their voices sounded softer and more feminine than those of any woman I had met as yet on my trek northwards.

The old chief, after watching me sitting in my deck-chair, said that he was sure he could do that, and turned me out and himself settled down in it, lolling back with great satisfaction to himself.

At two o'clock herds of camels began appearing from all directions, advancing on the kraal. They generally are driven back at sunset, but to-day they were coming in early because of the festival. It transpired that people had come in from several kraals near, with their camels, to celebrate this event.

There appeared to be an enormous number, but camels are most deceptive. I thought that I would take Omari in, so I asked him how many camels he reckoned were coming. He guessed three hundred thousand. I then said that there were not more than three thousand, and we started counting some of the herds, to get a rough idea. In this way I gathered there were only about fifteen hundred. Omari said that he was counting the head, hump, and tail as three separate animals.

Presently the two Tumals returned, bringing a branch. This they spat on, and then seized my hands and spat on them also, and gave me the branch. Knowing that this custom of spitting bestows a blessing amongst the Masai, I was not as incensed as I might reasonably have been expected to be, but merely retired behind my tent to wash my hands with a little of the precious water out of the *hans*. I asked Abdi to find out what was to be done with the branch.

It appeared, after questioning them, that at this festival everybody had a branch of this particular bush tied up over their hut, and they had brought one to put over my tent, so that I should not be left out in the cold. They then excused themselves and hurried back to the kraal, as the remainder of the day was to be devoted to feasting.

CHAPTER VII

THE RENDILE COUNTRY (*continued*)

WHEN it came to the point, it appeared that the Rendile really did not wish to sell camels. They hoard camels as a miser hoards gold. It was not a question of price, as I was prepared to pay anything within reason so long as I did not absolutely spoil the market. This is a point I am always very careful about, as I have so often met with preposterous demands on the part of natives who have been spoiled by rich travellers.

Just to save themselves trouble, and to make themselves appear great in the eyes of the savage, some of these people give ridiculous rewards for the least service rendered. The result is that the poor traveller or hunter who follows is treated with contempt, and cannot get any of his needs attended to.

On the other hand, I quite recognize that the country and goods of natives are their own, and that one has no right whatever to force them to give up their land or to sell goods which they wish to preserve for themselves. Many travellers get annoyed when they find that natives will not sell them their stock, and take it by force, thinking that this is quite justifiable if they leave presents in exchange.

Unjust action of this sort is generally deeply resented by natives, and remembered for years. The news spreads

quickly to all the neighbouring tribes, and may be the
cause of subsequent travellers being molested by the
people through whom they pass. One does not expect
to meet with gratitude or deep affection from natives,
but they are very sensible of just and considerate treat-
ment. Wherever I have been I have always been most
careful in all my dealings with natives of the country,
paying for everything received or service rendered, and
conforming to their wishes as much as possible, but, on
the other hand, allowing no impertinence or insolence on
their part. The result is that I could revisit any of the
places I have ever been to, and be received well, and in
most cases with open arms, by the inhabitants.

Here it became at once apparent that the Rendile were
not anxious to sell, or, at any rate, wished to haggle for
days before parting with anything. They at once offered
sheep for sale, some of which I bought, so as to encourage
a desire for my calicoes amongst the others.

The Rendile mark all their sheep and goats by a semicircle cut out of the front of either ear, in shape like a
large bite out of a piece of bread and butter.

Abdi and I put our heads together, and for two days
we talked solidly to the old men about different matters,
bringing in the subject of camels every now and again.
Every time we reverted to the subject of camels they said
there was no hurry, they would see about it in a few days'
time. They also harped continually on an ancient
grievance that somewhere some white man had taken
camels for nothing. At last, on the third day, some of
them said that there were a few men in the zariba who
wished to sell, and finally one camel was produced to see
what sort of price we would give.

It did not take long to fix up a price satisfactory to

both parties, but this having been decided on, the work
had only just begun, for calico was folded and unfolded
time after time, and measured again and again. They
were really most exasperating, the way they insisted on
slowly measuring out each bit of calico. If they thought
they had not made enough, they would start all over again
from the beginning.

Abdi's tact and patience filled me with admiration, as
I felt a hundred times like turning them all out of camp,
although I knew we must do our best to bear with them.
Finally one man insisted that two identical bits of calico
were of different quality, and wanted us to undo some of
our bales for him to choose from. This I did not wish to
do, for, as Abdi wisely said, " They always want all they
see, and we must only put a little out each day." I solved
the problem by tearing a bit off each piece, and, putting
them together, asked him to say which was torn from
which piece. After great cogitation he confessed himself
defeated.

The first deal was apparently satisfactory, for after it
had been concluded three more camels appeared, and
were bought for the same price. Only a few camels are
trained for loads by each man to carry his own or his
family's belongings. As want of grazing might cause
them to move at any time, they are naturally unwilling to
sell any of these, unless they have too many, which is
seldom the case.

Leshaulil told us that there were no more men in the
kraal who wanted to sell, but that the Rendile, at a place
called Arsim, a day's march away, had sent in to say that
they were coming into Disbahai, our present quarters, and
wished me to await them, as they had some camels to sell.

As I was loath to waste any more time in inactivity, I

left Abdi at Disbahai to arrange for the purchase of camels when the Arsim people arrived, and decided to visit the north end of Ol doinyo Mara myself, so as to sketch the country in that direction, and take some observations on Mount Kulal.

The heat and dust of this low country is so great that marches through the heat of the day are impossible, even for the Rendile themselves. I had asked for guides the night before, but they did not turn up, so I set out with a few of the men before sunrise.

We followed the foot of Ol doinyo Mara, and at our first halt Leshaulil and another Rendile came up breathless, saying that they had heard that we had started without guides, and so had hurried after us. I was very glad to see him, as I always found him pleasant and obliging, and ready to help us, whereas the other chief, though always most genial, never did anything for us.

At 2 p.m. we halted under the hill, and Leshaulil said that there was a water-hole on a terrace of rock above us. I sent some of the men up with Leshaulil, and they found a little water which had been fouled by a giraffe. They brought back a bucket and tank of this, which was very dirty and muddy.

At sunset we proceeded again, and marched three hours by moonlight, reaching a northern spur of Ol doinyo Mara, from which Kulal could be seen. I then ascended the hill above camp, and took observations, finishing up at 4 a.m. I returned to my sleeping men, and turned in till seven o'clock, when I commenced observations again.

At 3 p.m. we started back, arriving at Disbahai at midnight. The people of Arsim had not come in, as one of their women had just given birth to a child, so I decided to trek off there.

I had doctored many of the Rendile here for ailments, real and imaginary, and now the chief, a robust, jovial-looking man, came into my camp with a very long face, and said that he was very ill, and wanted some medicine. Various inquiries failed to elicit the nature of his ailment, so I asked how long he had been feeling bad, expecting to get the answer, "Since yesterday," or, "Since last night." To my surprise, however, he said that he had been ill from childhood until now. On imparting this information he shook his head and groaned.

As he had been perfectly fit before, I consulted the invaluable Abdi as to the nature of his affliction. Abdi said : "Oh, he has seen you giving out medicines here, and now he hears that you are going away, he thinks that he will never get a chance of obtaining some unless he asks you to-day."

There was one displeasing bit of news I was told here, and that was that the Reshiat, at the north of Lake Rudolf, had been attacked by the Abyssinians, and they had all taken refuge in the islands or on the other side of the lake. If this was true, it was a bad look-out for us, as it was in this country that we had our first opportunity of replenishing our supply of food. If the Reshiat no longer existed there, I did not know where we might be able to procure food.

A meeting of Rendile elders assembled to ask my advice, saying that, having heard this, they feared the Abyssinians greatly. Even now they were pushing down towards them. They had sent to ask the white men to help them against the Abyssinians, and we had not done so. What were they to think ? That we were in league with the Abyssinians, or that we feared them ? Now they asked me what they should do.

I replied : " You ask me why the white men do not come down here that they may protect you against the Abyssinians. I do not know what is in the heart of our chief, but I know this : yours is a very bad country ; there is no water and no food for us here. What white man would desire to come to your country ? What have you to offer him ? Will you build him a house to live in ? will you go and fetch his loads here from Nairobi ? will you offer him great wealth when he comes ? No, you have nothing.

" Now, as regards these Abyssinians, be careful not to embroil yourselves with them, as they are strong and numerous. Where you see one in front there will be a thousand behind.

" Now, this place is far from the white man's country, and he does not know what happens here ; and now I see your state is like that of which the Swahili poet Liongo* wrote : ' Before me is a lion, and behind me is the deep sea.' For before you are the Abyssinians, and behind you the white men. Now, my advice to you as a friend is this : If the lion advances towards you, fall back to the deep sea. Should it then be said by the white men, ' Why do you crowd into our country ?' say to them : ' We cannot do otherwise, for there is a lion in front of us.'

" Now, of these two things, the lion and the deep sea, which is the stronger ? Can the lion cross the deep sea ? No ; therefore choose the deep sea."

After this meeting, I spent the rest of the day buying *hans* and camel-mats, and wanted to trek off at 7 p.m., at which hour the moon rose. We procured a guide, who said that it was better to wait till the moon got up a

---

* Liongo was a famous chief, poet and bowman, who lived at Ozi, on the coast, several hundred years ago.

bit, pointing to its position at ten o'clock, and then we should get into Arsim early in the morning. His last words as he left our camp to go back to the zariba were : "Have no fear ; you just sleep, and I will wake you up at the right time to get into Arsim in the morning."

The men all went to sleep, but, having had experience of native guides, I sat up and waited. Ten o'clock came, and then eleven and twelve, and yet no guide. I sent Abdi over to the zariba, and he presently returned with Leshaulil, who had volunteered to replace the guide, and also some women to load our camels for us, as we had not yet learnt the intricacies of fastening the saddle-mats.

The Rendile use camel-mats much smaller than those of the Somali. These are kept in position by four poles fastened as in the photograph. These poles also serve the purpose of keeping the loads from rubbing against the animal's back and sides. They can also be used at the journey's end for making into a hut. The mat, called *herio*, as in Somali, is made of aloe-fibre, as is also the rope used for fastening them and the loads to the camels. The Somalis do not use aloe for the *herio*, as they say that it is bad for the back.

The camel is led by a rope passing round the animal's lower jaw, and not fastened to its nose, as amongst the Arabs, whilst strings of camels are formed by fastening the jaw-rope of one animal to the saddle of the one in front. In Somaliland and Arabia this rope is fastened to the tail of the leading animal.

We heard glowing accounts of Arsim, being told that we should be able to buy unlimited camels there, and that we should also find a running stream. Natives always give one such optimistic accounts of places to be visited ; it always appears that there is nothing whatever to be had in the place where one is, but always a march ahead almost anything can be obtained.

We felt very pleased to hear about the water, as we had had either to send for our water from afar, or buy it of the Rendile women during our stay at Disbahai. For five days now I had not been able to wash my hands or face.

The loading and preparations were not finished till 3 a.m., and then we trekked steadily till midday on the morrow, at which time we arrived at a big kraal at Arsim. The morning had been terrifically hot, and both men and donkeys were tired out.

On arrival, the *Legwanan* of the kraal, an old man called Ol lasarge, brought me a very nasty concoction of sour camel's milk, mixed with muddy water, in a dirty vessel. I was too thirsty to reject it, and after having drunk some, fully endorsed Abdi's opinion that a mixture of sour camel's milk and water was the surest means of quenching thirst. Certainly one would not drink more of it than one could help.

The water, we were told, was still two hours distant. As we wanted to procure camels, we decided to stop here amongst the kraals, and buy water from the Rendile. The reason that the Rendile live always at a distance from the water is to obtain grazing for their camels. Water-holes are so few and far between in this country that if all the kraals camped near the water-hole from which they draw water, the grazing would be finished in a day or two.

Ol lasarge was an old man who had become rather imbecile in his old age. He protested volubly that he would make all arrangements for me to buy camels, and do everything he could for me. He had a nice quiet *laibon* (medicine-man) called Beua, who, it transpired,

RENDILE MAIDENS

This photograph was taken in the valley of Arsim. The girls are dressed in skins, with numerous strings of big Somali beads round the neck, and bracelets of brass wire. They are wearing sandals, like all the natives of this country, as the ground is too hot for the bare feet. Their hair is in ringlets, and not done up in the crest or comb affected by the Rendile matrons.

was a relation of Abdi's. Abdi had become very *distrait* since his arrival here, and I then found out that he had discovered his mother in the kraal. It appeared that he had originally been a Rendile, and had been captured as a child by a raiding party of Somalis.

Beua told us that the old men of the kraal were just waiting to see what Ol lasarge did, and if, as they expected, he did nothing, they would themselves arrange for me the selling of camels. There were, they said, several men anxious to sell, but the chief would not let them. Finally one man came up, and said that he wanted to sell a camel, but that he was frightened of Ol lasarge, and so would bring it that night.

He had just gone back to fetch it, when Ol lasarge appeared, and, sitting down, said that he had taken a great fancy to me. On my arrival, he had given me milk, referring to the aforesaid milk and water, and now he would arrange for me concerning the purchase of ten camels, and, having settled everything for me, he would take me by the hand and lead me to the next kraal and arrange for everything there also. I was to do nothing myself ; he would fix up everything.

I sincerely hoped that he would not carry out this threat, as he had successfully prevented my buying camels here, and would probably do likewise at the next kraal. However, I replied that he had treated me as a son.

Abdi then said to the old man : " Our master has taken a great liking to you. He has heard that you have a daughter, and wishes to marry her. What dowry will you bestow on her ?" I then told Abdi to say : " Tell my father that it is growing late, and he is old ; let him return to his house before darkness sets in." We were anxious to get rid of him before the man with the camel turned up, but he stopped on ; and finally, on his way back, he met the camel being brought down for sale. The owner, when he saw Ol lasarge, turned round and hurried back, and so we lost our chance that night.

Next day we managed to buy the camel, and Leshaulil, who had been visiting a neighbouring kraal, came in with the news that they were anxious to sell some camels. As nothing was doing, we decided to go on, and Beua said that he would accompany us.

Leshaulil now wanted to return. He had done well by us, as twice, although himself a chief, he had taken the place of the missing guides, and now he had ascertained the whereabouts of camels for sale. Further than this, he had introduced me in favourable terms to the kraals here, as one who would not harm or take advantage of anyone. News of this sort spreads quickly, and we subsequently found that word was sent as far as Laipora that a " quiet and gentle white man " was coming up.

It is curious that amongst natives, so noisy in themselves, a quiet white man inspires confidence. A man that raves and storms is either laughed at or detested by natives.

At last, after prodigious trouble and incessant talking, and visiting different kraals, we managed to collect eleven camels in all. It seemed impossible to persuade anybody to sell me any more unless I seriously delayed my journey by trekking still farther to the east. I had hoped to obtain about fifty, so as to carry a food-supply and water in *hans*, and have plenty of spare animals, so as to be able to make forced marches. I now had to do the best I could with these eleven.

During this time we had been either buying our water or sending to the spring at Arsim, or another, called

El Laut. As these two watering-places, both of which had only brackish water, were the last this side of the waterless Elges, it now became necessary to make preparations to cross this waterless tract. It was impossible to take the donkeys across this stretch, even if they had not been played out, whilst several of them had died of tsetse. I decided to send what remained of the donkeys back to Nairobi.

I thought that I should have some difficulty in obtaining volunteers for the return journey, as the men would consider it a disgrace to be sent back before the journey was finished. To my surprise, however, there was no difficulty in finding men. The heat of the Rendile country had told on them already, as also the discomfort of always being far from water. Moreover, having heard exaggerated accounts of the Abyssinians from the local natives, they were beginning to fear that we should not be well received by them.

I did not hear till long afterwards, but it transpired later that a great number of the men talked of returning from here, and even of running away. Rumours were bruited around that they would have various limbs amputated and dissected on arrival in Abyssinia, and altogether, if I had known it, my chances of losing most of my men at this camp were great.

Some of the porters said : " But if we return without the master, and with no letter from him, how shall we explain our presence in Nairobi ?" Others said : " Oh, we will say that he died, or was killed in the way." Then some of the bolder spirits spoke up, and said : " You men have no hearts ; we are going with the master. We don't believe in your stories of the Abyssinians, but if it comes to dying in the way, then we will all die together."

8

From scraps of conversation I afterwards heard, it appeared that my boy Sadi, the weakling whom I had wished to leave behind, and a small man called Osmani, were the foremost amongst those who resolved to push on.

Abdi, of course, was not admitted to these counsels, or he would have immediately told me about them. However, of all this I knew nothing, so I selected five men to return with the donkeys as well as the Suk guide.

Of this personage, enlisted at Rumuruti, I have said nothing. He was a cheerful, genial individual. According to him, he always knew the country just ahead and just behind, but throughout our journey he had not felt competent to guide us during a single day. As Abdi said : "What strange people are those of this land ! Now, there is that Suk. He never knows the country till we have passed it, and then he says, ' Oh, I was living in a Samburr kraal there once,' or, ' Do you remember that valley we passed to-day ? We once had some goats we had captured from the Turkana there.' "

The other men were selected from the worst of my porters. A number of things had to be arranged : guides had to be procured for them ; food sufficient to take them to Rumuruti had to be issued ; money for the purchase of food from there to Nairobi, and a host of other small matters.

Finally, I wrote my last letters for home, and giving them final instructions for the journey and presents for the chiefs they were to pass on the way, I bade them good-bye, and turned my attention to our preparations for crossing the waterless Elges.

CHAPTER VIII

THE WATERLESS ELGES

ELEVEN camels may sound ample for one white man's caravan, but it was not so. I still had twenty loads of food for the men, which took five camels to carry. It was also impossible to pass through a country like Abyssinia empty-handed, and my trade goods and water-tanks were carried by the other six. My personal kit, instruments, books, medicines, etc., were divided up into light loads, and carried by the men who were not leading camels.

Six men were apportioned to the camels. At first they were very frightened of us, and still more so of Narok. When one of us came near, they would jump about and kick their loads off. They soon got accustomed to me, as I used to walk round at intervals during the night whilst they were kneeling down, coming a little nearer every time. It was a long time, however, before they became used to the sight of porters with loads on their heads.

A camel is always frightened of a strange object, even if it is only something inanimate. However, they are not so foolish as a horse, who will shy at the same thing every day, as, once they have learnt that anything is harmless, they will never be afraid of it again.

We soon mastered the intricacies of loading them in the Rendile way, but we were very much at sea at first. I had often seen Somalis catching camels and bringing them in, but never noticed particularly how it was done.

When they came back from grazing the first day, we wanted to tie them up to prevent them running off to one of the kraals during the night. We had the ropes and we had the camels, but we did not know how to get the latter in a kneeling position. When we tried to get the rope round their noses, they haughtily put their heads up in the air far out of reach ; finally, we had to get some Rendile women to show us.

The rope is first tied round the neck, and then the end is thrown over the animal's nose. With this end the head must be very gently pulled down till it comes within reach, when the lip must be seized with a quick movement. If any force is employed in pulling the head down, as we had tried, the camel tosses his head, and the rope slips off his nose. After one or two unsuccessful efforts, the animal will probably get cunning, and skilfully avoid the rope every time it is flung up.

Arsim and El Laut are two springs on the north side of General Matthews Range. On the mountain above this place a band of robbers were reported to have taken up their abode, making raids on the flocks of the people living on either side. After leaving the range, there is no more water, we were told, until a well called Laipera is reached. This lies at the north side of the Elges.

The Elges is uninhabited, except at the edge. On our side there was a kraal a few hours from the mountains, and to this we moved. We got the Rendile of this kraal to fetch a good supply of water for us from El Laut, three hours distant, and with this we filled all our *hans* and water-tanks.

The two chiefs of the kraal at which we were stopping

were half-brothers, and both were called Laisinfesha. The people of this kraal are peculiar in that they are the only Rendile who do not eat either camel or goat. When one of their camels is sick, they send for people of a neighbouring kraal to buy it before it dies. The only reason they gave me for the observance of this custom was that it was the dying injunction of an ancestor. A girl of this kraal on the day she marries a man of another kraal is released from the necessity of observing this rule.

While at Laisinfesha's a youth came into camp and began talking to Abdi. As he seemed very communicative, I, with Abdi's help, elicited much information from him about the Rendile. According to him and others whom I had questioned, the Rendile were formerly great warriors. In fights with the Somalis they asserted that they completely exterminated one raiding expedition. On another occasion everyone who took part in the fight on both sides was killed. I asked how the Rendile on foot managed to fight the mounted Somali, and was told that they are very fleet of foot, and on the rough and stony ground of the escarpments are able to move as rapidly as the Somali pony. They use spears, but do not carry shields, saying that a man who carries a shield is a coward. Formerly they possessed many ponies, but now they have practically none at all. In all the kraals I visited I only saw one.

I have mentioned the similarity of their language to Somali. A few of these Somali words seem to have travelled far afield. I do not know what the explanation of this circumstance is. To mention one instance, the Somali and Rendile word *rob*, meaning rain, is found as *robta* amongst the Kisii, Lumbwa, Suk, Nandi, Kamasia, Elgeyo, and Sotik, but not amongst some of the tribes who border on the Somali and Rendile, such as the Samburr and Masai. The Nandi, Lumbwa, and Sotik use the Somali word *bokhol*, for a hundred, unchanged.

I might explain here what the word *Lokkob* means, as it has been assumed by former travellers that there is a tribe of that name. *Lokkob* is the Rendile corruption for the word *Loikop*. Thus it was the old Laikipia Masai, now no longer existing, who were originally called Lokkob by the Rendile. Now it is used to denote the people who live in the Loikop country—viz., El-burrgu Masai and Samburr—while in its wider sense it is used to denote any non-camel-breeding tribe, such as the Reshiat and El-molo. The Turkana are known to both Borana, Rendile, and also Somali, as Samai der (the long spear-hafts).

Having obtained a guide, I decided to start across the Elges at night, as soon after moonrise as possible. Women came down to help us load our camels, and were rewarded with beads. The loading up took a tremendous time, and it was not till 1.30 a.m. that we got away.

Progress was very slow, as the men and camels were strange to each other, and loads kept slipping off. I had two camels carrying *hans* full of water besides the water-tanks ; but, as luck would have it, both these camels got frightened, and began prancing about. The men with them did not know how to stop them, and they both succeeded in spilling all the water they were carrying. One *han* also fell off, and the camel put his foot on it and smashed it. Another delay ensued to collect and fasten on the empty hans, which had come adrift. At last we proceeded, and some time after noon we found some fair shade, and halted.

Everybody was very knocked up with the heat, and

LOADING CAMELS

The method of affixing the camel mats with our poles can be seen here. The camel on the right is Mwana, the little white camel, who carried a load as well or better than many of the bigger ones. A bale of calico and a box of ammunition is the load on this side.

unable to eat anything. Owing to the accident to the *hans*, it was impossible to distribute any water till the evening, when I gave out a small bowl to everyone.

It was no use loading up yet, as we could not proceed in the dark, so we awaited the moon. Everybody went off fast asleep on the ground, myself included. Fortunately, the rising moon awoke me, so I roused up the men, and we loaded the camels and started off again.

This time they went well, and there were few delays. We marched till ten o'clock the next day, and then, as it was practically impossible to proceed farther in the sun on our small allowance of water, we halted. The only vegetation here was the low country thorn, and so we rigged up waterproof-sheets and camel-mats to shelter us from the sun.

The guide said that Laipera was two and a half to three hours farther, so we hoped to reach it that night. I gave out another bowl of water apiece on our arrival and another before the evening march, to be put in the water-bottles. This finished the water we were carrying.

The strip of the Elges we were crossing was a flat red sand desert, studded with the atrocious thorn-bush described before. There was no path, but the way was easy, except where we struck patches of this bush, in which case we had to make détours to avoid the thorn. Although the way we took was flat and good travelling, we could see on either side nasty jagged lava escarpments. We were told that the country above these, and, in fact, most of the Elges, consists of lava rocks, over which travelling is very laborious, as loose, jagged blocks and lumps of lava lie about in confusion everywhere.

We were loaded up again by four in the afternoon, and moved on till at sunset we met a lava wall crossing our front. We had seen no life whilst traversing the Elges, except a *dik-dik* or two, but here, under the wall of the escarpment, were some gazelles, of which I shot two. These animals are curious in that they have the markings of Sömmering's gazelle (including the white rump patch, coming well up into the back), whilst they carry the horns of the northern form of Grant's gazelle. This white patch showed up well in a young one which the men found in a bush one day whilst collecting firewood.

The Rendile call this animal *haul*, which is like the Somali word for a Sömmering's gazelle—*aul*. The two *haul* were slung across the camels, and we proceeded till dark, when the guide suggested that we should halt for the night. We had already covered the two and a half hours he had told us was the distance to Laipera, so I thought that the well must be close at hand, and wanted to push on and reach it at night, as we had no water left. The guide said that we could not go on. I asked why, and he replied, there were lions about. I told him not to worry about that, but to go on, and he refused point-blank.

I could not see any reason for halting, so I asked if the way was bad. He said no ; it was just like that we had already come, except that now there was a path. When we had struck the lava escarpment, we found a camel-road passing north and south just under it, and had taken this northwards.

I then asked Abdi what he thought of it, as the guide had given no reason for not wishing to go on. Abdi replied : " I think that he is afraid of losing his way in the dark, and does not like to say that he is not quite sure of the country."

THE HAUL.   THE GAZELLE OF THE RUDOLF DISTRICT

This is a variety of Grant's gazelle, known as "Bright's." It is distinguished by the shape of the horns, more like those of Peter's gazelle, and the markings, especially the white rump patch, like those of Sömmering's gazelle. Narok is seen standing over it with an air of proprietorship. The strange-looking object to the left is only one of my men bending over to wipe his knife.

So we had to bivouac there, but as we were all fearfully thirsty, and had nothing to drink, I said that we would start on again at moonrise.

The guide said that there was no use in starting then, as we should arrive in the middle of the night, for Laipera was quite close at hand; in fact, that if there had been a kraal here, the water-camels would load up, go to the well, draw water, and be back before the other camels left the zariba. As camels go out about 8 or 8.30, this meant that Laipera could not be more than an hour distant, and the guide thought it would be quite early enough to begin loading the camels at sunrise.

I did not wish to subject my men to even an hour of the burning sun, as already by seven it is very trying, especially as it strikes on the forehead. Moreover, we were all so thirsty that we did not feel like facing even the sunrise before we had had something to drink.

The atmosphere of this country is extraordinarily dry, and an hour or two after one has drunk one's mouth gets parched, and after going for half a day without water all the body seems to dry up. Our condition was worse, as the last water we had drunk had been brackish. This being the case, I decided to start loading the camels directly the moon rose. Although there was meat from the gazelles I had shot, it remained untouched, as it was, of course, impossible to eat anything in our present condition. I was glad, however, to think that there would be some ready for the men when we reached water.

While we were bivouacking here in the Elges there was a sound as of distant drumming. Although I had often heard native drumming, I had never heard any with quite the same rhythm or sound. The latter was very marked, being in two keys. One had plenty of time to notice this, as we heard it at intervals through the night whenever the breeze freshened from that direction.

I heard two of the men solemnly discussing whether this was caused by a devil or not. Their conversation ran something as follows : " This waterless, uninhabited part is a very bad country ; there cannot fail to be bad devils here." " Yes, there are always bad devils in such places." " But this drumming—do you think it might be a Rendile kraal ?" " Who would live in a place like this ?" " Oh, the Rendile live in bad places ; but this is not like any human drumming." " No ; no one but a devil could play a drum like that."

At moonrise the night watchman woke us, and by 2.30 a.m. all the camels were loaded, and we proceeded. We continued till dawn without seeing any sign of the well. I waited for the men to close up, and by the faint light of dawn could see them patiently toiling along under their loads or leading the camels, without exchanging a word with each other. The perfect silence of the generally noisy, garrulous porters impressed me more than anything else could have done with a sense of their sufferings.

As I led the way on again, accompanied by the guide, a rhino came trotting towards us. If he had passed to a flank, I should have left him alone, but he was coming directly at us, and I did not want my tired men and camels to be disturbed by having to bolt out of his path, so I fired at him with my Mannlicher. He rushed about twenty yards, hit through the lungs, and then stopped, when another shot made him collapse in a kneeling position.

This seemed to have an inspiriting effect on the men, as they immediately began to talk. When they came up, the rhino was still just breathing, and Tengeneza called out : " Bring a knife to *halal* him."

As many of the men were Muhammadans, the meat would not be considered lawful unless the throat was cut whilst the animal was still alive. With a rhino this is generally a farce, as they make certain that he is dead first, and then cut his throat and pretend that he is still alive.

One of the camel-men, a tall Mnyamwezi called Majaliwa, came up with a knife, thinking that it was dead ; but as he came near, the rhino gave a sigh, and he ran back. I asked what he was waiting for, and he said : " It is still alive." I said : " Of course it is. Who would think of *halaling* an animal which was dead ?"

Some of the other men called out, " Go on, go on ! Don't be afraid," but he still shrank back. Knowing that the animal would never rise again, I took hold of his anterior horn with both hands, and said : " Now cut his throat while I hold him for you." He came up and commenced operations, and at the same time I swung the head round towards him. He started away and drew back hurriedly.

I said : " Well, what is the matter ?" Majaliwa replied : " Oh, he is still alive !" " Of course he is, but I am holding him for you."

Majaliwa again advanced, and again I moved the head, rather less this time, as if the animal had grown weaker. He withdrew again, but by now the men standing near had seen through my little joke, and said : " Go on ! Can't you see that the *bwana* is playing with you ?" Majaliwa looked rather silly, and the men all laughed at him.

When the throat had been finally cut, we left the rhino

lying there, to be sent for later, and moved on. By this time the sun had risen, and I felt very glad that we had not taken the guide's advice and started now instead of earlier.

However, this little incident bucked up the men, and they were even friendly disposed towards the guide, whom they had been cursing the night before. He had proved himself a most willing youth, and worked as hard as any three other men at loading the camels, rushing from one to another to see if they were properly tied up, being the only expert in this matter with the party. However, in time and distance he was as vague and inaccurate as most of these people, a circumstance for which he could hardly be blamed, as these considerations, so vital to us, are of no account to him and his people.

We had now reached a lava country, but the way was still quite good. After an hour's march we came to some lava nullahs. The whole country looked most forbidding ; there was not a spot of green anywhere, and it did not seem possible that there could be any water near.

I was some way in front of the men, when suddenly I came over a lava ridge, and saw a gladdening sight, which I shall always remember. Just below me was a valley of black lava, without a twig or leaf of any kind of vegetation. At the bottom of this valley were a number of loaded camels kneelir   ·   a semicircle, while about them were bustling Rendile women. As I looked closer, I could see that they were rushing backwards and forwards with *hans*, which they received from a hole in the ground, and fastened on the camels.

This hole was Laipera Well, bored out of the lava rock, the water being about ten feet below the surface. The curious thing is that this is not the lowest part of the

LAIPERA WELL.

The sticks seen fence about the well, while a group of hans are seen on the brink waiting to be filled. Behind these stands Rakari, the cook, with Tengeneza to his right. The Rendile women are busy loading hans on their camels to take to their kraal. In the foreground is one of the scoops used to bale up the water out of the well.

valley, as from this place it descends to a still lower valley and a sandy watercourse. Yet this well is the only place at which water may be obtained for miles round.

I went down to the well with the guide, and, after having a long drink, I borrowed some of the Rendile *hans* and wooden vessels with which they scoop water out of the well. These buckets are passed up full of water. One man, standing at the bottom and filling them, hands them to another standing halfway up the side, and he hands them out to the women waiting for them.

I placed these vessels in a row ready for the men when they came in, so that they should have no delay in getting water. The guide then got down into the well, and worked away busily, filling the buckets and passing them up to pour into two wooden troughs lying alongside, so that our sheep could drink when they came in. These sheep are used to going without water for long stretches, and ours came in rather tired, but quite fit, though they had not drunk since Laisinfesha.

Having filled these troughs, he turned to and filled buckets for the Rendile ladies, and altogether made himself very useful. When the porters came in they seized up the *hans* and buckets, some of them holding a gallon or more, and drained them off, and then asked for more. I tried to explain to them what a bad thing it was to drink so much when suffering from extreme thirst, but as I myself had just drunk about two gallons, I did not feel that I was arguing on very firm ground.

The Rendile at the well said that we must come and camp at their kraal, which was only just over the rise at the other side of the valley, a stone's throw away. As there was no shade here, I thought it rather a good idea. We should then get milk, and perhaps be able to buy some more camels ; so I set out with them, and marched for a mile and a half. They then pointed out the position of their kraal as being the other side of a ridge, about five miles away ; so I said, " No, thank you !" and returned to the well.

It was now fifteen days since we had camped by water, as all the time we had been buying camels we were either sending for water or purchasing it from the Rendile. We were delighted to be once more near water, and not have to think of every drop we expended.

Now I could have my clothes washed and bathe, have my plates washed, and a variety of other things I had had to forego.

We found some diminutive acacias not far from the well, which had at first been concealed from us by the side of the valley. There we camped, and made ourselves as comfortable as the sun would permit, as seen in the photograph of our camp.

CHAPTER IX

THE BORANA

WE had not pitched camp very long before some of the Rendile came in to see us. We learnt from them that it was a comparatively short distance to Koroli, and that there were Borana at that place, and also plenty of water.

The Borana are new-comers in this part of the world, having been pushed down from the north. From what I gathered, there is no love between the Rendile and Borana, although they have not fought now for many years. The Rendile do not seem much of hands at fighting now, and I expect the stories of their prowess in old days were rather exaggerated. All the old fights described by natives are always so bloody, and their present fights so bloodless, that it is hard to reconcile the two.

I was told that the old Loikop Masai once invaded the Borana country, and reached the east of Lake Stefanie before being driven back. It was easy to see that the Rendile were not pleased with the encroachment of the Borana.

Before we broached the subject of camels, we had to listen to a long and voluble tale of how some Somalis had taken away some of their baggage-camels. As they had so few to spare, we at once saw that it was hope-

127

less to try and get any here. We asked, all the same, and they refused point-blank, but said that we were sure to get all we wanted from the Borana. This I doubted, as we had heard the tale of the land of plenty just ahead too often.

We spent a day here to rest, and also to fetch in the rhino meat. The first night I took observations till 1 a.m., and during the day took some more, which gave me a bad sun headache.

We started away from Laipera in the afternoon, and bivouacked in the road just after sunset. Our guide trotted out his story of lions in the way again, but we said that we had heard it before. We rose again with the moon, and proceeded to Koroli, at which place we arrived shortly after sunrise. The lava escarpment which we had struck at our last bivouac in the Elges is part of an enormous long lava wall which runs north and south, perhaps a hundred or more miles in length.

Below it is a sandy, absolutely flat plain, while if one climbs this escarpment, only about one hundred to two hundred feet in height, one finds oneself on a plateau of broken lava. This lava wall had receded from us as we approached Laipera, but had been gradually drawing nearer to us on our march till we met it at Koroli.

Koroli is shown on some maps as a mountain, but there is no sign of even a hill here, except this escarpment, which cannot be more than two hundred feet high anywhere, and is the edge of a lava plateau.

Springs exist at the base of the lava wall at three different spots, and from here flow into small swamps a few hundred yards from the cliff, and then the water is lost in the sand or evaporated by the sun.

CAMP AT LAIPERA

These were the only trees we could find near the well, which is situated in a lava valley to the left. The view straight in front is eastwards over the Elges, towards Rudolf.

KOROLI

Borana camels and goats watering. This water is brackish. The view looks westwards over the bare open plain towards Lake Rudolf. On this plain there is absolutely no grazing even for the camels. The white in the distance is not water, but a deposit of salt.

As we approached Koroli we saw a long line of stones laid in a row on the open plain. This, the guide said, was a record of the men killed in an ancient fight between the Turkana and Borana, a stone being placed for every man killed.

There were numberless Borana camels being watered at Koroli. The herdsmen were dressed like Somalis, in dirty white robes, and carrying a single spear with a broad blade. The Borana own only camels and sheep in this low country ; the cattle-owning Borana live in the higher and better-watered escarpments to the northeast.

There are three brackish watering-places, their names being "Big Salt," "White Water," and "Young Camel's Water" when translated. There are also two so-called fresh wells. The sand is very salt here, and the movement of these numbers of camels filled the air and wells with salt-laden dust. I tried one of the " fresh " wells, but it was dirty, brackish, and extremely unpleasant. The Borana, however, told me that it was particularly good.

West of this spot is a flat sand expanse shining white in the sun, and stretching without a break, and apparently without a twig of any vegetation, as far as the eye can reach. North of the watering-places is a cape or headland of lava projecting into the sea of desert. This is called by the Borana *Dufanka marti*, meaning " the big-eating camel passed." This is because formerly a camel ran away here, and they were not able to turn him back—a trivial incident to be handed down to posterity in the name of a place.

It was rather difficult to tell the expanse of the small swamps here, owing to the mirage. They were probably

9

not more than fifty or a hundred yards long, and only a few inches deep. The mirage gave the effect of enormous swamps, in which hundreds of camels watering were wading knee-deep. If there had only been a few date-trees, one might have imagined oneself in Arabia.

Practically all the water at which we had camped since passing the Lorogai was unmarked on the map, but water was known to occur fairly plentifully in the Samburr country. I was especially pleased to arrive at this spot, also at Laipera, as all the country we were in now was by report absolutely waterless. We had now traversed about eighty miles of this country, and found water in two places since leaving Arsim, which also was a watering-place unlocated before. Moreover, we had news from the Borana that there was still water ahead in the direction in which we intended to go.

After watching the camels being watered for a few minutes, we continued on our way. Some Borana kraals were situated on the lava plateau above, and it was there I wished to go. To reach them we had to ascend the escarpment by a path, which was nothing but a mass of loose lava blocks, thrown together by Nature. On arriving at the top, we had a very arduous trek over the lava till, at noon, we reached the Borana kraals.

The first we came across consisted of a collection of the usual camel-mat huts scattered about amongst the rocks. Circular walls had been built here and there of lava blocks, to form kraals for sheep and goats. All round was a sea of jagged lumps of lava, and in the midst of the group of hovels was a single leafless acacia, to which a horse was tethered.

A more desolate-looking encampment I have never seen, and it seemed very hard to imagine that any human beings could take up their abode in such a spot, far less that it represented to those that dwelt there " home." Not only was it their home, but most of them had never known any better or brighter spot.

The only inhabitants of the hovels when we arrived were a few old women, it being the custom of these people, as well as the Rendile and many others, to send all their men with the herds when they go to water. The reason for this is that such a time offers a favourable opportunity for an attack by another tribe wishing to loot stock.

The Borana here are the Gabba Borana, while another section, the Algan, inhabit the country a little to the north. The camels are grazed amongst the lava rocks, as a certain amount of grazing for camels crops up in the interstices between boulders. On the plain below there is no grazing to be had at all. I noticed that the Borana camels were very much thinner and in worse condition than those of the Rendile. These camels are used to travelling about on loose stones, and climbing up and down lava escarpments, whereas our Rendile camels did not like this work in the least.

There was no flat space on which to pitch a tent by this encampment, so we tried another kraal to the east, and here we found a little level space. There was no shade, and the heat and glare off the lava were very trying.

Some old men, dressed in robes and turbans of *maradufu*, came to call. I call them turbans, although they were fastened in a way I have seen no turban fastened before. A folded strip of *maradufu* was wound straight round the head, and looked more than anything like the napkin round the basin of a steak and kidney pudding. They brought with them a present of milk in very small vessels, and did not seem to be, on the whole, very hospitable.

The chief of this section is called Ali Koti or Harroduchi. Abdi, as he knew Galla, found that he could talk quite well with them. Their language is almost the same as Galla, although they differ from these people in some of their customs and names.

A curious circumstance is that there are Galla on the Tana River, in British East Africa, and in Southern Jubaland, and also in Abyssinia. The Galla of these two places are almost identical in language, customs, and names, although there seems to be no connection between them at the present day. They are separated by the Borana, a people with slightly different customs, having often different names from the Galla, as also by other tribes, such as Somali, Rendile, etc., who have quite distinct customs and language.

There being practically no trees in this part of the country, many of the Borana huts consist of a low, circular wall of stone, with a few camel-mats thrown over the top. For the same reason they do not have wooden vessels for drawing water from wells, as do the Rendile, but they use strong leather buckets.

Peculiar little hutches of stone were scattered about in the encampment. These consist of a few stones piled in a circle, with a flat boulder on the top for a roof. These are to put young sheep or goats in. I could not make out what the roof was for, as there was no rain, and even if there had been, they would not have troubled to make a roof for sheep or goats. Perhaps it was to prevent them climbing over the low walls. These rings of stone must last long after the encampment is left, as there is nothing to disturb them. I frequently noted sites of old encamp-

A Borana Goatherd

This photograph is taken on the top of the escarpment. The open space in the foreground was the only clear space in which to pitch my tent. In the background my camels can be seen approaching. Behind them the lava escarpment droops sheer on to the plain below.

ments by such stones even in the uninhabited parts I visited later, showing that some people must have been living there once.

The Rendile, when travelling without camels, carry their water-gourds. I did not ascertain where they obtained these, but they must get them from some other tribe, as there is no cultivation of any sort in this country. The Somali on a similar journey carry theirs either in skins (*sibrar*) or wooden water-bottles called *weisu*. The Borana, instead of the gourd or the *weisu*, make for themselves neat little leather water-bottles with stoppers. I tried to persuade the Borana here to sell some camels, but as they declined to do so, I had to go without.

Fodder for the mule was a serious consideration these days, as we hardly ever saw any grass. The Masai sais was very good about getting what he could. He would grope round the rocks with a sickle, and obtain a certain amount. When grass was very scarce, I used to eke out the mule's food with a handful of maize. However, his work was very light these days, as I hardly ever rode him.

During all the long and waterless marches I went on foot, as I was afraid that it would have a dispiriting effect on the men to see me forging ahead mounted. It was only when I had been up most of the night taking observations that I used to ride the next day.

I asked the Borana old men to find a guide for me, but they went off, and never sent one. However, a youth came into camp, and when he heard that we wanted a guide, volunteered his services as far as Maikona.

He subsequently fetched a friend to come with him. It is very seldom that one man will consent to come alone, the last Rendile guide we had being the only exception I remember for a long time.

These two guides turned up in good time in the morning, and proved to be by far the best we had during the trip. First of all, they knew the country, quite an unusual thing in a guide ; they also acted as guides the whole time they were with us by walking in front with me. They usually lurk behind, and disappear if one comes to difficult country, causing the whole party to have to await their reappearance.

From the Borana kraals we went westwards again, and after a two-hours trek over the lava we came to the edge of the escarpment, and saw below us Maidahad, a pretty little oasis of the wild palms called by the Swahili *mkoma*. The stones in the background of the photograph form the path. If the reader will look at them carefully, it will obviate the necessity of my giving an inadequate description of the process of travelling over such country.

We descended to the oasis, and spent the middle of the day there, and very pleasant it was under the shade of the palms, while the lava escarpment behind us sheltered us from the tearing hot wind and dust we had had to put up with daily. The water was clear and sweet from one of the wells, but there is not enough water here for the camels of the Borana ; moreover, the salt water of Koroli is considered better for them.

While sitting here and watching our camels I had occasion to notice how very daintily they drink, as they only just put their lips to the water, and can therefore drink without stirring up the mud, whilst a horse would probably put both feet in the water, and dip his nose much deeper. Camels make a fearful business of being watered, as they drink slowly and at intervals, with long rests between.

While sitting here some of the porters cut off the top

My Camels Drinking at Maidahad

Camels take drinking very seriously, and spend a long time before they are satisfied; drinking a little, and resting, and drinking again. They hardly touch the water with their lips, so as not to stir up the mud.

of a palm, and brought me the heart to try. It was white and rather bitter. An extravagant dish on the coast amongst Swahilis is the heart of a cocoa-nut-tree, which is obtained by cutting off the top, and thereby killing the tree.

While we waited here game appeared strolling towards the oasis—oryx, *haul*, Grevy's zebra, and ostrich—evidently waiting to drink. When they saw us they stared for a while, and then moved off. They awaited our departure, full of impatience, as they returned again and again to look at us. I felt sorry for them, but really could not oblige them by going to sit on the bare, sun-baked plain, so they had to wait till we moved off in the afternoon. We filled up the tanks, and marched on till sunset, when we bivouacked near an old zariba, which had been but lately deserted, as we could see by the birds flying round.

Just after we had composed ourselves to sleep a few spots of rain fell, and so I had to turn everybody out to stack the loads and instruments under waterproof-sheets. It proved a false alarm, however, for after a few spots it cleared up. I had just got to sleep again when the night-watchman awoke me to say that there was a very bad animal prowling round, and at the same time Abdi called out : " Come quickly, as it is very close."

I seized my rifle, and hurried to the spot, and could just distinguish a form slowly approaching in the dark a step or two at a time. After every two or three steps it halted. Abdi whispered to me, " It is indeed a lion," but I was not satisfied, as everything appears so enormous in the dark that a lion would have looked huge. This only seemed the size of a leopard, and so was probably smaller.

As it advanced again I decided that it was not a leopard, as it did not move in a catlike way, nor did it have the movement of a hyena. What could it be, then, that was advancing on us so fearlessly ? I thought over all the animals, bad and otherwise, it could be. It was not a wolf, as there were none here ; not a hunting-dog, as one would not be alone ; nor a jackal, as it was too large. Abdi said, " Shoot, shoot, *bwana ;* it is now amongst the men "; but still I did not shoot, as I did not want it to be said afterwards that I had got frightened, and shot at some ridiculous animal of whom no one would be afraid. The figure then began moving slowly round our camp, and passing quite close to some of the sleeping men. I moved also, and suddenly by the light of the fire saw what it was. It was only a dog which had got left behind when the inhabitants vacated the kraal near which we were encamped. Now the unfortunate animal was sniffing round in the hopes of finding something to eat.

I retired to sleep again, saying to Abdi : " Don't wake me up every time you see a dog, will you ?" Abdi said he was very sorry, so I consoled him with : " Quite right, I am glad ; you should always wake me up if there is anything about at night of which you are uncertain, and I also really thought it was a bad animal till I saw it move."

The moon rose late now, so that it was not till four that we could load the camels. Whilst this operation was in progress, I heard a breathing beside me. Thinking that it was Narok, I was just stooping down to pat her, when I thought better of it, and swung round the lamp in my other hand, just in time to see a large brown African cobra gliding away.

We reached Maikona early in the morning. This place consists of a collection of wells in a large patch of the bush, called in Swahili *msuaki.* This is a low-growing, widely-spreading bush, which grows in circular clumps of ten or twenty yards in diameter. The coast natives and Arabs use sticks cut from this shrub with which to clean their teeth.

The wells and patches of *msuaki* bush were situated on the plain in a bay of the lava escarpment. The lava wall circled round this spot, and then trended westwards to a cape called Buliashe, at which spot it turned northwards again. The ground at Maikona was covered with loose powder-dust, which made the place most uncomfortable to remain in during the day whilst the wind was at its height.

The guides wanted to return from here, but I was loath to let them go, as they had been able to give me very fairly accurate estimates of the length of each day's march, and much information about the country. To get other guides, it would have been necessary to delay our march and trek up the escarpment, where I learnt there were some kraals of the Algana Borana.

I therefore tried to persuade them to go on with me, and they consented under condition that they got plenty of meat, as they said that they did not like their present fare of a little mutton, and some beans and flour. The latter they were, of course, unused to, and thought very poor food. I promised to do my best, and so took my rifle and went out into the bush, and soon managed to shoot three gazelle ; half of one I gave them, while the rest I gave to the porters.

When the wind died down in the evening, it was pleasant to get the dust washed out of one's eyes, ears, and nose, and settle down to a meal which was not covered with grit. After dinner the porters sat chatting by the fires, and everybody was cheery, as they had some meat to eat, and we had not felt the want of water since leaving Laipera, and had quite recovered from the exhaustion of the thirst we had suffered while crossing the Elges.

Omari propounded the following puzzle during the evening :

THE MWALIM AND THE ORANGE.

Once upon a time there was a Sultan. Now this Sultan became very ill, and all the arts of the medicine-men were of little avail, till one day there came forth a sage skilled in the seeing of visions and in the preparation of potions and charms. Now this sage spake, and said that on a certain hill there was an orange-tree, and it was of an orange of this tree that the only medicine could be brewed which could cure the Sultan's illness. So the Wazir set out with his slaves, and went to the hill in question, and there he found one orange-tree growing in a rocky crevice, and on this tree was one orange.

He sent one of his slaves to climb the tree to gather the orange. When he reached the branch on which the orange was growing, he shook it, and the orange fell down. The Wazir went to pick it up, but it rolled away from him into a small round hole in the rock, and out of sight. When he came to probe the hole, he found that it was many yards deep ; nor could he see the bottom, or where the orange had gone.

Then he was much afeared, and said to himself : " Surely my life will be forfeit if I return without the orange."

Now on that hill dwelt an old *mwalim*, one skilled in learning and theology. So the Wazir betook himself to the *mwalim*, and asked him to devise some stratagem by which to extricate the orange. The *mwalim*, after great deliberation, bethought himself of a stratagem. So they went together to the place, and by dint of the *mwalim's* device they extricated the orange.

Then was the Wazir very glad, and he took it to the sage, who forthwith brewed medicine of it and cured the Sultan. So the Sultan, on being restored to health, bestowed great favours on his Wazir, and the latter, in the hour of his prosperity, did not forget the *mwalim* who had helped him in his need, but exalted him to a high place under him.

Question.—What was the device of which the *mwalim* bethought himself ?

Answer.—He and the Wazir and his slaves filled the hole with water, till finally the orange floated to the top, and was taken out.

This reminded me of another puzzle I had lately heard at Lamu, which I will here repeat.

AN ARAB PUZZLE.

Two poor men, Hassan and Abdullah, were sitting beside the road. Now Hassan had five loaves of bread, and Abdullah had three loaves. They agreed to feed together, so Hassan crumbled up his five loaves, and Abdullah crumbled up his three loaves. As they were dry, thěy mixed all the eight crumbled loaves together, added water to them, and cooked them.

They had just finished cooking them, and were about to commence to éat them, when there rode past the son of a rich merchant. Now he was returning from hunting, and was very hungry. When he saw the poor men sitting down, just about to feed, he saluted them, and said :

" Peace be with ye." They answered : " And with you be peace. Draw nigh, O our master."

The merchant's son said : " I feel a great hunger. May I share your repast ?" They said unto him : " Eat, lord." So they made way for him, and he sat down. Then he said : " By Allah, I will not eat unless we all eat together !"

So the poor men said : " The lord's graciousness to his slaves is only exceeded by his generosity." So they all sat down and ate of the food, each man eating his fair portion of the meal. When it was finished, the merchant's son arose to go his way. He opened his wallet, and, taking forth eight golden dinars, he placed them in the plate, and mounted his horse and rode away.

Now Hassan took up the eight dinars, and he gave three to Abdullah, and five he kept himself. Abdullah said to Hassan : " I do not agree at all, for the stranger gave the eight dinars to us both ; therefore we should divide them equally, each man taking four." But Hassan said : " Did I not provide five loaves, whereas you only provided three ? Therefore, I take five dinars, and you take only three."

But Abdullah would not agree, and claimed a half-share, for he said that they had both invited the merchant's son, and the merchant's son had given the eight dinars between them, and therefore that they must be divided equally. Hassan refused, so Abdullah went to the *kadhi* (judge), and accused Hassan before him.

Now the *kadhi* was a man well versed in the laws of equity and the Sheria (Muhammadan law). So he searched his books and pondered over the case for two days. On the third day he gave judgment. How did he settle the case ?

Answer.—The *kadhi* gave seven dinars to Hassan, and to Abdullah he only gave one. For each man had eaten a third of the eight loaves, which equals two and two-thirds of a loaf. The merchant's son gave the eight dinars for his share only. Abdullah ate two and two-thirds of his own three loaves, and thus only contributed one-third to the stranger. Thus Hassan contributed two and one-third loaves of the stranger's portion. So the dinars must be divided in the proportion seven-thirds to one-third, or seven to one.

After having heard Omari's story, and a few others too indifferent to repeat, the natives turned in, and I was left to write up my notes. Meanwhile Narok prowled about, returning at intervals to see how I was getting on, and if it was yet time to turn into the tent.

CHAPTER X

MORE UNKNOWN WATER-HOLES

WE were glad to leave the dust-laden air of Maikona. The next water-hole, according to the guides, was called Gamra. The caravan proceeded to this place, while I ascended the escarpmènt north of Maikona, and then followed on their track.

I came up with them in a few hours, resting beside a pool of water which welled out of the desert. This was surrounded by *msuaki* bushes, while in the centre of the shallow pool on an island was a construction of dead branches. I asked the guides what this was, and they said that Abyssinian hunters had been down here, and had made this little shelter in which to await animals drinking at night. Heaps of bones lying all round the oasis testified to the fact that they had in this way performed great execution.

We drew our drinking-water from two little wells just above the pool, and found it sweet and good—a pleasant change for us, as the Maikona water was brackish. Amongst the bones lying round the oasis we noticed those of several rhinoceroses and oryx, and also a lion and ostrich.

A nice shady place had been prepared for me to sit in by cutting away some of the under branches and making an arbour in a thick *msuaki* clump.

142

In the afternoon we moved off again, and. after rounding Buliashe, the cape of lava mentioned before, we followed along the escarpment northwards. I tried to take observations from this point, but, as had often been the case before, I was defeated by the mist, dust, and haze.

We trekked on again till at dusk we came upon a large patch of desert, encrusted with a thick layer of salt about half an inch in depth. This was practically pure salt, and lay on the ground like thin ice, while our feet broke through it as we walked. This lone country must, I suppose, at some time have been under water strongly impregnated with salt, which was deposited on evaporation. We bivouacked for the night amidst the salt, but were unable to light a fire, as there was no firewood or anything combustible.

Next morning we moved on, and soon came to a bay in the lava escarpment, sheltering a thick forest of *mkoma* palms, called Karauwi. This forest was dense near the head of the bay, growing sparser near its mouth. We passed through the less dense parts to the other side, where the guides said that we should find water.

The three-day-old spoor of an enormous bull elephant led into the recesses of the *mkoma*, he evidently having come at night to drink. Presently we met the same spoor coming out again, and heading straight away towards some hills under Mount Kulal, called Asi or Esie, which we could see to our west.

I should have dearly liked to have been able to stop and hunt this old fellow, for I could pretty well tell from the size of the spoor that he must be a big tusker. However, I dared not delay on the way, as I was very anxious about the men's food, more especially since we had

heard that the Réshiat had fled from their former
villages. Already the men were on half-rations whenever
I could obtain sufficient meat to make up for short
rations.

As we passed through the palms we came on little
patches of real green grass, and on this buffalo had been
grazing. The guides said that there were a few old buffaloes who lived in the dense recesses of the palms, and
only came out here to graze at night. They were bad-tem-
pered old fellows, and so the Abyssinian hunters had
given them a wide berth. After passing through several
of these little green grass glades, we came to the stream
from which they got their moisture. It rose in the dense
bush, opened out here, and then was quickly lost in the
arid desert beyond.

We found a beautiful shady camp on the green grass
at the water's edge, and then discovered that the stream
was a hot one.

I meant to have had a go at the buffaloes that day,
but as I had only had one hour's sleep the night before,
and was feeling very upset from the brackish waters we
had been drinking, I thought that I would take a nap
in this delightful spot. The result was that I only awoke
in time to take my observations before the sun set.

This peaceful spot was the most pleasant camp we had
had since leaving Rumuruti. There was beautiful shade
from the palms, and we were protected from wind and
dust, whilst the green was most soothing to our eyes,
tired out with days and days of the white glare of the
desert.

Next morning we started loading the camels at 4.30,
and as dawn broke I determined to visit a few of the
glades, on the off-chance of seeing a buffalo. It seemed

a fairly hopeless chance, as the camels had already been roaring over being loaded for nearly an hour, and the men shouting and bustling about.

I took Tengeneza, and we proceeded cautiously to investigate some of the glades. As we were proceeding in this way, Tengeneza, who was behind me, suddenly stopped. His eyes had been sharper than mine. As he said afterwards, he saw something dark amongst the bushes.

I did not notice, however, that he had stopped, and went on another five yards, when I suddenly saw the enormous hind-quarters of a buffalo not fifteen yards distant. His head and chest were concealed by a low *mkoma*, and as he was quite close to this, he might even now have seen me through it, although I could not see his head. There was no chance of getting a clear shot, and in another second he might have the alarm, so I decided quickly to shoot. I had a double ·450 in my hand, and, guessing where his chest would be, took a step forward to get clear of a branch in front, and, aiming for the bush, fired.

He plunged into the undergrowth and disappeared in a second, and the next moment the bush two yards to my right seemed to open, and with a bellow he appeared. I had no time to think what to do, or to raise the rifle to my shoulder, but jabbed it against his chest, pulling the trigger of the second barrel. At the same instant I stepped to one side, and he swept past, pushing the rifle aside. The next moment we heard him groaning and struggling on the ground twenty yards behind us. Tengeneza had been but five yards away on the other side, and the beast had passed between us, but he had stood his ground without moving. This gave me another

10

proof, had any been required, of the stanchness of my gun-bearer.

We pushed through the palms to where we heard him struggling on the ground, and another shot despatched him. He was a fine bull, with nasty sharp horns, well curved.

We had to delay starting, so as to cut up the meat, but that was of little importance, as the next water-hole was only about seven miles on. Buffalo meat is much appreciated by the men, and they were able to fill themselves for several days on this large addition to our food stores.

Having transferred the meat to the camels, we moved on, and after one and a half hours came to a bay in the lava wall, in which I subsequently found a hot stream called Burgi. This and Karauwi are not visited much by the Borana.

Passing Burgi, we came to another bay of *mkoma* palms and *msuaki* bush, and saw camels being driven from the escarpment out on to the plains. This was Kalacha, in which place there are several wells and a small pool. The camels belonged to the Borana, and were going to drink at a salt oasis a mile or two out on the plains. By game tracks on our path I had ascertained that we had passed several swamps on our way since Maidahad, but our guides had told us that the water was undrinkable for human beings, indicating this by drawing a finger across the throat.

Our guides wanted to return from here, saying that they were now far from home, and did not know the way in front. We learnt from a few Borana watering their flocks that there were some kraals on the escarpment five hours distant.

Abdi went off to see the chief of these kraals and obtain guides, and also to purchase *hans*, if possible, as the Rendile had only sold us their very old and rotten ones, all of which, save one, had cracked and broken on the way.

Whilst Abdi was away, I occupied the time investigating Burgi and the salt oasis at which the camels drink. I also started studying the Amharic characters, as it was necessary that I should begin to know something of this language before reaching Abyssinia.

Abdi, after being one day away, returned with a chief, two guides, and some old men, but he had been unable to buy any *hans*. I then made presents to our old guides, and also gave them some of our female goats and sheep.

The Borana were very emphatic at first that we could not go on any farther; finally, we elicited the information that if one went on northwards, we could camp at the following places :

First day : Ragi.
Second day : Hirimat.
Third day : Naga Laga. Here we should turn up a dry river-bed, which breaks the line of escarpment, and proceed to
Fourth day : Balessa (in Had watercourse).
Fifth day : Had watercourse.
Sixth day : El Had.

At El Had was, they said, a deep well. This made six days without water—a much greater distance than we could traverse.

Then an old man said that we could get water at Balessa by digging. There used to be a well there, but now it was filled in with sand. This sounded more hopeful, so I asked about it, and he added, as an after-thought : " You will have to put eight men into the well."

Abdi was at a loss to understand what he meant, but, after much questioning, it transpired that a well must be dug deep enough to permit of eight men one above the other passing up the water. I asked how deep the well must be, and he pointed to a tree one hundred yards away, and said : " As deep as from here to that tree." Imagine one arriving thirsty after a four-days march, and having to dig a well three hundred feet deep in sand before being able to get water. The chief had the sense to tell the old man that he was talking rot, and that it would take fifty or a hundred men a month to dig the well.

The same genial old man said that we did not need a guide to go to El Had ; we should find it all right if we just trekked on. I asked about Lake Rudolf, but none of them had heard of it, except the chief, who said that his father had told him that once he had been a long way westwards on a raiding expedition, and reached a big lake called Ganal.

I next tried to elicit information concerning the country westwards, but without success. At last they told me that seven years ago they had lived at a place three days to the north-west, called Horr, but they had been driven from there by the Turkana. There was water at Horr, and it could be reached in two very long days or three short days. I asked how far it was from Horr to El Had, and they said it was three days also.

Thinking that I had solved the problem of how to proceed northwards, I decided to go to that place. The conversation had been very boring at first, as to every direction I suggested the Borana shook their heads, and replied, *debitch*. At last I asked Abdi what was this *debitch* they were always talking about, and he told me it meant a waterless tract.

The new guides, having seen me giving presents to the old ones, said that they were very pleased to come with me ; but if I intended bestowing on them any sheep for their services, I had better give them to them now, as they would suffer by being taken a hard march to Horr and El Had and then back again. I did not like paying anything in advance, before they had proved their capacity, so I gave some sheep to the chief, and said that I would send him back some *maradufu* and other presents by the guides, and that then he was to give them the sheep. If they returned without presents for him, he would know that they had run away or behaved badly, and that in that case he must keep the sheep for himself.

We started away from Kalacha in the afternoon, and soon after leaving met with thick powdery dust, in which the feet sank in six or eight inches—a circumstance which made marching very slow and tiring for the porters. I was also confronted by another problem, which worried me almost daily, and that was how to protect one's forehead and face from a setting sun with a gale blowing from the east. To gain any measure of protection, one must pull one's hat right down over one's eyes, and in this position a hat refuses to stop on when a strong wind is blowing from behind. The result is that one gets the sun in one's eyes, and consequent sun headaches.

We trekked from two o'clock to nine, and then a shot was fired from behind, and we halted to see what was the matter. One of the men came up to say that a porter had succumbed from thirst. I asked what had happened ; they replied that he had suddenly fallen down in a faint, and when they looked at his water-bottle, they found it empty, so they had not been able to do anything for him. I asked why they had not given him some of the water out of their bottles, and they said that all theirs was finished too.

It is useless to try and teach them providence, as an hour or two after leaving water, directly they feel a little dry, they drink up the contents of their water-bottles. I then sent back my water-bottle to him, and presently he was brought in, evidently having had a touch of sun. I made it a point never to touch the water in my bottle till the next ration was served out, when I would drink it, and put the new water in my bottle. On occasions, however, on the march, when Narok was very done, I had to give her a little out of my bottle, as she could not go for many hours in the sun without suffering extreme exhaustion.

This episode curtailed our march that day. On the next morning we started before sunrise, and, after crossing another tract of loose, soft dust, steering for an isolated little hill called Daban Dabli, we arrived at a long line of *msuaki* bush. Beyond this we struck a country of sandhills, amidst which our guides · wandered about, looking for Horr. After an ineffectual search, I saw a good many birds hovering about, and, steering for them, reached a broad, shallow valley in the sandhills. By this means I found a small salt swamp, and when the guides saw this, they recognized it, and said that the fresh-water *sokota* was close by.

One of them found an ostrich-feather, which had got caught up in a little bush, and took it to wear in his hair. Unfortunately, he dropped it on the bare flat surface of the ground, and, the wind catching it, it began scudding along like a small boat at sea. Thinking that he would easily catch it, he ran gently after it, making ineffectual prods at it with his spear. But the ostrich-feather sailed faster and faster, and he, unwilling to lose his treasure, went flying after it, presenting a most comical sight as he kept prodding away at it. Finally, the ostrich-feather outran him, and so, throwing down his spear, he set off, running over the plain, the feather always leading, till he must have gone a mile or more. Finally, he got left a very bad last, and had to give up, utterly blown, while the feather disappeared in the distance, going at a terrific pace.

In this valley we saw in the distance a great brown object, which we could not make out. As we drew nearer, we found that it was the carcass of an elephant, on which a great part of the skin had dried. Unfortunately, the tusks had been abstracted—probably by Abyssinian hunters. The atmosphere is so extraordinarily dry that skin and flesh shrivel up, instead of rotting and decaying. I often noticed animals a portion of whose skin had dried on to the carcass. Particularly was this the case with the body of a rhino we had seen at Kalacha, on which the skin had dried practically intact, except for a big hole in the stomach, which birds had picked open to get at the entrails.

The guides took us over the slope to the west of this valley, and in the next dip we came across a patch of reeds about fifty yards broad. The edge of it was much trampled by game, and very muddy. In the reeds I saw something lying, and found the skull and bones of an oryx, which had been killed, evidently by a lion, the night before.

Not far from this patch of reeds, on either side of the shallow depression, was *msuaki* bush. The leaves of this bush had formed the staple food of our camels for some time now, but it is not good for them, as it is too green, dry food being much better for them.

We passed round to the west side of the little *sokota*, and there, as yet sheltered from the sun by the reeds, we found cool and sweet water welling up. As I stooped down to drink, I caught a faint distant purring sound, from where I could not quite make out, but fancied it was from the patch of bush several hundred yards behind us. I said to Tengeneza : " Perhaps the lion who has killed here is in that patch of bush ;" but later on, in the selection of a suitable site for camp, I forgot all about this incident. On a little rise above the *sokota* were situated about half a dozen acacias, giving poor shade, but better than nothing.

The guides had said that Horr was marked by a single tree, so I asked which of these was the single tree. They replied : " When we were here seven years ago, there was only one tree ; that was why we did not recognize the place."

This water was quite the best we had tasted since camping on the Morendat on the second day of our trek. So we camped under the acacias, quite satisfied with the spot now that it had been found.

The description the guides gave of Horr before they left Kalacha was most misleading. For a long time Abdi and I were under the impression that they were talking of Lake Rudolf. They told us Horr was a place with very much water. We asked if it was as big as from where we were sitting to a tree a hundred yards away. " No," they said ; " it is a very big water."

" From here to the other side of the valley ?" we asked, indicating a distance of about a thousand yards.

" No," they replied ; " Horr is a very big water."

" They must mean Embassu Narok," I said to Abdi. He agreed, and we then cogitated how we could ascertain for certain. At last I hit on it. " Ask them if there are any fish in the water."

They said, " No," but that it was a very big place, and the water flowed down in four different directions.

In reality, the little *sokota* was not more than about fifty yards across. They also described the water as being like that at Koroli, which was the nastiest water we had met with.

My first anxiety on reaching this spot was to obtain more meat for the men, as the buffalo was now finished. If I could not shoot anything else, I should have to give out a full ration from our now fast-diminishing store. There were plenty of oryx and zebra about, but it was impossible to approach them on the flat, bare plain. However, in the afternoon they began to come towards the water. I thought that if I could approach through the patch of *msuaki* bush, it might be possible to get within a hundred and fifty or two hundred yards of them, as they came up to the *sokota*.

Telling the men to draw all the water they wanted at once, and not to visit the *sokota* again till I returned, I set out with Tengeneza, the latter carrying my big bore. The *msuaki* grew in patches and clumps in the sand, and it was easy to walk between them. As they were in places low, and also on a hill gently sloping towards the water, my whole attention was concentrated on seeing the distant game through and over the bushes without being myself seen.

If I had been hunting in my usual way, and watching the ground, I should have probably noticed some spoor, but I was absolutely engrossed in the distant oryx, as it meant starvation to the men if I could not keep up the meat-supply.

Suddenly, as I walked round a *msuaki* bush, I was startled by a duet of deep bass grunts right at my feet, and two lionesses sprang up and plunged into the bush. If they had waited another second, I must have trodden on them. I threw up the Mannlicher, aiming between the shoulder-blades of one of them as they bounded off grunting; but as I was about to press the trigger, the other whipped round, growling. For a moment I thought she was about to spring, and hurriedly transferred my aim to her chest, thinking the while that I must make deadly sure of a steady shot through her heart, or my Mannlicher would not stop her. In a moment, however, she sprang sideways behind a shrub, and I had lost the pair of them.

I ran after them through the bush, but only came out into the open in time to see the two disappearing in the distance. If Tengeneza had carried my Mannlicher and I the big bore, things might have been different, as I should have risked a rapidly-aimed shot, relying on its stopping power.

We still had a few sheep left, so I gave out the remainder of these. Next morning before sunrise a visit to the *sokota* was productive of an oryx.

During my wanderings round camp that day I struck another little *sokota*, consisting of a small patch of thick reeds, in the midst of which was a pool of clear water. I was led there by following fresh lions' spoor, and, examining it, found that three parties of lions had drunk the night before. Evidently this was a favourite place for them, but no other game-tracks led to the water, as this little patch of reeds was encompassed by bush and a few *mkoma* palms. The game preferred the *sokota* in the open plain, where they could see all around, whilst here a lion might be lurking in the bush close by, and catch them at their drink.

There was a group of palms about thirty yards from the spot at which the lions drank, so I put my men on to build a platform there, on which I might pass the night. I spent the day reconnoitring round Horr, and just after sunset went down to await the lions. Tengeneza insisted on accompanying me, although I felt sure that he would go to sleep ; also, the platform was rather small for two. However, I was glad to have some company, especially when I found that, owing to the small height of the palms, they had not been able to make the platform high up and safe, but only just above my head.

We waited silently for a while, Tengeneza looking out in one direction, and I watching the reed-patch. Presently I heard the deep and comfortable breathing of slumber coming from Tengeneza's side of the platform. After watching for about two and a half hours, I suddenly saw a shadowy form standing by the patch of reeds about thirty yards away. It had not " come," but seemed to have grown out of nothing. It was perfectly still, and I could not make out if it was anything, or just the result of continually straining the eyes to see in the dark.

I watched it till suddenly it moved, and then I saw that it was a lion facing me. I kicked Tengeneza, so as to prepare him for the report of my rifle, and then fired. There was a roaring grunt as the lion disappeared headlong into the bush. It only went a short distance, and then the noise suddenly ceased.

I could not tell if I had hit him or not. It was too

dark to see one's sights, but, as he had answered to the shot, it was probable that he was hit. Tengeneza assured me that he was hit, but this did not convince me, as he was sure to say that to please me. When I told him how I had first seen him, he replied : " Lions at night are often like that : they are invisible, and then they suddenly become visible."

We waited about a couple of hours more, and then we thought we heard a sigh. Nothing more appeared during the night, and with the first streak of dawn we descended and examined the tracks by the water.

We then followed them, and found, to our delight, that there was a blood-spoor. After going about twenty yards, it disappeared into a thick patch, so we cautiously made a détour, and struck the track at the other side. Now the blood was fresh, whereas before it had been dry, so he must have passed the night behind this place, moving on just before dawn. This looked as if he was badly hit. We followed the spoor back, to see where he had been lying. We found the spot under a bush, and there was a big pool of blood. We then followed the spoor on for a couple of hundred yards, and it entered a small patch of thick bush. We circled round this patch, but no spoor led out, so we knew he was in there.

My cautious tactics were to walk round and round, peering into this thick patch, ascertaining, at least, some of the places where he was not. This did not please Tengeneza, who, when we got opposite his place of entry, said, " Come on ; let us go in," and began marching in.

It was impossible, of course, to let Tengeneza precede me, as it would have ruined my reputation with the men, so I took him by the coat and pulled him back behind me. At the same instant I caught sight of the lion's head glaring at us from under a bush. If Tengeneza had rushed in, he would have been had for a certainty.

I fired at him, and he immediately collapsed. We went in, and, peering under the bushes, saw him stretched out. Tengeneza said : "He is alive. Why are his eyes fierce ?" And so they were, as he had a yellow glint in them, and at the same moment he moved a paw. We retired a few yards hurriedly, but soon his eyes glazed over and his limbs stiffened out.

He was a red-maned male, but not a very big specimen. He had been lying in a little depression behind a thick branch resting on the ground, and so only his head had been visible. The first shot had passed through a front leg, high up, and then through the stomach, while the second hit him in the neck, stunning but not killing him immediately.

I now wanted to push on to El Had without further waste of time, but the guides absolutely refused to go on, saying that we could not possibly reach the place from here, as the country was too bad, being all lava and rocks. I asked them what they had come here for, and they said because I wanted to come, but we could not go any farther ; we must turn back now, and perhaps we could get up into the Borana country from Maikona, but there was no way on. The country was too bad to travel at night, while the sun was too hot to travel by day, and not even the Borana would attempt the journey at this time of the year. If a man carried nothing but water, he would drink it all up before he got anywhere. This last remark very aptly described trekking in this country.

El Had, they said, would take a man without a load five days to reach, and the way led over lava. Moreover,

the water there was uncertain. I was very annoyed with
the guides, as they evidently did not know anything
about the country, and did not even know of the other
water-hole at Horr ; for, besides the lions' water, the camel-
grazing party had found a third fresh-water *sokota*.

When they suggested that we should turn round and
go back again, and refused to go on, I told them that they
could go back, as they were not wanted. So I sent them
off with only a small present, as they had come under
false pretences.

The next thing was to decide what should then be done.
I wanted to get northwards, if possible, but, failing this,
would strike across country westwards, and make for
Lake Rudolf. The first thing was to investigate northwards, and see if there were any signs of water, as I had
no faith in the guides' statement that there was none
either northwards or westwards. They had never even
heard of Rudolf.

I was not able to spend much time in these investiga-
tions, because of the food question. All I found was a
mass of sandhills, and in the far distance I could see a
lava escarpment. I secured a zebra for the men, which
kept them in food, with their usual half-ration of flour.
In the bush at Horr there were a number of vulturine
guinea-fowls, and whilst I was looking at the country
round, and shooting meat for the men, Tengeneza secured
some of these for my table.

Finally I had to give up the idea of proceeding northwards, and turn my attention to the consideration of
whether we should be able to reach Lake Rudolf with the
water we could carry. The porters were very horrified
when the guides were dismissed, and thought that our
last day was near. They could not possibly understand

that I could work out our position, and know where we were with reference to the lake. Also, being very bad hands at finding their way about, the idea of even returning without guides appalled them.

I called up Abdi and Omari, and told them that I was tired of the waterless country, and so was going to the lake, and soon we would be in position to camp by water every day. As I knew that the men were very fearful of our future movements, I instructed them to explain this to their men.

Whilst I was engaged on my calculations Abdi appeared, and asked me to come and see what Tumbo had done. I went to look, and met the resourceful Tumbo staggering up from the *sokota*, carrying an improvised water-skin made of the skin of our last sheep. This and a second one were christened Tumbo's babies.

If there had been any doubt in my mind as to whether we should undertake the long march to the lake, it was this incident that finally decided me.

CHAPTER XI

TUMEPONA WATER-HOLE

OUR own position I had worked out on the map, and as the position of Lake Rudolf was known, it was possible to measure the distance as the crow flies. The part of the shore for which I intended to steer was the little bay just south of Longendoti Mountain.

Although one knew the distance and the direction of the point to be reached, it was impossible to guess what kind of country lay between us and the lake. Assuming that it was fairly good going, and that the men kept up their spirits and marched well, I calculated that the water we could carry would give us each two small bowls a day, with a little extra for the porters carrying loads. In a temperate climate such a small ration of water per diem would have been no hardship, but here it was miserably inadequate.

A serious consideration was the nature of the country. Fortunately, the moon was nearly full, so that we could take advantage of practically the whole night for marching; but if we met with very broken country, with steep lava escarpments and ravines, it might not be possible to proceed at night. As a long march during the day was out of the question under such a powerful sun, this would effectually stop us.

Still, I had another resource to fall back upon, and that was, should we meet with such country, to leave all our loads behind us, and try to make the lake with just our water-tanks. Having arrived there, we could then send back the camels and a small party, with all the tanks, to fetch in our loads. Such a course would, however, entail serious delay, and might be fatal to our food-supply.

The chief difficulty to contend with was the slowness of the men and camels picking their way at night over loose stones or through dust and volcanic débris. This made the fatigue and length of time of the marches actually performed out of all proportion to the ridiculous little distance they appeared when plotted off on the map. My great fear, too, was that the men would lose heart, in which event we most certainly should not reach our destination.

I knew that nearly all the men and Omari were in favour of taking the guides' advice and going back. Abdi, however, was, as usual, quite ready to do as I wished, and, I believe, almost as anxious as I was to push through to the journey's end at all hazards. Besides being pleased at Tumbo's resource in making the water-skins, I gathered from this that Abdi had imbued his men with the proper spirit.

Before starting, I did my best to cheer up the men, and make them put their faith in me, addressing them as follows :

" You have heard the guides say that we cannot reach water northwards, and we have tried that country, and it is bad. Of the country westwards they know nothing, and admit that they have never been there. Even if they had, of what use would they be, for they

could not even find the water at this place, where they say
that they themselves used to live ?

"They did their best to cause us trouble and suffering
in coming here. Of what use are the guides of this
country ? Do you not remember how in the Elges they
told us that we should reach water on one day, and we
did not ? Now I have sent these two guides away, and
have decided to become myself the guide of this caravan,
and lead you of my own wisdom.

"The place to which I have decided to go is Em-bassu
Narok (Lake Rudolf), for there is much water. If you
say, How can I know the way, when I have never yet been
there ? I tell you that the wisdom of the white man is
greater than you can fathom.

"Had I wished to go there from the first, I could have
led you there, for other white men have been there, and
the way is written in books of learning. The reason I
came here was that no white man had yet been here, and
I wished to find a new country.

"We have found a new country here, and now I have
measured the stars, and find that there is a way to Embassu Narok. But I will not deceive you : the distance
is great, and there may be bad country in the way.
If I told you that it was near, and that we should have
plenty of water in the way, then would you recognize
my words as those of a fool.

"No ; we shall have but little water in the way, but
much water when we reach there. This is my plan, and
when you hear it you will recognize that my words are
spoken with wisdom. We will leave here this evening,
when the strength of the sun is but little, and will march
all through the night and as long as we may to-morrow
morning, making but short halts on the way.

" All this we must do on the water that is in our water-bottles, but when we halt to-morrow, then each one will have a bowl of water, and those that carry loads will have a bowl and a half. In the evening we will have another bowl to put in our water-bottles, and will march on all through that night. Next day will be the same, and we will march through the next night.

" On the following morning you will not have water, but you will have the sight of Embassu Narok to gladden your hearts, and we will march that day until we reach it. And the place that we shall reach on the lake will be the old camp of another white man, and I will give you a sign by which you may recognize it from afar. There will be white sand, and thick bushes like those called by the Kikuyu *nyambura*."

This last touch was put in from Von Höhnel's description of their camp, which was amidst what he called " succulent bush " growing in sand. This succulent bush I afterwards learnt was the shrub called by the Swahilis *msuaki*, already referred to.

The preparations for the journey were soon made. I looked up the declination of the moon in the nautical almanac, selected the equatorial stars which would serve our purpose, and jotted down their declinations in my pocket-book. I also noticed a rocky peak in the distance, which might serve to guide us, as our direct route passed under its southern end.

The new water-skins and other water-vessels were filled, the only remaining *han* was put aside for the use of the mule, and two bottles were filled for Narok, to last her till the first issue of water, when she would draw the same rations as everybody else, or a little more if she showed signs of great exhaustion.

Finally, the camels were loaded, and after a last drink from Horr *garba*,* we started.

The first part of the journey led over sandhills, and then we struck a sandy watercourse, where we rested for a little, and continued over an absolutely flat plain, composed of level, smooth rock. We had lost sight of the rocky peak soon after starting, but as the night wore on I hoped to see it against the sky-line.

In the early hours of the morning we struck a belt of bush and another watercourse. On arrival here I was immediately aware by the scent that there had recently been elephant at this place, and, looking carefully, I discovered their spoor by the light of the moon. As we pushed through this bush patch in the utter stillness of the night there was a sudden loud crashing sound, and then the familiar "puff, puff" as a rhino we had disturbed crashed through the bush in front of me and blundered off.

I was glad to emerge from this bush patch and reach the open plain again, as the way was easier, and the chance of large pachyderms careering round in the dark gave both myself, the men, and the camels the jumps.

The non-appearance of the peak had puzzled me, but presently the reason for this became apparent, for a long black form loomed up in front of us. As we came near it rose higher and higher, till we could see a long lava escarpment, running north and south, silhouetted against the sky-line, and concealing from view the setting moon.

At the base were game tracks, and I felt certain that under this escarpment, either to north or south, must be water—probably water-holes of the same type as those under the escarpment we had left behind us. However,

* Horr *garba* is the Borana name for the Sokota nearest our camp, meaning the "rush (grown) Horr."

a search for these would entail camping here, and if the search was unproductive, or the water proved salt, we should then be compelled to return to Horr, and so waste valuable time.

Behind us the plain was still lit up by the moonlight, but here under the escarpment we were in shadow, so that our way up was difficult. I selected a spur, and began climbing this. The escarpment was composed of masses of loose bits of lava thrown together, but here they were rounded fragments, whereas on the other side of the plain the lava was sharp and jagged.

As I was getting near the top of the slope I suddenly stopped, for I was semi-conscious of something moving just in front of me. Seeing nothing, I lay down, to get a better view, and then made out a shadowy form against the sky-line, moving diagonally across my front.

Tengeneza, who had been just behind me, came up and lay down beside me, and as he did so the form separated into two, and we could see two long bodies advancing obliquely across the spur to the left. Then they passed into a depression, and were lost to sight.

I stood up to try and get another glimpse of these figures, and at the same time Tengeneza caught hold of me, and pulled me back, so I knew that he had formed the same opinion as I had. He whispered to me : " There are no horns, so they must be either lion or rhino ;" to which I replied : " I don't think that they are rhino."

Presently we advanced up the spur, and from the nullah below us on our left we heard a rasping purr repeated a couple of times, which told us that they were lions.

We waited for the men and camels, then proceeded to the top of the escarpment, and found that the moon was setting. After travelling a short distance, our path being

made difficult by the loose boulders of lava, we came to
steep nullah across our path. As it would have beer
impossible to get the camels down this in the dark, we hac
to stop here till the dawn. Forming the camels into a
circle, we made them kneel down, and unloaded them, anc
we lay beside them on the rocks to get what rest we could

I gave out a little water to the porters who had beer
carrying loads, but the others had to do without. I had
just settled myself down when Abdi came to me, and saic
that three lions were sitting down close by on the other
side of the camels. He was sure that they were lions.
I said : " If that is the case, we will fire a volley at them."
This may sound rather unsporting, but I could not afford
to run the risk of losing a camel, or having the men disturbed, when they wanted all their strength for the
morrow.

I went and lay down where Abdi directed me, and
certainly saw three forms, but what they were I could
not tell, as they appeared perfectly stationary. I said
to Abdi : " I don't believe that those are lions, for they
do not move." Abdi said : " No, not now, for they are
sitting watching us; but I saw them move before you
came here." As he seemed so certain, I gave the order
to fire, and a volley was fired, but the three objects still
remained stationary. I gave the order to advance, and
we advanced about fifteen yards, and lay down again.
The three objects were gone.

We returned to our first position, and there they were
again! How small we felt! The objects we had been firing
at were three little tufts of grass not ten yards from us.
I went back to lie down, cursing Abdi and myself for being
two excitable fools.

After an hour and a half's sleep dawn broke, and we

loaded up the camels again. The going was bad, but we could now see how to pick our way. We proceeded till, as the sun became unbearably hot, we saw a valley below the escarpment, and some thorn-trees, which would afford a certain amount of shade.

We descended from the escarpment, and struggled on till we reached the shelter of these trees. On the way a curious object appeared in the distance, which I at first took to be a Waller's gazelle, but which through glasses proved to be a tall, thin, white ant-hill. We had not seen one for perhaps two months, and I remembered that Von Höhnel remarked on meeting with white ant-hills for the first time near Longendoti. So I pointed this out to the men, and said : "There is a sign that we are in the right way, for it is written in a book I have here that there are no white ant-hills along the Embassu Narok until the camp is reached for which we are making."

When the camels had been unloaded and turned out to graze, we dealt out the ration of water from "Tumbo's babies," as the men called the water-skins. One had leaked on the way, and both had rotted, and the smell of the water was vile. The men did not seem to mind it much, although it nearly made me sick to smell it. Tumbo's sage remark was : "The water itself is quite good and sweet ; it is only that it has the smell of the skin in it." Fortunately the skins were emptied before it came to my turn, so I did not have to drink this water.

After having had their ration of water, the men lay down, and immediately went to sleep, food being, of course, quite out of the question, as our mouths and throats were so dry that it would have taken gallons of water to wash down the least fragment of food. I was not so lucky as the men, as I could not sleep, and lay on

the sand, moving about to try and keep in the small
patches of shade from my tree, with head and eyes
burning from the heat and thirst. Narok kept me
company, and moved with me from one patch of shade to
the other with her tongue out. Every now and then she
would go and lick her empty water-plate, and look at me
beseechingly.

Before we started on I made an effort to go out and see
if there were signs of water to be found anywhere in the
valley on one side, while Omari went in another direction.

In the afternoon we loaded up again, and after a ration
of water had been given out to last through the night, we
proceeded. As there was a steep escarpment to be
ascended on the other side of the valley, I proceeded to
choose a good route for the camels to climb. I also
wanted to see what the country was like on the other side.

I reached the top, and, leaving Tengeneza to mark the
way for the camels, went on, and hit on an old elephant-
path leading westwards. As this was the direction in
which we wanted to go, and would, moreover, avoid the
worst country, I was overjoyed, and determined to stick
to it through the night for as long as possible.

The men were a long time coming up, and then progress
was painfully slow, as they straggled tremendously.
Every quarter of an hour or so I had to wait for them to
close up, and threaten them with all sorts of punishments
if they did not step out. The camels lagged up the
escarpments, and the men struggled on listlessly, hardly
noticing what I said.

The moon was bright, and the elephant-track proved
very fair going. As we trekked along we suddenly came
on a circular wall of stones, showing that at one time
there must have been inhabitants here, perhaps Turkana.

Then two other elephant or rhino paths converged with the one we were on—a favourable portent.

Suddenly we dipped down into a little nullah, and as we reached the bottom I heard a lapping sound from close by. I rushed to the spot, and found Narok with her nose poked down a long crack in the lava, and there was water the whole length of this crack, which was about ten yards long by a foot broad.

I immediately knelt down to try the water before informing the porters, for it might have been salt, and I did not wish to disappoint them. It was sweet and pure, but I did not wish to show any unseemly joy at finding water, or let them think that I was at any time uncertain as to whether we should ever reach Rudolf. So when the leading porters came up, while the sais was calling out, " Water, water !" like a maniac, I said, " If anybody wants any water, there is some in that hole there."

The porters hardly believed at first, but when they realized they threw themselves down beside the water, crying out : " Tumepona bwana tumepona !" (We are saved, master—we are saved !). Whilst they were drinking I went on and inspected the sandy bottom of the valley beside the lava crack, and found fresh traces of elephant—in fact, so fresh that they must have been digging in the river-bed as we came up. There were one or two holes scooped out in the sand. At the bottom of two of them was a little muddy water.

I came back to the men, and said : " I think we will camp here ; we have, of course, plenty of water to go on with, but as there are elephant here, it would be rather a good thing to stay."

On the other side of the sandy watercourse we found a little ring of thorn-trees round a nice level place for the camels to kneel on, so, after the porters had drunk their fill, we unloaded here, and food was given out. We had had no food since leaving Horr, so I now gave out a full ration, and promised to obtain some meat for the men on the morrow in addition to their ration.

After having fed, I had just got to sleep, when I awoke with a start, and seized my rifle. The camels were standing up, and some of them were gurgling, which meant danger, and at the same time the night-watchman rushed up to me, and said that there was a rhino in the middle of the camp. I hurriedly shoved on my boots, but before I could get up I heard " puff, puff, puff " going off into the night, so, after taking a turn round to reassure the camels, I went to bed again.

Camels make excellent sentries at night, as they are quick of ear and scent, and always stand up if there is any danger about. Somalis say that the only things an old male camel will stand up and gurgle for at night are a lion, a rhino, or a strange man. If it is only a strange woman, they take no notice. They always seem wonderfully tractable with women, and allow strange women to load them, whereas they are often afraid of a man to whom they are not accustomed.

After these doings there was not much left of the night, but we slept till after sunrise. I decided to stop here to-day, and start next afternoon, as it was necessary for the camels to get some grazing, for on the march they get little or nothing. It was also necessary to obtain some meat to buck up the men, and help eke out the rations. An elephant would have suited us nicely, but my first duty to the men was to shoot anything I saw, at the risk of disturbing any elephant in the vicinity with my shots.

There was little to be obtained in the neighbourhood

CAMP AT TUMBOONA

The extraordinary effect, as of snow, is produced by the bright sun on the white sand. It was into the little ring of thorn trees here seen that the rhinoceros who disturbed us at night found his way.

except gazelle, and the occasional elephant and rhino who visited the water. The gazelle were not plentiful, they were very wary, and there was not much cover under which to stalk them. The result was that I spent a very long, hot, tiring day stalking and crawling on my stomach over hot lava rocks, but managed to bag five gazelle, to the joy of the men.

During the day I saw a party of five cheetah, but they saw me first, and bolted off. No fresh elephant or rhino tracks were met with.

An examination of the watercourse showed that there was no other place up or down stream at which water came to the surface, so our luck was great in striking it here.

By the tracks in the river-bed it appeared that rhino often visited the water-hole at night, and one of the men said that during the night he had gone to fetch a drink, and saw two rhino there. So after dinner that night I crept out to the water-hole, and had not been there very long before I saw two great forms coming down the dry river-bed.

I crept back, and waited opposite the water, but presently heard them digging in the sand above me. When I tried to approach them, my boots made such a noise amongst the stones of the nullah that I returned to camp, changed to a pair of rubber-soled boots, and came out again. As I pushed through the bush just behind camp, I saw the rhino dimly outlined on the other bank. They had evidently heard something to alarm them, or seen or smelt the camp-fires.

As they were about to depart, I crept across the river-bed, and got them outlined against the sky. I could not see my sights, and should not have fired, but I thought what a blessing so much meat would be to make up our short rations, and so was tempted to try a shot just as they were going. The result was that I sighted too high, as one generally does at night, and the bullet passed over them. They bolted, and presently I heard something else coming through the bush. Thinking that it might be another, I sat still in the river-bed, but it was only Kitabu and the night-watchman. I asked them what they were doing, and where they were going to, and they said : " Oh, we heard you fire, and came to see if you were all safe."

I was much touched at the solicitude of these good, faithful souls, especially after the way I had been swearing at them the night before to get them along.

CHAPTER XII

WE REACH LAKE RUDOLF

IT was not possible to delay here any longer, so I gave it out that we were going to start again. Omari came to me with a very long face, and said that the men would never agree to go on ; they were frightened that they would die of thirst on the way, and would never consent to leave the water.

I did not wonder that the men felt mutinous after all they had endured, when they thought of facing a waterless march again to a destination unknown. I said to Omari : " The men can stop here as long as they like, if they eat nothing the while. Will they consent to that ?'

Omari replied : " How can we live without food ?" to which I answered : " Just so ; that is why we are going on."

The country in front of us appeared to be a broken, intersected country, difficult to travel over. If the men got too depressed, they would go so slowly and lag so at night over this broken ground that they would cover no distance at all. I could see that they were very down and played out with the heat, as they did nothing but sleep all day. When I wanted men to come out with me or to fetch in meat, no volunteers sprang up as usual; the headman had to go round and stir them up.

I called up the men, and addressed them as follows

"Now I see that you have all become as women, and your hearts have turned to water. You say in your hearts, 'The *bwana* is going to take us out into the waterless country, and there let us die'; and when I say that Embassu Narok (Rudolf) is near, you do not believe me.

"Now, how am I going to get a caravan of women to Embassu Narok ? I shall get there, for my heart has not turned to water, but you—how shall I get you there ?

"This is what I am going to do : I am going to prove to you that my words are true. I shall start from here to-night, alone, and in my hand I shall take a bottle, and I shall go down to the lake and fill the bottle, and bring it back here on the third day.

"When you taste the water, you will know that it is the water of Embassu Narok, for it is not sweet like the water here, but bitter. Now, if I do not come back, you will know that you were right, and that I have lied to you about the lake. But if I come back in three days, I shall come back evilly disposed towards you, and will make you all carry sixty-pound loads, as you do in our country, and I will reduce your rations, to make up for the time you have wasted. What say you ?"

They murmured amongst themselves, and then said : 'We will follow you." This would have sounded better if they had not added : "We cannot be left by ourselves."

Then I said : "Well, if I let you come with me, you must step out, and not loiter on the way. Now, listen. We will march this afternoon and through the night, and to-morrow you will see Embassu Narok ; but it will be far off. I told you that you would see it on the third

day from Horr, but we have stopped here on the way.
Now, see if my words do not come true."

We had no longer " Tumbo's baby " to augment our
water-supply, but the distance was short, and if only the
men stepped out, we ought to do it easily enough. We
started away by an elephant-track, and at first all was
easy going, but, as the afternoon wore on, we had to
leave our elephant-track, which went off northwards.
Seeing that the country ahead would probably be rather
rough, I pushed on with Tengeneza and the sais to see
what it was like.

At sunset we were a long way ahead of the caravan.
Just in front the view was restricted by a lava rise. As I
wanted to select a good line before it got dark, I mounted
the mule, and went forward to reconnoitre the ground,
telling the sais and Tengeneza to light a fire of some dead
grass and sticks, to guide the porters.

Having ascended a small hill, and seen as much as
possible of the country to the front, I returned, and found
that the pair I had left behind had displayed the typical
African's devilish cunning in doing the wrong thing if it
is possible to do so ; for in a perfectly open country they
had selected the only patch of bush there was, and lit
the fire behind this, so that its light could not be seen by
the advancing caravan.

I felt most annoyed to think that the porters might
even now be worried as to where we were, and perhaps
had wearied themselves unnecessarily. It is no good
ever getting angry with natives, as they will then pretend
that they are hopeless idiots, and understand nothing you
say—an attitude which often makes one lose one's
temper, and then they score, as that is what they wished
you to do.

So on this occasion I merely said : " Men of wisdom and learning, masters of guile, and sons of a sage, how are the porters going to see your fire ?"

When the porters came up, we proceeded by the light of the moon, and spent a dreary night trudging over the lava till, shortly after midnight, the country became so intersected and broken that it was impossible to select a route. We therefore lay down to rest.

When dawn broke, I awoke the men, and while they were loading the camels, ascended a small peak near, thinking that from the top a view of the lake would be obtained. To my disappointment, however, nothing could be seen except a lava ridge, about a mile in front of us. I consoled myself by thinking that, when we reached this ridge, we ought certainly to see the lake. So we proceeded, picking our way over the broken lava and always keeping our general bearings by the sun, so that we should hit off the lake just south of Mount Longendoti.

When we reached the ridge, it was necessary to choose a good line of ascent for the camels. On arriving at the top, I eagerly looked for the lake, but only another lava ridge just in front was visible. Again we had to make a détour to descend, and again we climbed a ridge, and again I was disappointed of my view of the lake.

Now the sun was mounting up, and the lava rocks so unbearably hot that it was impossible to rest the hand on them. Every moment I expected to hear that some of the men were unable to proceed any farther, so despondent had they grown, and still the promised lake was not in sight.

We laboriously ascended another ridge, and as I reached the top, a most magnificent view opened out before me.

There, far away below me, was Lake Rudolf, glistening in the sun, and stretching away to the right and left as far as the eye could reach. The country between me and the lake was laid out like a panorama, and I could easily select the best course to follow, which led down by a line of spurs to a broad nullah, and thence along the bottom to within a few miles of the lake.

I took but a momentary glance at this picture, and then, as the descent immediately in front was too steep for the camels, turned off sharp to the left along the top of the ridge, to reach the line of spurs I had selected.

The tired porters and camels struggled up to the top, and then turned along the ridge to follow me. So much had they lost heart that they did not even notice the lake for some time, but just plodded wearily along. Suddenly I heard a murmuring of voices, and knew that they had seen it, and the sais rushed forward, saying : " Look, master, look !"

I replied : " What's the matter ?"

" Look there—look down below !"

I affected to look at the foot of the ridge, and said : " What is that you are so excited about ? It must be elephants. Where are they ?"

" Don't you see Embassu Narok ?"

" Oh, that !" I replied. " Have you only just seen it ? What did you imagine I was climbing up to look at while you were loading the camels ? I told you that you were going to see Embassu this morning, and now you have seen it, you come and tell me the news, as much as to say, ' You are not a liar, after all.' "

This, said in a loud voice to impress the men, had the desired effect, for I heard them murmuring to each other :

12

" He knew all the time, yet he has never been here.'
" The white men who measure stars are like that."

I told the men who carried the theodolite afterwards
that, while measuring stars at Horr, I had found a very
good one, which had led us to the water at Tumepona
first, and then taken us on to the lake. This, told in
confidence one night, was sure to have been repeated to
everyone.

Although we could now see the lake, there was still a
long way to go, and we picked our way down the spur
till we reached a dry, sandy nullah. Here was a thick
tree, giving good shade, called in Somali *garas*. Abdi
was very pleased to see this tree, as he said that he had
not seen one since leaving Somaliland.

I found afterwards that the bush called " succulent
bush " by Von Höhnel was nothing more than our old
friend the *msuaki ;* but from his description, I jumped to
the conclusion that it was what the Kikuyu call *nyambura*. I had told the men that this would be a sign by
which they would recognize our camp on Rudolf. I
fancied now that this *garas* tree might be the " succulent
bush " referred to, and it was necessary to explain to the
men that my words had so far come true, so that they
would have more faith in me another time.

So I said to Abdi : " Behold, this is the tree of which I
spoke, and which I found written in one of my books of
learning. We have no names for these trees in my
language, but I saw written, ' a thick tree, on which was a
berry,' so I said in my heart, ' It is indeed the *nyambura*.'
Now I see that it is the *garas* tree."

We gave out water, but it had grown so hot in the
metal tanks that it was impossible to drink it immediately
it was poured out. At three o'clock we moved on again,

and as we reached the lower country the travelling grew better, and near the lake it was quite flat and good. The sun set, and we travelled on, content to think that we should reach the lake during the night. At last we came to an old level of the lake, marked by a hippo skull, but we had some way to go yet.

The way now led over dry, sun-cracked mud for a couple of miles, and at last we reached a fringe of grass and reeds and the lake. We waded in, and tried the water, but it was very vile. Especially was it bad here, as the water was very shallow, and the mud had been stirred up by numerous wading birds and ducks. We then looked for a spot in which to lie down for the rest of the night.

At dawn next day we searched for a suitable camp. I could not locate Teleki's camp in the thick " succulent bush," the only bush being a long way back from the lake. His camp was probably in that bush, but since his time the lake had receded considerably, and so that would have been much too far for the porters fetching water.

We found bush only growing near the old margin of the lake, and between this and the actual water there was from two to three miles of dried, sun-cracked mud, most trying to walk over.

During our trek up Rudolf we had only the option of either camping miles away from the lake and getting a little shade, or camping near the water on the bare, dried mud in a shadeless camp. The only exception was where the shore was steep and rocky, for at such places the subsidence of the lake—a matter of only six or eight feet, perhaps—did not materially increase the distance of the water, as it did on the almost level plain.

We could see such a place a mile or two to the north,

where a little cliff—the tail-end of Mount Longendoti—bordered the lake, and on the top of this was a little clump of bush.

I had had to give out a full ration during the night, but to-day I hoped to obtain some game, and save our fast-diminishing food-store. So I directed the caravan to proceed to this spot, while Tengeneza was to try and shoot a duck for me. After trying for a hippo before sunrise. I went to look for game, taking with me a porter, who. from his slow gait, bore the nickname of Kobe (Tortoise).

By a fortunate chance, I was able to surprise a herd of zebra in a little dip, and, firing, dropped one of them On looking round for the tortoise, I found that he had lagged behind, and wildly beckoned to him to come and perform the last rites. Instead of hurrying up, he stood still. After I had shouted and whistled for some time he began slowly advancing again. I pointed to the zebra and proceeded, hoping to get another.

However, the animal, who had been lying as if dead suddenly got up, and galloped off, and we never saw him again. I must have hit him in the neck, "creasing" him. After an ineffectual effort to obtain something else I made for camp, and asked Omari why he had sent a tortoise with me instead of a man. The porters were very annoyed when they heard what they had missed, as they love zebra-meat, because it is so fat.

As the game only come down to drink at the lake, after wards going inland to graze, it was no use trying again till the evening. Omari said that there were a lot of fish near the shore, and suggested that we should try to net them with calico. So some lengths of calico were given out, and we waded into the lake, some holding the calico, and others driving fish into it.

We were not very successful, as we did not catch anything bigger than an inch or two in length ; but we got some nice little fish like whitebait, which made quite good eating. The men soon got bored with this, however, as whitebait was much too delicate for their palates, which required to be tickled with a few pounds of meat apiece. I tried fishing with a line, but the first fish that came broke it.

The wealth of bird-life on the lake is remarkable. A few yards from the shore there is one long line of aquatic birds the whole length of the lake. The east side is generally very shallow, while I believe the west side is deeper, and the banks more precipitous.

In most places where we camped one could wade out several hundred yards into the lake, and still the water would only be knee-deep. This shallow water, containing multitudinous small fish, affords a capital fishing-ground for the aquatic birds. Sometimes great flocks of geese and ducks may be seen together, and connecting these flocks is one continuous, unbroken line of other birds, such as pelicans, plover, cranes, divers, cormorants, and a multitude of other fish-eaters. After the utter silence of the uninhabited solitudes through which we had passed, the Babel of quacks and caws in the early morning, and the splashings of the birds, was most refreshing.

In the afternoon some *haul* came near camp, and I secured some of them. Whilst we were clearing a spot for the tent, an unopened tin was found, which showed that some white men had camped here. It was opened by Sadi in great excitement, and he pronounced it to be tea. When they tried it, however, it proved to be hops.

I was able to assuage his disappointment, as I had brought a lot of spare tea, which I distributed at intervals amongst the headmen and boys, whilst for the porters I had tobacco and cigarette-papers. The latter I did not produce until I knew that everybody had run out, which was not long after leaving Rumuruti. Tengeneza had shot some ducks, and so, with one of these and white-bait, the dinner was excellent, although it was marred by the filthy water.

From Von Höhnel's account of Teleki's trip I gathered that it was impossible to follow the lake-shore here, as Mount Longendoti rises too precipitously out of the water. His party proceeded behind Longendoti, and reached the lake again at Alia Bay.

On this march they obtained water by digging at the first camp, and then had a trying, waterless march till they found a little water, but not sufficient for his numerous followers, in a basalt ravine. I was not sure if I should be able to locate this spot from his description, so we had to be prepared to march to Alia without water.

With this in my mind, I announced to the men that we must push on that night, and would have to leave the lake, but would meet it again on the third day, or perhaps the second if we marched well. They implored me not to leave the lake, but to follow it up, so that we might have water every night. I then asked them : " Who found this lake ? Was it you or was it me ?"

They replied : " It was you, *bwana.*"

" And did you see it on the day I said you would, or did you not ?"

" Yes, we saw it."

I said : " Then it is my lake to leave if I wish, and on the day that I say you will see it again, you will see it."

They replied : " But cannot you follow the shore, so that we may have water every day ?"

I answered : " Is there anyone amongst you who knows the way ?"

They replied : " No ; how can we know the way in a strange country ?"

Then I answered : " If there is none here who knows the way, you must take my counsel, for I know the way, and my plan is this : We cannot follow the shore, for there is a mountain that rises out of the lake. Had you been baboons, you might have taken that way, but you are only men. Therefore we must pass behind this mountain. We will travel to-night and to-morrow, and then we may find a small spring of water in the mountains ; but this spring of which I speak may be dried up, so we may not be able to find it.

" On the next day we will journey on and reach the lake again. There you will certainly get water the day after to morrow, and you may also have some to-morrow."

This point having been settled, it only remained to decide on the hour of departure most suitable to the phase of the moon. This proved to be two o'clock, so I gave the order for the camels to commence loading at midnight.

CHAPTER XIII

A LUCKY FIND OF WATER

ACCORDING to Von Höhnel's map, we had to round the southern end of Mount Longendoti, and then march parallel with this mountain, which runs due north and south. We rounded the end, and then I endeavoured to strike northwards, but we struck a stony country, intersected with ravines, which made very indifferent travelling at night, as it was impossible to select a good line. As we topped the edge of one of these ravines, the most appalling roar suddenly burst upon our ears from close at hand. Wondering what this unknown savage beast could be, I slipped the safety-catch of my rifle, and prepared for the worst. Then the sound tailed off into the loud, raucous bray of a Grevy's zebra, and I felt rather foolish at having been startled by nothing.

Von Höhnel mentions several times how he and Teleki often mistook this sound for a lion's roar. I was not struck with the resemblance myself, the sound being more like a very powerful donkey's bray than anything else. So great is the resemblance that the first time I heard this sound at night, which was at Lesirikan, I thought that some of our donkeys had broken loose, and called out to Abdi, who was sleeping by them, to count them. This braying sound is sometimes commenced with a roar like that of a camel.

As the country was so intersected near Longendoti, I thought it advisable to give that mountain a wide berth, and so struck eastwards till we reached more level country, and then northwards again. In this way we met with very fair country, over which we marched well. High ground gradually began to appear on our right, and as dawn broke we found ourselves following up a valley about four miles broad, between Longendoti and this high ground. On our right was a many-peaked hill of white and yellow earth and lava.

Close under this hill we could see from the trees along it that there was a watercourse. At one spot the trees looked green, and so I sent the sais off to investigate the river-bed at this place, and see if there was any chance of obtaining water by digging. I told him to follow up the river-bed, which came from the direction in which we were proceeding, and to stick a spear into the sand at intervals, and see if it was moist at the tip.

In every other direction the country looked most forlorn and desolate, being covered with little flat-topped hills and miniature plateaux of ashes and volcanic débris, looking like the mounds of waste thrown out from mines more than anything else. Some of the mounds were of soft, powdery volcanic ash, which flew up in clouds when trodden on. This afforded a proof how very minute the rainfall must be in this part, as one good downpour would have washed away a mound of this description. In front of us the valley narrowed as the high ground on the right neared, and finally met with Longendoti. For this point of junction we steered.

Shortly after dawn Narok, trotting along briskly, as she did before the sun rose, came over a little lava ridge, and suddenly came face to face with a civet-cat, which had been lying in a little hollow in the lava, caused by an air-bubble when the rock was in a molten state. The civet-cat jumped up, with bristles standing erect, a truly fearsome-looking object. The two animals stood facing each other, not two yards apart, each struck with the unwonted appearance of the other. What would have been the next act in this little drama I do not know, for at that moment the civet-cat saw me close by, and turned and fled, Narok giving chase, but being very careful not to make a tremendous effort to catch it.

Presently we met with a herd of *haul*, and I had a shot and wounded a good male, but he made off. Narok followed, and pulled him down three times, but each time I was afraid to fire for fear of hitting the dog. Finally the *haul* got away and disappeared over the stony rise eastwards. At the same time the sais came back with the news that he could not find any signs of water.

The chase had taken us about a mile and a half from the caravan, and as this had all been performed at a run, I felt more dry and thirsty than usual, and decided to break my rule and drink from my water-bottle for the first time during a march. Then I thought of the filthy Rudolf water, now hot and puggy in my water-bottle, and what a pity it was that, having made up my mind to an excess, there was nothing nice to drink. Then a brilliant idea struck me : I would put some cocoa into the water, just as it was, and shake it up. This I did during the rest of our trip up Rudolf, and although it did not quite disguise the taste, it made it ever so much better.

As we proceeded, a steep-sided ravine in the side of Longendoti came into view. It did not look like Teleki's basalt ravine, but might contain water, so I sent Masharia, the Kikuyu, to investigate. Just beyond this was another deep ravine, also in the side of Longendoti, and it was from this that the watercourse in the valley took its origin.

Directly I saw it I thought that, if there was water in the neighbourhood at all, it would be there, so I led the caravan straight across to it, although it was somewhat out of our way. My idea was that, if there was no water, we should find shade under its precipitous sides in which to pass the middle of the day before moving on in the afternoon.

As we drew near we passed the watercourse, which had taken a sharp turn towards the mountain, and here, in the sandy bed, was a little tuft of grass, greener than any I had seen for days. This was a good sign, but on the bank above there was a better one—converging game tracks leading into the ravine, and on one of these was the fresh spoor of zebra. Zebra do not walk into a ravine like this without reason, so I had high hopes, although I did not mention them to the men.

The track led us into the ravine on a little ledge of rock above the watercourse, and just inside I saw below me a wall of black rock across the ravine, and at the foot of this a little pool of green water. The sais was with me, so I told him to go down and see if it was fresh. When he tried it he said it was sweet and good, so I went out and shouted to the men outside not to follow the rocky path I had taken, but to bring the camels up the sandy floor of the watercourse. As they entered the ravine below me, I said : " There is the spring I promised you."

I wondered whether this was Teleki's ravine. There were no columns of basalt here, or broken pillars lying

about on the ground, as he had described. Perhaps
Teleki's basalt columns were higher up this ravine. Anyhow, the water looked green and dirty, and there might
be better water farther up, so I started up the narrow
ravine, which wound into the heart of the mountain,
enclosed by perpendicular walls on either side. Here and
there was a wall of rock to be climbed, but generally the
bottom of the watercourse formed a flat sandy road
winding into the hills.

This ravine in the black lava rocks reminded me
irresistibly of the winding nullahs above the upper tanks
of Aden. The only living things to be seen here were
a few ravens, birds which truly love the solitude.

After proceeding a mile or so, I thought of my poor
camels, waiting to be unloaded. As no one had followed
me, all being much too engrossed in sampling the water,
I had to return myself to arrange for pitching camp.

The wind blew straight into the ravine, and animals
came in here to drink, so if camp was hidden away somewhere inside, it might be possible to secure a zebra, or
perhaps even a lion, at night by sitting over the water.
Thinking out this problem on my return journey, I chose
a spot inside the ravine where camp-fires would be
invisible from the outside. When I got back to the water,
I found a steep, stony path on one side of the wall of rock,
but the camels might not be able to mount this. Anyhow, we would try.

The individual temperaments of camels differ much
more than do those of horses, and by now we knew the
character of all our camels well. So I consulted with
Abdi as to which should be made to essay this feat first.
Finally, we decided on the two camels led by a fat little
youth called Yusufu. These were our two quietest ones,

and one of these had been used, so the Rendile who sold it said, to carry children from one kraal to another when changing quarters.

" The breaker of vessels," as I called the camel which had upset and broken *hans* in the Elges, would probably give the most trouble, so I gave orders for this one and a few of the most troublesome to be unloaded outside. Then, with smacks and " Oh-oh's !" (the noise made by the Rendile to encourage camels, meaning " Gee-up!"), we induced the whole caravan to go up the steep path and into the watercourse beyond. The men then brought in the spare loads, and we pitched camp on the sandy floor.

As there was only a thin layer of sand over the lava rock, it was impossible to drive in pegs, and so the tent-ropes had to be tied to blocks of rock.

The water had appeared very foul at first sight, looking thick and greenish, while the rocks around were covered with droppings of birds and baboons. However, now I came to taste it, I found that its appearance belied it, for it was cool and sweet, infinitely superior to the filthy water of Rudolf.

In the afternoon I sallied out, accompanied by Maja-liwa and two of the men, to look for game. We had a long and tiring walk over the volcanic débris, and saw nothing. Turning round, disgusted, we made for home, but on the way Majaliwa spotted two *haul* on a distant lava ridge. They had not seen us, and, knowing how short were our food-supplies, I determined to do my best to shoot them. There was but little cover to be had, and the stalking entailed a long and painful crawl over the sharp and baking lava rocks. Several times I got up close enough to shoot, but as they were moving all the time, they passed out of sight before I could get a steady aim. At last I got up again, but this time the alarm was given by four other gazelle, which had, unknown to me, formed part of the herd. They all bolted save one, which stood a moment, and I bowled him over, and then, jumping up, fired three long shots into the remainder, and bagged two of them. Majaliwa and his followers did not give them much chance of getting up again, but dashed at them and finished them off. I said : " You don't take so long over that as the Tortoise." " No," replied Majaliwa ; " no more Tortoise for us. We are all very hungry."

Leaving the three men to cut up the meat, I went off to make a little détour on my own account before returning to camp. Just north of our ravine was another, and out of it issued a similar watercourse, flowing eastwards, the only difference being that, after flowing for a few miles, it took a sharp bend to the north, instead of to the south, as did ours. Between these two watercourses was a neck of high ground joining Longendoti to the hills eastward.

I wondered if this could be Teleki's basalt ravine, and so paid it a visit. The sandy watercourse led into a narrow, deep-cut ravine, with perpendicular sides, but there was no resemblance to the picture given in Von Höhnel's book, and so I decided that it was not his ravine. A lion spoor led up the sandy bed of the nullah, and if I had hit this off in daylight, I could have followed him to his retreat.

Now, however, the sun had set, and so I hurried back, as I might not be able to find my way over the lava ridges in the dark. It was dark before I reached the ravine, and I came out on the high cliff above it, and saw a search-party going out with the lamp to look for me. I called to them to show me the way down the cliff, and when they had done this, despatched the lamp to meet the party bringing in the meat.

The three gazelles would only feed the men for one day, and so that night Tengeneza and I sat over the water-hole, hoping to obtain a zebra or a lion. Such was the difficulty in securing meat for the men in this country, and while continually on the move, that, had the two animals presented themselves together, I should have had to choose the former. Tengeneza went to sleep at once, making no pretence of keeping awake.

At eleven o'clock I woke him, and we returned to camp. At five next morning the night-watchman woke me, and Narok and I went to see if anything would come to drink in the morning. Nothing, however, came, although Narok once pricked up her ears as if she had smelt something.

We started away again the same day. The pool of water was now sensibly diminished, and would not have supported us for more than a day more. Shortly after leaving camp we met a zebra, which I was lucky enough to bag. We cut him up, and fastened the meat on the camels. He was full of water to bursting-point, and must have drunk within the hour. As he had not been to our ravine, it was only left to me to conclude that there must be water in the second ravine in which I saw the lion's spoor.

We followed parallel with the watercourse flowing northwards. Towards evening it suddenly entered a ravine, and, on looking down, I immediately recognized Teleki's basalt ravine, with the broken columns of

different sizes lying on the ground. The caravan passed
above it, but Bakari, the cook, and I descended and
searched for water. The place described by Von Höhnel
was easily recognizable now, but there was not a drop of
water, although there had been a little fairly recently.
Some doves sat cooing on the walls, and their presence
is generally a sign of water, but an exhaustive search
failed to bring any to light.

Many times during the last two days I had tried to
picture Teleki's enormous caravan travelling through the
selfsame desolate waste as we had just traversed, till the
picture had grown quite familiar to me. It was hard,
however, to imagine this lonely ravine peopled by his two
hundred followers, pushing and jostling each other,
shouting and fighting for the little water there was, as
described in the account of his travels.

We proceeded northwards, bivouacking that night, and
reaching Alia Bay next morning. Here Teleki and the
other travellers who have passed met with two fishing
villages on little flat islands a few hundred yards from the
shore. There was not a sign of the Elmolo, as these
people are called, or any trace of human habitation. The
Elmolo consist of a mixed community of fisher-folk,
drawn from the outcasts of different tribes living round
Rudolf, such as Reshiat, Turkana, and Samburr.

We followed round the bay to its north side. It
seemed to have shrunk considerably, and when we reached
here the reason for the absence of the Elmolo was apparent,
for their islands were now dry land, and half a mile from
the lake's margin. Being a very weak community, a
village on the mainland, where they were open to the
attack of anyone who chose to raid them, was not
according to their taste. On their islands they were

perfectly immune from attack, as none of the people likely to visit this spot are able to obtain canoes.

I was much disappointed at not meeting these people, as I wanted to have an opportunity of making inquiries as to their customs and habits, and also their language and origin. Their canoes, I suppose, are made on the Omo River, as there is not a tree on any other part of Rudolf out of which so much as a pig-trough could be made. When we had passed through this desolate, uninhabited part, and once again reached human beings, we heard that the Elmolo had taken refuge on Centre Island, one of three rocky peaks situated in the middle of the lake.

Round the edge of the lake here was a certain amount of grass, but between this belt of grass, several hundred yards wide, and the old shore of the lake was an expanse of dried, sun-baked mud, several miles across. Over this dried mud travelling was especially loathsome, as the feet sank into the cracks and the caked surface gave way as one trod on it.

The hot wind of the Borana country was not so powerful here. One also discovered that it was the sweeping over the lava and sand plains which made it so hot. Here, in the grassy fringe of the lake, if there was only a hundred yards of grass to the east of one, the heat of the wind was not oppressive ; in fact, by comparison, it appeared quite cool.

In Alia Bay the only kind of bushes close to the water are a few tamarisks, only a foot or two in height. To obtain anything better in the way of shade it would have been necessary to camp four miles from the lake. This being the case, we chose the site of an old Elmolo village on which to pitch our tents, as here was a little patch of sand rising above the level of the sun-cracked mud.

13

The wind sweeping over this expanse was scorching in our shadeless camp, and my camp-table was so hot under the tent that I could not bear my hand on it. There was a considerable quantity of game — oryx, zebra, topi, and *haul*—but it was impossible to get near any of them on the absolutely flat, dry mud.

One of the porters, going through the grass patch to draw water, said that he ran up against a buffalo, which chased him ; but when I went down to look at the spoor, I doubted the story, as I could only find tracks of a few days old. Natives see no difference between an old spoor and seeing an animal, and I have very often had natives rush in to tell me that they have just seen an animal when in reality they have only seen spoor.

Tengeneza brought in nine ducks' eggs which he had found. Curiously enough, natives seldom, if ever, eat eggs, and amongst different tribes there are various superstitions concerning the eating of them. These were a godsend to me, as I had not tasted eggs since leaving Rumuruti, two months ago.

In the evening there was a plague of small green flies off the lake. These flies are especially bad at certain times of the year on Lake Victoria, and sweep up with the wind in clouds, covering everything in their path. They effectually stop reading and writing at night, as they put out the lamp, and cover books and paper in myriads.

On checking the food-supply, I found that there were only three bags left. This meant but four days' full rations, or eight days' half rations. I had been unable to obtain any game on the bare plain here, and we could not be less than eight days reaching the Omo River. Our position for food now was thus as serious as our want of water had been. Had there been elephant or rhino in plenty, as in Teleki's time, it would have been easy to secure enough meat and to spare ; but, alas ! these days were past, and now only remained keen-eyed oryx, gazelle, and zebra on the perfectly bare, open plain.

My porters begged me to let them rest here a day or two, but this could not be done   To them the future was as nothing, so long as we had a bag or two of food left : they were content to dwell in the present only.   To me, however, the daily increasing dread of seeing my last ration given out before we had reached an inhabited country was an ever-present source of anxiety.   Long after the men had turned in to peaceful slumber I used to measure off the marches remaining before we reached the Omo again and again, and wonder if even there we should obtain the food we required so badly.

CHAPTER XIV

THE LAST OF THE UNINHABITED TRACT

I was heartily glad to leave our shadeless camp at Alia the day after we arrived there. The usual method of travelling now was to fill up water-tanks and start soon after twelve o'clock, and travel through the afternoon till it grew dark. So, as we often left the lake for a few miles, cutting across from bay to bay, we did not trouble to reach the water's edge that night, but just bivouacked wherever we happened to be.

The following morning we started on with the moon, which now rose late, and trekked as long as we could into the next day, or till we found a very favourable camp near the lake. We then halted and pitched camp, remaining till the following noon. Thus, although we marched each day, and bivouacked and camped alternate nights, we had every other day a rest of twenty-four hours in camp. This mode of progression was less trying to men and animals than an early start every day.

Shortly after leaving Alia Bay I secured a *haul*, an oryx, and a greater bustard, all of which we fastened on the camels. We then went on till dark, and bivouacked some distance from the lake. Shortly after dark we heard a lion roaring as he came from inland towards the lake, presumably to drink. The lion generally kills first, and then drinks in the early hours of the evening. In these arid plains I noticed that they usually drank shortly after dark.

We moved on next morning before dawn, and at ten o'clock found a dry watercourse, with some thorn-trees and a certain amount of shade, so we decided to camp here, although it necessitated a walk of a couple of miles to draw water. The reason we camped so early was that, shortly after starting at night, we had heard the sound of distant drumming coming from the north-east. The rhythm was exactly the same as that we had heard in the Elges.

Just before dawn the sound ceased. As any kraal here must in all probability draw water from the lake, I expected to cut across some tracks of either men or camels, but there was not a sign of any human being, nor had there been since we left Kalacha. This drumming puzzled me, and so we camped early, and I sent search-parties in different directions to look for smoke or human footsteps, while I set out to augment the meat-supply.

Grass and game were now more plentiful than they had been for a long time, and, moreover, the country lent itself more to stalking. I obtained a gazelle and a fine bull oryx, and so—for another day, at least—I was able to save my food-stores.

Tengeneza very kindly kept me in ducks, but I regretted much that, now there was such a glut of birds for the table, I could not enjoy them as I might have done in a colder climate. Owing to the disturbing influence of the lake water and the heat, I was unable to eat more than a couple of slices off a duck's breast daily. The extraordinary aridity of the atmosphere dried up the remainder of the bird to such an extent that it was uneatable the next day.

The search-parties returned, having failed to find any signs of human beings, and the porters were confirmed in their own conclusions as to the origin of the mysterious sounds we had heard.

Having had a short day's march and a good feed, the men's spirits had risen considerably, as could easily be told by their noisy conversation during the evening. Happy-go-lucky children, they had no thought about the time when our food-stores would give out, or misgiving lest I should not be able to shoot them meat in the future. With their stomachs full, they lived only in the present, and forgot even to anticipate the heat and burden of the morrow's march. Narok also found it pleasant enough : a good feed and plenty of water, and a cool, refreshing breeze off the lake—what more could she want ?

I alone amongst the whole caravan felt anxious as to the future, as I watched the camels growing weaker daily, and worked out a hundred times how long our remaining food could last, and what distance we should traverse in that time.

I am afraid that I must have been very trying to the men these days, as the constant anxiety about food, the daily petty worries and difficulties to be overcome, and a bad knee, which prevented my sleeping at night, combined to make me very irritable and cross. The men, however, if they noticed this, with characteristic good-humour, failed to be annoyed by it, but went about their work much as usual, sometimes forgetting the most necessary and daily duties, such as refilling the water-barrels, and at other times surprising me with their willingness and obedience.

Although they ignored my irritability, they did not treat Omari with equal tolerance. Omari was willing and hard-working, but, somehow, he could never make the porters do as he wished—on the contrary, he seemed to act on them as a red rag to a bull. He was constant in his complaints of their refusal to carry out my orders, and I tried again and again to support his authority, but without success. I had only to give an order through him to feel certain that it would not be carried out, whereas if I gave it myself, or through Abdi or Kitabu (the second in command of the porters), it was, with rare exceptions, immediately performed.

If I had abandoned earlier my attempt to establish Omari's authority, much friction would have been saved. Again and again I would find something wrong, such as an empty water-barrel left in the sun to warp and crack, after which it would, of course, leak. I used to say to Omari : " Have you suffered so little from thirst that you wish to destroy what vessels we have ?"

Omari used to reply : " Oh, master, I have told them to fill it, but they won't hear my words."

To this I would reply : " Whom have you told to fill it ?"

He would say : " The porters."

To this I answered : " You cannot give an order to a whole caravan to fill one barrel ; you must say, ' So-and-so and So-and-so, fill that water-barrel.' Then, if they refuse, come to me, and say, ' So-and-so and So-and-so have refused to fill the barrel,' and I will have them beaten at once."

Then perhaps I would go out and call two of the nearest men. " Fill that barrel at once, and when it comes to distributing the water, your share will be that which has leaked out, and mine that which remains."

With a cheerful laugh they would run off and do as

they were told, the more eagerly in that they felt that they had somehow scored off Omari. I felt sorry for Omari, but he grew more and more hopeless as time went on, till at last I had gradually to treat him as the figurehead he was, and trust to Kitabu to perform his duties.

Next day we trekked on after noon, and towards sunset struck a wide, bare plain, at the other side of which we could see *msuaki* bush. I was lucky in getting an oryx on the way. Level with the bush at the other side of the plain two round domes rose out of the lake. I looked again and again at these strange, distant objects, without being able to make them out. In the jagged lava I had never yet seen a rounded rock, and so felt convinced that they must be huts of Elmolo, transferred from their abandoned village, on the site of which we had camped.

It grew rapidly darker, till at last they were lost to sight ; but we trekked on in the dark till we reached the line of bush. Here I carefully selected a site for camp, and arranged a position for each fire, so that it should be invisible to the occupants of the supposed huts, and so not alarm them unnecessarily.

I decided not to trek the following morning, but to try to establish communication with these people, but directly dawn broke I saw that they were only rocks. I went to inspect them, and found that their tops, about ten feet above the water, represented a former level of the lake, and so had been rounded by the washing of the waves.

It was now too late to trek on in the morning, so I came back and had breakfast, and then started fishing. The water was too clear, and the only fish I hooked was lost by one of the men, who, in his excitement to help me, seized the line out of my hand. As I stood in the shallow water of the lake I saw large fish as dark blue objects darting about in the shallow water, but they refused all my allurements.

It was so pleasant, standing in the lake, with the generally hot breeze cooled to a certain extent by the water, that I decided to give the men and camels a long-promised rest. We had changed camp daily since Tumepona, so that there had not been much rest for either. After spending the whole morning in unsuccessful fishing, I tried to get a hippo, but these animals would not come near enough to the shore for a shot.

Not wishing to return empty-handed, I thought that I would try to shoot some of the big fish. Waiting for a favourable chance, and aiming rather low, to allow for refraction, I fired, and up floated a large fish, weighing ten pounds or so. In the evening I was able to return to camp with sixteen large fish, some four feet in length, which served to eke out the half rations on that day.

Next day we started at 3 a.m., and shortly afterwards reached a lava ridge, and then a deep nullah. Had we been trekking in daylight, no doubt we should have been able to avoid this bad country. As it was, the only feasible route offered to me was to follow the edge of the nullah down to the shore. A ghastly trek along a mass of loose lava boulders ensued, till at last we passed the lava strip, and came out on the usual flat country which forms such a great part of the lake shore.

At every camp we had noticed the water gradually getting better, and that which we had obtained whilst passing along the lava shore was infinitely preferable to anything we had as yet essayed, as there was no vegetation, and, consequently, no fouling of the water by birds.

After reaching the flat shore again, we found a sandy margin to the lake, in which there were signs of nests, one bird, laying eggs about the size of a pigeon's, apparently burying its eggs. I searched in vain for eggs, but could find nothing but innumerable broken ones, some more successful egg-hunters—probably in the shape of crows—having been before me.

We trekked on till about noon, when we camped in some very fair shade, for which we had been steering the last few hours. In this patch of good-sized thorn-trees and other bushes I noticed many nests built by some cunning bird, which fenced about the whole of the exterior of its nest with thorns pointing outwards.

At 2.30 a.m. next morning we trekked on, and as we topped a rise, saw a fire, apparently quite close, but it proved to be at the opposite side of the lake. Shortly afterwards we heard the strange drumming sound we had noticed before, but this time much nearer. I stopped to listen and consult about these sounds, while the porters discussed them in awed whispers.

I did not want to delay the march by wasting the valuable cool marching hours of the night whilst I went to see what these sounds betokened, and, on the other hand, did not like to let the caravan proceed without me. I conferred with Abdi, while Tengeneza, hearing our discussion, said : " Master, pay no heed to it ; it is no human drumming we hear." Abdi replied : " Leave alone that talk of devils—it may be men ; and I am ready to go and look for them."

Finally, we settled that Abdi should go to look for the cause of the drumming, accompanied by Majaliwa, whilst we proceeded. I told Abdi that we would follow the lake till we came to the first watercourse flowing into it, and would there await him.   On arrival at this watercourse, I had an ineffectual hunt for meat, and returned to camp.

I had long suspected that there were two usual lake-levels—a wet-weather and dry-weather level—and was able to ascertain this for certain here, for this and other watercourses stopped before reaching the present level of the lake.

It appears that when the heavy rains break in the Abyssinian mountains, a great volume of water is discharged into the plains below, the Omo overflows its banks, and all the plains north of the lake are under water.   Lake Rudolf then fills up, and these watercourses, which perhaps only contain water once or twice during the year, flow into the lake when it is at this higher level.   Long before it sinks they have dried up again, and so, after the subsidence, no trace of them is apparent below the high-level lake margin.

However, in addition to this yearly change of level, there also appears to be a marked diminishment of the lake.   Teleki passed at much the same time of the year as I did, but in his time the lake was much higher, as was proved by the Elmolo villages, on the site of which we camped.   Again, the dome-shaped rocks of which I spoke prove an ancient level of the lake, much higher than any of the marks of recent wet-weather levels observed by me.

When I returned to the camp I found that Abdi had come back, having seen nothing.   He said that they heard the drumming in front of them, and proceeded towards the sound, when it suddenly came from their left hand.   They then went in that direction, and shortly afterwards heard it behind them.   He did not know what to make of it.

The men shook their heads, as much as to say, "We

told you so," and Sadi said that we were all very lucky not to have been led astray, as many caravans had been lost in this way. They have heard the demon's drum, and followed it miles into the bush, thinking that it was human beings, till they have been utterly lost.

I did not know what to make of them, and decided to investigate myself next time, but unfortunately never had the opportunity. Of one thing I was fairly certain, and that was that it was not made by human beings, or we should certainly have come across the tracks of either themselves or their stock. We had not seen the tracks of human beings now for just on a month, except some month-old tracks of Abyssinian hunters, and I had looked very carefully for any such signs. Directly we arrived in an inhabited part I picked up tracks at once.

Abdi's account seemed to indicate that the noise was made by something which moved rapidly, and so I came to the conclusion that it must have been caused by some kind of bird. If this was the case, the sounds, although seemingly distant, must have been in reality quite close at hand. However, this theory was received with polite incredulity even by Abdi in the light of recent events. Sadi, it appeared, knew all along that it was a Komazi, as he had often heard one at his home in Malindi.

So as not to unduly bias the reader, I will now give a short dissertation on Swahili demons, at the end of which he will be able to weigh the facts for himself, and decide whether the balance of evidence is in favour of the Komazi or not.

There are a variety of devils known to the Swahili, both male and female. Every big lake and the sea possesses a devil or devils of its own, who sit at the bottom, and are in some cases accountable for storms and waves. It is sometimes necessary to propitiate these with offerings of beads and flour.

Almost every tree of extra size, such as an enormous baobab or sycamore, is the habitation of a devil. The bark of such ancient trees is often valuable as a medicine, but before tampering with such a tree it is generally thought advisable to leave a small offering to propitiate the devil who inhabits it.

Of the devils who live in solitary places, the two chief are the Ngoloko and the Komazi. The Ngoloko is a male demon, with one eye and two hands, of which one arm is very long, and the other very short. On the middle finger is an enormous nail, with which he kills people by clutching the throat. He has one leg like a man and the other like a donkey, while his ears are also like a donkey's. He lives in the bush, feeds on blood and honey, and has female buffaloes as wives. The Ngoloko sometimes assumes the form of a man, and if he meets anyone asks and gives the news, and then seizes his victim all unawares.

The Komazi lives near the sea or a big lake. He has but one leg, with which he takes enormous hops a few miles at a time. It was this hopping of the one leg that had, according to Sadi, been mistaken for the beating of a drum. He had often heard one hopping about on the rocks at night at Malindi, " ding di-ding," exactly like a drum. The Komazi has two eyes, but the slits are vertical instead of horizontal.

The Yaos have a devil called a Chitowe, who answers more or less to the description of the Komazi. We heard once that a Chitowe was coming up to pay us a visit at a station I was in. Great consternation prevailed amongst all the natives, as the Chitowe brings sickness in his path.

A hut had been built for him about thirty miles from our station, and he arrived there one night, as was apparent the next day, for he had taken the food prepared for him. However, he returned from there to Lake Nyassa, from whence he had come.

After resting during the middle of the day, we once more urged on the tired camels, and proceeded till nightfall, when we bivouacked as close to the lake as we could find a convenient spot. On the way I shot two topi and a greater bustard, so the meat-supply for that day and the next was assured. The lake had been gradually narrowing, and now the Luburr Mountains on the opposite side were to be clearly seen. During the night I woke suddenly, as there was a slight noise, and at the same moment a cat-like animal, probably a serval, leapt past me, and darted into a bush behind my head. Next day the porters solemnly assured me that there had been a leopard in the camp, which they had driven away.

We arose before dawn, and proceeded through a country of scattered bush. As we reached the north of the lake the bush gradually became thicker, and the view to the east opened out till we could see distant mountains towards Lake Stefanie. During the whole length of the lake till now there had been no view eastwards, as the landscape was bounded by lava ridges only a few miles distant. As we proceeded through this bushy country I suddenly discovered the tracks of a few men, and, investigating, found that they had come from the north, slept the night under a patch of *msuaki* bush, where they had been eating berries, and then returned northwards again. This naturally caused great excitement amongst the men.

Presently we came to a bay bounded by sandhills, on

Tom

On the extreme left is a porter called Kilimanjaro, because he is so tall. He is carrying my plane-table and maps. Tumbo is seen in white clothes on the right; one of the other men has made himself a halo of zebra mane.

which the *msuaki* grew thickly. As the shore rose here steeply, these clumps of bush were quite close to the water.

As we trekked along the shore we felt a westerly wind for the first time during our journey in daylight. Coming as it did over the lake, the breeze was cool and fresh, and made marching a pleasure after the days and days in which we had suffered from the scorching east wind.

The *msuaki* here were covered with little berries, which were now ripe, and tasted sweet, but hot, like nasturtiums. The same bush on the coast does not bear this berry. I selected a site for the midday halt, deciding to push on again in the afternoon.

My men cut me a shady bower in one of the *msuaki* clumps, and in this house I was sitting when I heard excited talking amongst them, and one of them rushed in to tell me that a man had been sighted. I went out, and saw a naked savage, with a bundle, strolling along the side of the lake. On his head was something white we could not make out.

I told the men not to show themselves, and then selected Masharia, the Kikuyu, and another man who had just thrown off his clothes, as the two nakedest among the men, and sent them to entice him into camp. I impressed on them the necessity of doing nothing to alarm him. With the native's usual distrust and fear of a stranger, they wanted to take rifles, which would have been certain to frighten him. I told them that they could always run back to camp if he threatened them with his spear, so they went forth.

The man, when he saw them, stopped, and as they beckoned to him, gradually approached. When he came near they pointed to camp, and he accompanied them back quite fearlessly. He put down his load, which con-

sisted of a certain kind of earth in a basket, evidently for
the making of salt, and walked into my bower.

I motioned him to sit down, and gave him some beads,
with which he seemed very pleased. The white thing
we had seen on his head now proved to be a closely-fitting
cap of white fur, which we afterwards heard was made from
a hare's under-side. This gave the wearer a most curious
appearance, as the cap fitted so closely that at a short
distance it looked as if the fur was the hair of the wearer.

Abdi tried to converse with him, but he did not understand either Samburr or Galla. The men crowded round
to stare at this curious individual, a link with what to
them was civilization.

He did not seem particularly uneasy, but he did not like
to find himself the centre of so much interest, and waved
to the men to stand aside; so I made them withdraw, and
leave him alone with Abdi and myself. We gave him
some of the meat of the topi, which one of the men cooked
for him. Great amusement was caused, as this naked
savage did not care for it half cooked in the careless
manner in which my men prepared it, and sent it back
to be further grilled.

The men reported two other human beings passing,
and, going out, I saw two men creeping along, thinking
that they were concealed by the grass, knee-high at the
edge of the lake. I beckoned to our new friend, and by
signs conveyed to him that he was to call these men.

He went down towards them, and I regretted for the
moment that I had let him go, as, if he did not like our
looks, he might not come back at all. However, I was
consoled to think that he had left his load with us, as he
would probably come back to it; and so he did, as presently he returned with a fellow.

This man was rather shy at first, and would not understand anything we said. After he had recovered from his alarm, Abdi finally made him understand a little Borana. I could not make out who these people were, and thought that they must be Turkana from the other side of the lake, who had come across in canoes.

I had grown so accustomed to the idea that we should not meet the Reshiat here, who, the Samburr said, had been driven away by the Abyssinians, that it never dawned on me that it could be these people, and I puzzled over who they could be. When they were asked who they were, they replied, " Goliba," a name I had never heard before. They said that they had not come in canoes, but had walked along the bank, and that their villages were two days to the north.

This was good news; and then we asked about food, and they said they had plenty at their homes—an unusual assertion for a native, who usually, however good the harvest, pretends that there is much hunger in the village. We were naturally overjoyed to hear this, but it would be rash to count on the food as a certainty. Anyhow, we must take every precaution not to alarm these people, but to do everything in our power to establish friendly relations with them as soon as possible.

Thinking that it would be as well not to appear too suddenly in their midst, we decided to keep one of these men as a guide, while the other was to go ahead and inform the chiefs of our arrival.

So, taking out some presents from my stores, I despatched him of the skullcap to precede us with gifts and friendly messages for his chiefs, while we followed afterwards with the man who could talk a little Borana.

14

CHAPTER XV

THE RESHIAT

WHEN I gave the word to bring in the camels and load them up, some delay was caused by one of them having run away. This wary old animal used to graze peaceably with the rest, but directly they were rounded up to be driven back to camp, knowing that it meant an afternoon march, he used to bolt off as hard as he could. To-day he had given the men the slip, and it was some time before he could be found.

As we skirted round the bay we met with the remains of an enormous fish washed up on the shore. Only the head and tail remained, the rest having been eaten by birds, but from these two fragments I estimated his total length at eight feet at least.

We now found a track along the side of the thick bush, and followed this, while in front of us many natives were seen hopping in and out of the bush, or bathing on the sea-shore. By way of allaying any fears they might have had, I preceded the caravan alone, and apparently un-armed, by about six hundred yards. I say "apparently," because, although I had nothing but a whip in my hand, I had a repeating-pistol in my belt under my coat.

In front I saw a lot of natives congregating under a tree, whilst others were running up from the shore to join them. A turn of the path left a tongue of bush concealing them from view, and I marched on, wondering what they would do when I rounded the corner and suddenly came into their midst.

Had I wished to keep them in view, I could have left the path and kept along the edge of the lake. However, such conduct would have been liable to be interpreted as fear on my part, so I stuck to the path. As I rounded the tongue of bush, and knew that I was coming face to face with a large party of natives, I could not resist putting my hand nonchalantly on the butt of my pistol under my coat. Such misgivings as to the reception I should receive seemed foolish enough in the light of future events, but at that time I still had not realized who these people were, and thought that they might be a section of Turkana, or Donyiro, who had moved across to this side of the lake.

Any fears I might have entertained were immediately set at rest by a youth coming forward alone to meet me, bearing a handful of grass as a peace-offering. He greeted me with " Soro, soro," the Wallamu greeting.

This giving of grass is a widespread custom in Africa. I have only noticed it amongst cattle-owners, but am not prepared to say that purely agricultural natives do not do the same. As it is generally impossible to ascertain the origin and inner meanings of any ancient custom from natives themselves, it is only left to us to conjecture on such matters. If one arrives at a village almost anywhere in Africa, the first thing that happens is that a present is brought and accepted by the stranger. The original meaning of this, I take it, is a peace-offering or sign to show that the stranger is to expect peace and hospitality, and not war and treachery.

In the bush there is no present ready to give the stranger, and so grass is the most handy substitute. The reason why grass is chosen instead of anything else might have two interpretations. Grass is held in great veneration by some of the cattle-owning people; for instance, among the Masai, if a boy is being beaten by his father, he sometimes plucks up grass as an appeal. Then the father ceases to beat his son, "for the Masai love grass, for it is that which is given by *Engai* (God) to make their cattle fat." Therefore a gift of grass is not in the eyes of the giver a gift of some worthless substance, but something wherewith to rejoice the heart of a cattle-owner.

The other significance it may bear is that the grazing grounds of the giver are at the service of the stranger to whom the gift is given, and so it is an emblem of a larger gift. However, if these are the original reasons for the action, I do not suppose that the average native is aware of them, any more than the average European knows why he bares his teeth when he sneers.

When I reached the end of the bay I waited for the caravan to overtake me. A promontory formed the northern side of the bay, and the guide wished us to follow the lake shore outside the bush.

However, this would have been a long way round, as I saw that the tracks there were few, while through the bush there were numerous cattle and goat tracks, which made me think that the villages were nearer than the guide had led us to imagine. Moreover, whilst I had been waiting for the caravan, I had seen two small girls, who, directly they saw me, had fled along one of these tracks. I argued that their natural instinct would be to run towards home, and not away from it, so that the village must be in that direction.

This being the case, I told the guide that I knew the way, and was going to take the shortest route, as I saw no object in rounding the cape. The guide should have shown some surprise at this statement, but natives always seem to expect the unusual in white men, and so he appeared to think it quite natural.

I led the way into the bush, but here the maze of paths trodden by herds of goats grazing was so intricate that I should have been at a loss to find the way if it had not been for the footmarks of the two girls, easily distinguishable in the soft sand amongst the larger footprints of full-grown men and women.

It appeared that at this time of year the Reshiat used to come down here to eat the *msuaki* berries, now ripe, and that the numbers we had seen were all picnicking on the seashore. We found numerous little recesses and shelters, made of boughs, hidden in the bushes.

After emerging from the bush, we reached a park-like country of acacia-trees, amongst which were a few goat kraals. These kraals were for goats and their herdsmen only, and were in the bush a few miles from the villages, being moved about to suit the grazing. Into one of these kraals a herd of goats was being driven—a sight which moved the stock-loving Somali more than had the sight of the first man seen.

"Allah is great!" Abdi exclaimed; "to-day we have seen goats for the first time for a month."

The guide wished us to camp here, although it was not yet sunset, and it seemed evident that the villages were near. I then gathered the reason that he had wished us to take the circuitous route by the cape. He was afraid that we should reach the villages the same evening, before they had received timely warning of our approach. I immediately yielded to his wishes, and we pitched camp in this pleasant part of the country.

It was as we were encamped here that I for the first time realized that these people were the Reshiat. The men were in high spirits that night at the prospect of arriving at villages the next day. I gave them out the usual half-ration, which, with the meat of one of the topi of the day before, was ample for them.

I might have given them a full ration, but as now we had but one bag left, I thought it more advisable to keep this until we saw how soon the Reshiat would be able to bring us in food.

I was intensely interested at the prospect of seeing these people, but I could not help regretting that the solitudes had been left behind. There was a charm about those uninhabited tracts that appealed to me much more strongly than the prospect before us. We had just hurried through them, driven by force of circumstance, with no time to explore or enjoy them. How I longed now to be just starting back, with a large supply of food and unlimited time at my disposal, to wander and hunt in their unknown recesses !

Of hunting on the journey I had been able to do nothing, all my spare time having been devoted to crawling about on my stomach after the common gazelle and oryx of the plains. What magnificent opportunities for hunting elephant, lion, and buffalo I had had to abandon, owing to insufficient time and the necessity of keeping up the constant food-supply of the men !

Next day we started early, and had not gone very far before we saw some old men advancing towards us, accompanied by our white-capped friend of the day before. In their hands they bore small gourds of milk. Our acquaintance of yesterday rushed up and seized me by the hand, and opened his gourd of milk. This was a luxury

I had missed for a long time, but I feared that it would prove to be the usual curdled stuff in a filthy, odoriferous receptacle. To my surprise, I found comparatively clean, pure milk in a clean gourd, and I drank it on the spot, while the old men kept pressing me to take more. The remaining gourds I gave to some of the men, choosing Abdi and the sais first, as they came from cattle-owning races, and so would appreciate it more than the men to whom it was an unknown luxury in their homes.

We were led to the first village, which is situated on an arm of the lake, which had now dried, leaving only a pool in the middle. All round the pool we saw a great mass of cultivation planted on ground which, during the wet season, is under water.

The old men selected a site for our camp, and then produced a woman who could talk the Samburr language. We immediately opened a market for food, and the Reshiat began bringing in half-gourds full of white *sorghum* (or *jowari*, as it is called in India). They were very poorly off for beads, and so readily sold their food for blue Masai and large white beads. It was rather interesting to think that most of the few beads they were wearing must have once belonged to either Teleki or Neumann.

Directly I saw that there was going to be no difficulty about food, I gave out our last bag to the men.

I had no idea that Abyssinian stations existed so far south as this, but we were now told that there was a post of the Siddam (as they and the other tribes to the south call them) not so far off. In the afternoon I was told that two Abyssinian soldiers were visiting the Reshiat village, so I sent for them. One of these, who proved to be a Danakil, came and gave us a lot of information.

He said that there was a post quite close by, and that there were about forty soldiers there, under two *azach* (sergeants or subalterns), one a Muhammadan and one a Christian, as half the men were Muhammadan and half Christian. He knew Galla quite well, so Abdi could talk to him easily. He could not make out where we had come from, and Abdi told him of the march we had made, and how we had come from a very far country. He asked for some calico, saying that they were far from home, and found it difficult to get enough to make their clothes, so I gave him a piece.

I had been diligently learning up the Amharic characters and language, and tried to say, "How do you do?" to him, but failed, as I afterwards discovered that it was not pronounced as spelt. I next wrote it for him, but he could not read or write. He went back to his post, and that same night came back with a little honey and some coffee as a present for me.

Meanwhile, during the afternoon, a patrol from the post passed and visited us on the way. They looked very clean and smart amongst the naked Reshiat, wearing trousers and long shirts of white calico, with a sash and red bandolier round the waist, and heads and feet uncovered. They had been told by the Danakil that we were here, and they, too, were very curious to know where we had come from.

They wanted to know why we were camped here, and not at their post, and made us promise to move our camp next day and come over to them. They also said: "Why did you not send and tell us that you were coming, and we would have met you with food?"

They apologized for having come empty-handed, but soon rectified this omission, as they turned to some of the

Reshiat who had brought in food for sale, and, taking it out of their hands, presented it to us. I put it on one side, and, after their departure, handed it back to the owners.

Abdi had appeared rather incredulous on the journey when I told him that I was learning the language of the Wahabashi (Abyssinians), but now that I wrote a few words and showed them to one of these men, he was much astonished to find that he could read it. Finally, they departed, saying that they were making a round, but would be back at the post next day, and would then see us again.

That night I gave out to the men, in addition to what they had already received, as much of the food we had bought as they could eat. The sais was talking loudly about a certain bird, and that he would give it a present of honey if he had any. I asked what he was talking about, and he said that there was a bird known to the Masai that, if it cries on the left flank, denotes danger or evil, but if on the right, good luck. It was this bird, it appeared, which had led us to the Reshiat.

As night drew in we heard leopards in several directions grunting in the bush. The Reshiat had told us that there were plenty here, but no lions.

The porters feasted far into the night, filling themselves to bursting-point. The last thing I heard before going to sleep were the most horrible groans, coming from the side on which Abdi and the camel-men slept ; then the voice of Abdi saying : " What is the matter, Yusufu ? Are you ill ?"

" No ; I am only pleased that the master has given us so much food."

" But what are you groaning about ?"

" I am pleased ; but oh, this stomach of mine !"

I noticed afterwards that the little fellow, never very thin, was strangely distended, and remained like this till the day he fell ill and died.

Next morning we followed round a bay, marching at the foot of the sandhills, and at the edge of the wet-weather level of the lake, now dry and covered with cultivation. After an hour's walk we climbed the sandhills, and found on the top the Abyssinian zariba. Platforms were erected at different points as look-out posts, and on one of these sat a man, who directed us to proceed round the zariba. A motley crew of soldiers emerged, headed by the Abyssinian *azach*, a tall, good-looking man, wearing a soft black felt hat.

He conducted us to a camping-ground, and then they withdrew and sat on one side. Presently Abdi, who had been talking to them, came to me, and said : " They are asking if you have a letter. They say that no man can travel through their country unless he bears a letter from the Sultan."

I affected to think for a bit, and then replied : " Well, what shall we do now, Abdi ?"

Abdi had seen a thousand difficulties crop up on the journey, many of them seemingly insurmountable at the time, although they may sound trivial enough in narration, and, all these having been successfully overcome, he had great faith in my powers of resource. He thought for a while, and then said : " You can write their language. Why do you not write out a letter, and give it to them, saying that it is from their Sultan ?"

I had ready in my pocket-book a passport, obtained through the kindness of the authorities, so I pulled this out and gave it to Abdi, saying : " Here, show them this,

and see if it will do." Abdi took it to the *azach*, and great
was his astonishment to see all the Abyssinians rise to
their feet directly they recognized Menelek's seal, and
continue standing whilst the *azach* read it out to them.

Azach Kalile, the head Amhara in the post, brought us
some sheep and goats and some grain as a present. I
accepted the grain, but refused the sheep and goats, fearing that they had been taken from the Reshiat for my
benefit.

During the whole of my journey through the outlying
provinces of Abyssinia, I was always very chary of
accepting such presents. It generally meant that they
had been taken from the natives of the country, who got
nothing in return, while the Abyssinians, having given
something that did not belong to them, received my
presents in exchange.

Azach Kalile expressed himself very hurt at my refusal, and came back at intervals all through the day to
see if I had not altered my mind. Aba Gibi, the head of
the Muhammadan soldiers, whom we had seen the day
before, returned with his patrol in the evening, and
immediately came to my tent to know why I had not
accepted the sheep.

The *azach* and another Abyssinian were very interested
to find that I could write Amharic characters, and spent
a great part of the time I remained with them instructing
me in the language, writing words for me in my vocabulary,
and reading through my grammars.

In the afternoon I heard a strange voice speaking
Swahili, while the porters were convulsed with laughter.
Presently Omari brought a Reshiat up to me, and said :
" Behold, here is one of these savages who can speak
Swahili." I turned round and saw a perfectly naked

man with Omari, who, when he was addressed, replied in fluent Swahili. I could not help laughing, as it seemed to me as curious as if a naked man had suddenly come up and addressed me in my own language, for none of my men spoke English, and so Swahili sounded to me as strangely familiar amongst all the different tongues we had met on our journey.

I asked him where he had learnt Swahili, and he said that he and another Reshiat had been taken away by a native ivory trading caravan. I asked him where he had been to, and he replied : " I don't know—Bagamoyo or Dar as Salam, somewhere on the coast." Omari suggested that he ought to be ashamed to go about naked after he had known better, but he said : " No ; it is good to be like this."

From this man I obtained a certain amount of Reshiat words and other information, but not as much as might have been expected, as he could only keep his attention fixed on answering my questions for about half an hour at a time. After that time his attention used to wander, and his answers became vague, and he had to be given a long rest. To the raw native it is a very serious brain-fag to have to keep the attention fixed on anything for the shortest intervals, however hard they may try.

The second time the Swahili-speaking Reshiat came to see me he brought with him a chief of the nearest kraal, who asked me what presents I was going to give him. I replied that I was a stranger, and had not yet received a present from him, and so it was not likely that I should give him a present first.

To this he replied : " You are right. The Siddam go into their zariba at sunset, close it up, and do not come out again till sunrise, for they are afraid to walk about in the dark. I will come to-night and bring my present, for at that time the Siddam will not see me here."

At sunset the *azach*, who had been giving me an Amharic lesson, said good-night, and all the Abyssinians retired into their zariba, which they carefully barricaded. Shortly afterwards, Menyi Imorsha, who was the present *makansi* (or chief) of the tribe, as well as of the nearest kraal, came stealthily up to my camp. He sat down, and, with great secrecy, produced a large gourd of honey, saying to Abdi : " Tell him not to let them "—pointing to the zariba—" see it, as every day they ask us for honey, and we always say we have none. Don't let them see as much as the gourd, and to-morrow night at the same time I will come and fetch my gourd back."

I had a long and interesting conversation with the *makansi* and his old men, as he understood Samburr, and so Abdi was able to converse easily with him, whilst I was able to follow the conversation.

All I knew about the Reshiat so far was gleaned from Von Höhnel and Neumann's books. I will give a short résumé from these books, so that the reader can see in what respects they agree with what the men told me.

Teleki and Von Höhnel arrived with about two hundred followers, and camped on the sandhills somewhere near my present camp, and there built a strong zariba. They say that on their way to the camp they passed a lot of human bones, and that the Reshiat told them that these were the bones of some Samburr who had built a kraal near them, and then had stolen some cattle, and so the Reshiat had killed them all.

Von Höhnel talks of the *oromaj* (saying that this word means chief, or medicine-man) of the Reshiat, who always carried with him a long stick. The Reshiat refused to let them proceed northwards, saying that the people there were *mangati* (which word he translates by " wild beasts ")—a circumstance they were at a loss to explain. They visited Lake Stefanie, leaving their ivory buried with the Reshiat, and then came back, fetched their ivory, and returned the way they had come, by Rudolf.

Neumann visited the Reshiat several years later with a caravan of donkeys, with which he had proceeded up Lake Rudolf. Unlike his predecessor, he did not build a fortified zariba, but lived on terms of great friendship with the Reshiat, and finally built a hut in their own kraal, in which he left many surplus loads, intending to return at some future date to claim them. It was on the Omo River that he was badly mauled by a female elephant, and as soon as he was able to be carried, he was brought back to the Reshiat, in which locality he spent a period of convalescence, until he was able to walk, when he returned by Lake Rudolf, the way he had come.

I will now tell the reader what the Reshiat told me. I will not attempt to elucidate it, but leave it for him to pick out the bad from the good. Nor will I bore him with the hundreds of questions I asked to elicit this information, but just give a summary.

The first white man who ever visited the Reshiat was Bwana Nyamayangu (Neumann), who came up with donkeys ten years ago. After that came two white men, twelve years ago, with a great multitude of porters. Yes, they were quite certain about the times and the order of precedence (showing that Neumann had left the greatest impression).

These had buried some ivory with them, and gone off,

and came back again to fetch this ivory. No ; they had
refused to let them go on, as all the tribes to the north
were *mangati* (enemies, not "wild beasts," as Von
Höhnel has it), and so they were afraid of embroiling
themselves with them.

The last fight they had with any other tribe was with
the Turkana, one hundred and forty years ago. Yes ;
they were quite certain that it was one hundred and forty
years ago. No ; the speaker was not then a young man :
he was an old man, as he was now ; but he was sure of the
date.

It had happened like this : The Turkana had fought
with the Samburr to the south of the lake, and, to get
away from them, the Samburr had trekked up here, and
built a kraal near. The Turkana had followed them up,
and made war on them here. On the day that the
Turkana had arrived, the chief of the Reshiat happened
to be in this Samburr kraal, visiting them, and was killed
by the Turkana. When the Reshiat heard of the death
of their chief, they turned out and joined forces with the
Samburr against the Turkana. However, the Turkana
overcame them both, and got away with some of their
cattle. The bones still to be seen on the sandhills were
a record of that fight. The name of the old chief who
used to carry the long stick was Longoramai (hence Von
Höhnel's *oromaj*).

Shortly after Neumann left, the Abyssinians came down
in force, and they took flight to the islands at the north
of Rudolf. They subsequently made peace with them,
and they returned to their own village. The Abyssinians
gave them back some of their cattle and flocks, but what
saved them was that they had a lot of tobacco buried,
and this they took to the Turkana west of the lake, and

with it bought sheep and goats. Some of these sheep and goats they afterwards exchanged for cattle with the Abyssinians, but they had not the number of cattle they used to have formerly. Now, if one saw a herd, it belonged to many men—two or three to one man, and two or three to another. Formerly whole herds belonged to one man.

Then Abdi asked if Neumann had left any goods here, and they replied, "No." They asked after Neumann, and the deceitful Abdi said that I was his brother. At this they evinced great interest, and, after a long consultation in their own language, they said : " We cannot lie to you. Bwana Nyamayangu did leave some goods here, and no doubt his brother has come to fetch them. He built a hut and left his things there, and then locked it up and went his way. Shortly after he had gone, the Abyssinians came, and we fled away, and when we came back, we found the goods no longer there."

I asked about the Elmolo, and was told that the Rendile had attacked them first, and subsequently some Abyssinian hunters, and so they had taken refuge on Centre Island, or South Island—I could not quite gather from the description. Their language, they said, was more like that of the Amarr (or Amorr) than any other. These people live to the east of the Reshiat.

Next morning the Abyssinians came to see me, and brought back the sheep, and also an ox, saying that they had now discovered why I would not accept the sheep, as it was too small a present for me, so they had brought an ox as well.

I explained to them that the customs of different countries differed. In our country we made each native pay a hut-tax ; in theirs there was no hut-tax, but the rulers took from the inhabitants what they needed in the way of food and supplies. This was all right for the rulers of the country, but I was not of that country, and therefore I had no right to expect food from the inhabitants of the country. The grain I had accepted, to show my friendship for them ; but a big present I did not wish to accept.

They replied that the sheep were not taken from the natives for nothing, but were bought with coffee from the Abyssinian station of Bako, and therefore I need have no fear of accepting them. When I heard this, I did not resist their importunities any longer, and accepted the sheep, but declined the ox.

My porters had been licking their lips at the prospect of sheep since the day before, so now that I had accepted them, I immediately distributed them amongst the men, who made short work of them.

Most of the former travellers who had passed through Abyssinia so as to visit the Omo River had come by way of Lake Margherita and the north of Lake Stefanie, and so I had always intended to take a route rather north of this, to strike new ground. From what the Abyssinians told me, it was evident that there was such a route, and that a big Abyssinian garrison at a place called Bako would be passed on this route in about a week's journey from Reshiat. However, I was sorry to hear that part of the Abyssinian Boundary Commission had returned from the Omo by Bako to Addis Ababa, and so this route would no longer be new ground.

My men had been very nervous about the Abyssinians before we met them, and now they disgusted me by the cringing servility they showed them. Omari tried his hardest to ingratiate himself with them in Arabic, as

15

both he and some of the Abyssinians knew a few words of this language, although Omari's, spoken with a Bantu accent, was not very easy to understand. He made himself especially ridiculous by addressing a small, ragged urchin, who was sent down with milk for me, as *sheikh*.

On the second evening that I was encamped here there was a plague of lake-fly, and also of jumping insects (grasshoppers and crickets), which hurled themselves about the place with the utmost abandon. This is supposed to be a sign that the rains are near.

Shortly after the Abyssinians had retired into their zariba and shut themselves up for the night, my friend the *makansi* brought up his wife to see me. I gave her some beads, at which she was very pleased, and also gave the *makansi* and his elders some presents.

Evidently the only two white men they have had to deal with—Neumann and Teleki—both made a very favourable impression on them, as they told me that when I came they were overjoyed to hear that another white man was coming, and hoped that they might sit with us, instead of with the Abyssinians, for they said : " We are become as donkeys and beasts because of these Siddam, who have taken our country ; and now that we hear that you are leaving us to-morrow, our hearts are sad, for our state will be as it was before you came."

I must say, however, that the Abyssinians treat their subjects very much better than any other African tribe I have met would treat a subject-people.

A few notes on the Reshiat might be of interest before closing the chapter. The males are generally perfectly nude, except for their head-dress, as seen in the photograph, whilst the females wear skirts of skins. The

THE RESHIAT OR GOLIBA

Some of their fancy coiffures can be seen. They are almost as elaborate, but not as massive, as those of the Turkana. On the right one of my porters can be seen doing up his blanket into the turban on which the load is supported. The figure next to the left of the group of porters is holding one of the long thin basket-work shields found amongst these people and the Samburr.

hare's-skin cap worn by many of the young men I have already described. This generally has a socket on the top, in which an ostrich-feather, or else a long, whip-like ornament, is worn. Others wear chignons of hair and plastered mud, like the Turkana, but not of such massive size. Some are uncircumcised, like the Turkana, whilst others are circumcised. They told me that the latter state was customary in the tribe, but I fancy that recent intercourse with the Turkana has led some of them to adopt their customs. The women wear the hair plaited or in ringlets.

They possess but few beads or ornaments, and practically no cloth. Circular wrist-knives are worn, as described in connection with the Turkana. The men of this and the other tribes to the north on the Omo River—Murule and Kerre—carry about with them small wooden pillows like miniature one-legged stools, on which they sometimes sit.

The Reshiat can often be seen standing on one leg, with the sole of the other foot resting behind the knee-joint and knee, at right angles to the body—an attitude which has often been noticed amongst Hamitic people. The people that do this are Somalis, Masai, Rendile, Samburr, Alui, Bari, Madi, and many other non-Bantu people of Africa.

Although this attitude has been remarked on by several writers as indicative of a certain type of native, I have never seen another curious custom referred to in this respect. This is the manner in which meat is eaten : A large piece is held in the left hand, the end is seized with the teeth, and a piece cut off while in this position by a knife held in the right hand, at infinite risk to the nose and lips of the consumer. Although I have often seen this act performed by such tribes as rest on one leg, I have never seen a Bantu native eat meat in this fashion.

The Reshiat are the only Africans I have yet met who make a practice of eating donkey-flesh, and the large number of these animals they breed appear to be used for food only, and for no other purpose. They do not wander about as do the Rendile and Samburr, and so do not require animals to carry their goods from one place to another.

The prospective husband pays twenty cattle for a girl, and four to six for a mature woman. The women here and amongst the Rendile struck me as having better figures than those of the natives to the south. Some of them had quite slim waists, while the usual Bantu woman is barrel-shaped.

The Reshiat each carry one spear, with a long haft and blade, often protected with the leather sheath mentioned before. They do not usually carry shields, but occasionally a long one of thin basket-work is seen.

Having rested the men and camels a day and a half here, it was necessary to push on, in spite of the protests of the *azach*, who wanted me to stop for a long time with him. Not only was the time at my disposal short, but I also feared the approaching rains, which are very heavy in the mountains of Southern Abyssinia, and render travelling in this season specially arduous and uncomfortable.

So I said good-bye to the Abyssinians, and started off for the Omo River. Azach Kalile, my Amharic instructor, bade me a very affectionate farewell. As the camels moved off and I hastened to take the head of the caravan, he seized my hand in both his, and walked with me for about half a mile, without releasing it, much to my embarrassment.

He had treated me exceedingly well, and I really believe that his kindness to me was prompted purely by nice feeling, and not out of hope of gain. I cannot say the same for the other Abyssinians in the post, or the majority of those I subsequently met, nine hundred and ninety-nine out of every thousand of whom were ceaseless in clamouring for presents, while they would do nothing for me. The *azach*, on the contrary, when I made him presents on leaving, begged me to remember that I had a long journey before me, and must not expend my goods too freely.

After expressing all sorts of good wishes for the journey, and hopes to see me again, he finally turned back to the zariba, while we slowly wended our way northwards to a place on the Omo called Murule.

CHAPTER XVI

THE OMO RIVER AND NERI DESERT

SHORTLY after leaving the Abyssinian post, a long, dark line of trees came into view on the left. This was the Omo River. During the day's march this line receded from us, and then approached us again. We bivouacked that night just before reaching a spur coming down from the Bashada range.

Some Abyssinians were driving sheep to Bako, and were supposed to be showing us the way, but as they proceeded so slowly, we left them behind. Next day we crossed the tail-end of the spur, and then saw the line of trees marking the Omo winding round to our front. The whole of this country appears to be under water during the rains.

On reaching the trees we had seen in front, we found that either bank of the river is enclosed with a belt of thick vegetation and tall trees—about one to two miles broad. Passing through this belt, we selected a well-shaded camp on the river-bank, which was here high above the water.

A lion was roaring in this thick patch, while shortly after we had started in the morning we had seen a very big spoor, perhaps of this selfsame animal.

Just before entering the wooded belt we had seen a greater bustard, which I stopped to stalk and shoot.

While doing this, the Abyssinians came up, and showed us the path through to the river.

The spot at which we camped was called Murule, this being the name of a tribe who live about here. We did not see any of them, as they appear to live chiefly on the opposite bank. The river itself was very low, but by the breadth and depth of the banks one could see that it must have about ten times its present volume of water during the wet weather.

Narok, who felt the heat very much crossing the bare, flat country we had just traversed, wanted to rush into the river to cool herself. Fortunately, I stopped her in time, and found a shallow spot in which to let her wallow, attached to a cord, so that she could not go far in. A crocodile at the other side of the river immediately began sailing across towards her, but when I raised my rifle to fire, took fright, and quickly sank out of sight.

On leaving Murule, it was necessary to follow the river along outside the wooded belt, as the latter was too thick to force a way through. We found the track followed by the Abyssinians in their goings to and from Bako. The open country soon gave way to a dense jungle of thorn, aloe, and cactus, through which a way had been cut by the Abyssinians. As it had only been cut to suit men and donkeys, our camels met with some difficulty in passing through, as overhanging branches caught their loads and the cross-poles with which the camel-mats were kept in place.

After about ten miles' march through the bush, we suddenly came out on an open spot on the river-bank. On the left was a village, and on the right an Abyssinian post. I steered towards the village, and a pleasant-looking chief came out to greet me. At the same time a group of soldiers came across from the zariba and took me over to it. One of these men could speak a little Arabic, so I could make myself understood by him.

We passed the zariba, and descended a little dip, where was a solitary tree, and he chose an absolutely shadeless site for a camp on the other side of this on some sand-hills.

Under the tree which appears in the photograph a small market was held. Here I saw for the first time natives from Bako. These had come down with grain, to exchange with the local natives for salt. The men were absolutely nude, but had their hair dressed in waves and puffs, as seen in the next photograph. The hair was well kept, and not smeared with mud, as amongst all the peoples to the south. The coiffure looked exactly like that of some European women. The Bako women, on the other hand, generally have the head shaved, and wear an extraordinary sort of kilt made out of strips of wild palm-leaves.

The bag hung up in the tree is the skin of a goat stuffed with grass. This is hung up to dry, and then scraped and pounded till it becomes soft, when it will be used as a bag for coffee or grain.

The name of this place was Karo, and the village I had seen that of the Kerre. As I should have plenty more opportunities of seeing Abyssinians, and probably of a better class than those here, and no other opportunity of seeing these people, I was anxious to camp near them.

Especially did I want to avoid the shadeless camp which the Abyssinians had chosen for me. So I waited till the camels came in, and then we marched across to the village, and the chief I had before seen soon found a pleasant place in which to camp.

There are plenty of fish in the river here, and some of the children play games with the fish, which the latter thoroughly enjoy and enter into the spirit of. Each boy provides himself with a long line of plaited aloe-fibre, and an iron hook shaped like the diagram, and pointed at the end.

The boy then takes enough baked dough or pulse for a meal for two full-grown men. With this he goes down to the river, and, sitting on the bank, baits his hook with bits of dough, in this way accounting for half of it, and during the time occupied he himself eats the other half.

Having baited his hook, he slings his line in the water, and immediately thousands of fish rush at it ; the quickest gets the bait, and the fisherman draws in his hook to rebait. No secrecy, stealth, or silence is required on the Omo River ; the fisherman proclaims his presence with loud noise and splashing of cumbersome tackle, and all the fish flock round. Hour after hour the patient fisherman continues to rebait his hook, throws it out again, and after the hundredth part of a second rapidly pulls in his line, as if his life depended on it.

Perhaps once or twice in the course of a whole day's fishing some unwary fish gets caught on the point, and is sufficiently lazy not to trouble to wriggle off the smooth-pointed hook.

After watching some time I essayed the art, but with an ordinary fish-hook. My first efforts were unsuccessful, as miserable little unhookable fish ate the bait before I could get a chance at a big one. Presently, however, I began to learn where to cast for the big ones, and succeeded in catching thirty fish, much to the chagrin of the local fisher-boys.

I stopped a day at Karo to give the camels a chance of grazing, as the camel-grazing was good, and mine were now miserably thin. During this time I learnt about several curious customs from the chief of the Kerre. The men are completely nude. Many of them wear a false back to the head, which gives them a most curious appearance. The hair is plastered with mud, and pulled over a shape or puff fitting on the back of the head. When the coiffure is complete it looks like part of the head. The whole is surmounted by ostrich-feathers, or long wires poked into the false back, and standing upright.

The Kerre live on the banks of the Omo about Karo, while in the hills to the east are two small tribes called the Banna and Bashada. All these three tribes are in the habit of strangling their first-born children, and throwing the body away. The Kerre throw it into the river, where it is eaten by crocodiles, and the other two leave it in the bush for hyenas to eat. The only explanation they give of this custom is that it is the decree of their ancestors.

Talking to Abyssinians about this afterwards, they said that they had tried to break them of the habit, but found it impossible. They also declared that it was only illegitimate children who were treated in this way. However, I think that they were mistaken on this point, as I asked most carefully, and was told that for a certain number of years after marriage children would be thrown away, and after that they would be kept. The number of the first children who were strangled, and the period of years during which this was done, appears to be variable, but I could not understand what regulated it.

There was one point, however, about which they were certain, and that was that the first-born of all, rich, poor, high and low, had to be strangled and thrown away. The chief of the Kerre said, "If I had a child now, it would have to be thrown away," laughing as if it were a great joke. What amused him really was that I should be so interested in their custom.

When I first heard of the custom amongst the Kerre, I conceived the idea that the crocodile here might be held in veneration, as it is by at least one other tribe I have met, and that this might be a sacrifice to a deity whose visible form took the shape of a crocodile. However, I asked most carefully about this, and could discover no connection between the crocodile and this custom. It just happened that the river was handy to throw the babies into, but if they were on a journey or inland they would be thrown into the bush.

There are numbers of crocodiles in the Omo River, and they are very bold where black men are concerned, although they are more frightened of white men. I have seen a man sitting on the shore, and a crocodile come up to the edge of the river and look at him with hungry eyes, only fifteen or twenty yards distant, no doubt wishing that he would come a little nearer to the edge of the water. I have never heard of a case, however, of a crocodile entering a hut or village at night, as is told of the South American cayman, or alligator. These reptiles are so

236 OMO RIVER AND NERI DESERT

slow and clumsy on land that it is difficult to imagine
them doing anything of the kind.

From the above it will be seen that the Kerre are a
people whom it would be worth the anthropologist's while
studying, for the customs narrated above are, to say the
least of it, unusual. Those I am about to describe are
perhaps equally uncommon, though to the general reader
less interesting.

The Kerre men eat together, instead of each man eating
with his family. I believe also that the women eat quite
apart from the men, but of this point I am not certain.
A large dish of pulse is cooked, and the men sit round,
each helping himself from the common dish, and eating
with a wooden *spoon*, instead of with the hand, as is
customary amongst even civilized natives, such as coast
Swahilis and Arabs.

The men sleep at night on raised platforms in the open
air, several on each platform. The floor is covered with
stalks of millet, and these platforms are situated in the
village close alongside of the huts. The women sleep in
the huts, and are only joined by the men if it rains.

They have a few cattle, and the milk of these they sell
one to another in exchange for millet-flour, at the rate of
about one measure of milk to twice that measure of flour.

Neither the Reshiat nor Kerre disfigure the ears, as is
customary with most East African tribes, and to a lesser
degree with the Bako.

I have already remarked that natives of Bako bring
down grain to exchange for salt. I was told that there
was a plain covered with salt to the west of the Omo,
which from its description must be like that which I
traversed after leaving Maïkona and Gamra. The salt
from this plain supplies all the natives of the surrounding

BAKO NATIVES AT KARO

These are a party of natives who have come down from Bako. The central figure shows the palm-leaf kilts worn by the women. The figures on the left are servants of the Abyssinian soldiers. The inflated skin hung up is a goat's skin drying, which is afterwards made soft and used as a receptacle for coffee, beans, etc.

country. Apparently the Kerre are to a certain extent
purveyors or middlemen, receiving it from the west side
of the Omo, and passing it on to the tribes to the north-
east.

The Reshiat represent characteristics of both the
Turkana and the Borana, and so are links in a chain which
may in time, as more becomes known about the peoples,
connect most of the northern tribes of non-Bantu people.
The Kerre bear slight resemblances to the Reshiat on one
side, the Turkana on another, and the Banna and Bashada
on a third.

The Donyiro, living to the west of the Kerre, are a
people who it is said also bear a great resemblance to the
Turkana.

Whilst on the subject of these different tribes I want
the reader to wade through a few dry facts about the
distribution and characteristics of certain others. By so
doing he will, if not before familiar with those referred to,
be able to follow, I hope, with more interest my very
meagre accounts of the tribes subsequently met with.

A large part of Central and Southern Africa is inhabited
by negroid tribes universally admitted to spring from one
stock—viz., the Bantu. Although there are a great
number, each with its own languages, customs, and
manners, the similarity between all these peoples is very
marked—generally speaking, short, tubby men and
barrel-shaped women, with coarse and flat features (but
not so flat as those of the pure Negro) and woolly hair.

Their languages bear such an extraordinary resemblance
that it is only necessary to hear a few sentences, and a
practised ear will immediately detect that it is a Bantu
language, although the words may be absolutely un-
intelligible.

The many marked similarities of these languages would fill a chapter or two, so it will suffice to say that their most curious and unmistakable peculiarity is the " concord." Nouns are divided into a number of different classes, each of which has its prefix, both singular and plural, and almost every word in the sentence must agree with the noun subject by the addition of the same or a similar prefix.

The northernmost Bantu race on the east coast is the Kikuyu, who live, roughly speaking, between Mount Kenya and the Aberdare range. Side by side with these live a non-Bantu people, the Masai, immediately distinguishable by language and characteristics as springing from a very different stock—long, thin, wiry men, with Hamitic caste of countenance and greater intelligence than the Bantu.

On the east shore of Lake Victoria, to the west of the Masai, live the Kavirondo, a people differing from the Masai in language and many other respects, yet differing from them less than they do from the Bantu peoples. After crossing the lake we come to the Baganda and Banyoro, northern outposts of the Bantu races.

On the other side of these, on the banks of the Nile, we meet with people almost identical in language and other respects to the Kavirondo—viz., the Acholi and Alui. Following down the Nile, we meet with different tribes of Kavirondo-like people, the Madi and Bari, till gradually these merge into the Dinka and Latuka, the latter more like the Masai. It is therefore supposed that the Masai originally came from this neighbourhood, and pushed down, perhaps viâ Lake Rudolf, to their present quarters.

East of the Upper Nile, and north of Lake Victoria and

the country of the Kavirondo and the Masai, we get various tribes, such as Turkana, Suk, Elgeyo, etc., who are neither Masai nor Kavirondo, yet who bear resemblances to both. We thus obtain many links in a chain connecting the Kavirondo and the Masai, two fairly different peoples, and pointing to a certain similarity of origin.

So much for these peoples, whose origin is still shrouded in mystery. Now to turn to the Hamitic people of the north. We have the Abyssinians, chiefly Amhara and Tigre, an intelligent people who, from ancient history, ruins, etc., we know reached a fairly advanced state of civilization. This was probably brought about by the connection known to exist in old times between their country and ancient Egypt and Arabia. Since then they, for many centuries, lapsed into semi-barbarism, but always maintained a little of the arts and culture they had acquired.

East of the Abyssinians are the Somalis, a highly intelligent but utterly uncivilized race, who probably represent an admixture of Arab blood with some uncivilized race.

South of these peoples we have the Galla, a race less civilized than the Abyssinians, but amongst whom traces of an ancient civilization exist in the form of inscriptions and monuments.

Now, although the intercourse existing between ancient Egypt and Abyssinia is known, it is not known how far such Egyptian influence spread into what is now Southern Abyssinia, or how far Egyptian blood is responsible for the non-Bantu races. Somalis may represent a mixture of Arab with black blood, and Masai may represent a blend of Egyptian and black blood.

In such a case it would only be natural to expect the tribes farther to the south to show less and less traces of Egyptian blood and intelligence, and more characteristics of the black savage. Exceptions to this would, of course, be such tribes as have changed quarters *en masse*, as the Masai are supposed to have done.

I fear that I have not sufficient knowledge of my subject to be able to draw valuable deductions from my very meagre observations on the tribes through which I passed. Perhaps, however, a more long-sighted reader will be able to see in my subsequent descriptions of peoples such as the Uba and Wallamu not merely a bare narration of characteristics and customs, but hints at a subject of much wider interest—the possible origin of these people, and the light they throw on the ancient civilization of these parts.

An interesting bit of information I gained on the Omo River was that a new illness had arrived last year in this neighbourhood. From the description the natives gave me of it I had no doubt left in my mind that it was sleeping-sickness to which they referred, although I had no opportunity of seeing a case.

I am afraid that if this news is true, the banks of the Omo River will fast become depopulated, and such tribes as the Reshiat, Bume, Kerre, and Marsha, will soon cease to exist, as no precautions are likely to be taken. I am at a loss to understand how this cursed insect could have reached this neighbourhood, as it only follows the course of great rivers and lakes. I suppose that it must have come in the wet season viâ the Sobat and swamps of the Nile, as it is already infesting the upper waters of the latter river.

The Abyssinian in charge of the post of Karo was ill

A BAKO NATIVE

Natives from Bako come down to Karo on the Omo River with coffee to exchange for salt. The man shown here is carrying his coffee on his back, and his gourd of water and provisions for the journey in his hand. Notice the way the hair is dressed in puffs and waves.

with fever when I arrived, but came to me afterwards, asking for medicine. After giving him some quinine, I asked to be supplied with some guides, as I was tired of waiting for the party with the sheep, or of finding my own way. After a lot of talk, we obtained an Amhara soldier and a Bashada native, who can be seen in the photograph with the Bako man.

From information we received, we had one other camp on the Omo, and then had to cross the Neri Desert to the foot of the mountains, after which we should reach the mountainous country of Southern Abyssinia.

At the other side of the flat country which bordered the Omo we could see a series of peaks, amongst which was the distant flat-topped mountain of Bako, rising some ten thousand feet. South of this were two remarkable peaks, perhaps eight thousand or more feet in height. These were both shaped alike, though several days' journey apart. They rose up as square, rocky-topped blocks, with precipitous sides looking like enormous battlemented towers.

We had only one more waterless stretch to cross, and three more days to endure the heat of the low country, and then we should be refreshed by the cool air and running streams of the mountains. My men were overjoyed at the prospect before us. As for myself, I should have preferred to cross the Omo and make my way through Kaffa and by the Sobat to the Nile, for the country ahead was too civilized for my taste.

Often, however, as I saw Narok dragging herself along with tongue out, while the mountains were already in view, I wished that I could tell her that she had only a day or two longer to suffer from the heat and thirst.

Led by our new guides, we left Karo, and followed a

16

narrow path, which had been cut by the Abyssinians in the dense aloe and euphorbia bush. After about ten miles we suddenly emerged from the jungle into a field of millet, and at the other side of this field we could see the banks of the Omo again.

Narok, who had been ranging ahead, was halfway across the field, and making for the river. Fearing that she would rush into the water in her usual manner, I shouted and whistled to her. She turned round and wagged her tail, and then trotted off again, unable to resist the attractions of a plunge in the water.

Tengeneza and I started running after her as hard as we could, but as I reached the bank I heard the most pitiful cries. A moment afterwards I arrived at the river's edge, and saw poor Narok but a yard or two from the bank in the jaws of an enormous crocodile.

Contrary to my usual practice, I had not my rifle in my hand, and had outrun Tengeneza, who carried it. Even before the latter, who was but a yard or two behind, had come up I had whipped out my pistol, and put five shots into the brute; but it was too late, for it and the dog both sank together. All that was left for Tengeneza to see was a swirl on the water and a little line of blood. Even though the crocodile was dead, there was no hope, for now heads were popping in and out all round.

I took the rifle from Tengeneza, and put a bullet into every head that showed itself anywhere near, and then, after waiting some time, we silently moved on. The name of this place was Lebuko, and we were going to camp here. I felt now that I must get away from the scene of this sad occurrence, and so we moved on another four miles along the river to a place called Múgije.

The men showed their sympathy for me at the loss of

my only companion by remaining quite silent all day, for which consideration I felt most grateful to them.

The poor camels which had served us so long and so well were now quite done up. The grazing along the river-bank had not agreed with them, and they now showed signs of giving in. Many of them had been carrying but nominal loads during the last few days, and now, when I came to inspect them carefully, I found that nearly half were unfit for use.

As one of the porters was ill, we rested at Múgije for a day, and during that time I made up my mind which loads I should throw away to relieve the camels. After careful consideration, I discarded two water-barrels, some beads, some of my food-stores, and some medicine. The men had, on the whole, been remarkably well ; practically the only trouble I had had to deal with had been a few sores and cuts, besides hunger and thirst.

At Múgije there was a small zariba, in which were two Abyssinians, whose duty it was to collect taxes from the Marsha tribe living on the opposite bank. These men profited largely by the loads we discarded.

While we were at this place several Bako people passed to and fro, either going down with grain or coming back with salt, and I had occasion to notice how they carried their loads. The load is made up and tied round each end with a strip of leather or aloe, and a loop is left in this on either side. The porter then lies on his back on the top of the load, and slips his arm through these loops. He is unable to rise with the load until a companion has pulled him forward into a sitting position. He can then rise by himself, while the load rides on his back like a knapsack. In British East Africa both the Masai and Kikuyu carry their loads on the back, but the former support the weight by a strap passing across the chest, whilst the latter use a thong passing round the forehead.

From Múgije it was necessary to cross the Neri Desert to the foot of the mountains. Putting the sick porter on the mule, we started at 10 a.m., and by 10 p.m. we had only marched six miles, so played out were the camels. Another circumstance which made travelling difficult was that it suddenly commenced to rain, and the surface of the path, especially where there were little watercourses, was so slippery that the animals could hardly stand up.

At one time I returned to see what the delay was about, and found that there was a small nullah in the path, only a few yards across, which completely defeated the camels, so slippery had its sides become. The men were sitting down, resigned to wait there for ever, not one of them having taken the trouble to look round for a better path. I soon found a way round through the bush, which was not so steep, and less slippery ; but now darkness was falling, and it was with great difficulty that the camels could be induced to push through the bush. Finally, it was necessary to cut a way for them with axes.

My men had been praying for rain for the last month or two, and I had often said to them : " One day Allah will grant your prayer, and then you will see that our state will be worse than it is now, for the country we are going to has very bad rain." Now my words had come true, for from here onwards our progress was impeded by rain and mud, swollen rivers and marshes, till we finally reached the desert again, in the Danakil country.

However, this shower was only the forerunner of the

A Bako Man

On the road with all his stores or the journey and a load on his back. To the left is our Abyssinian guide. Between these two is our Bashada guide.

heavy rains we were to come in for, and next day the path soon dried up, leaving a few pools here and there, for which we were thankful, as otherwise we should have only had the limited supply of water left in our remaining tanks.

The country was more open the next day, and we saw a certain amount of game, giraffe, topi, and hartebeest. The giraffe were stalking across the road, quite unconscious of our presence, till I tried to snapshot them, and then they got the alarm, and before I could get the camera into action they had disappeared into the bush.

After a whole day's march, we reached the foot of the hills and the wooded banks of the Neri stream. The water was muddy and warm with the rain-water off the hot earth.

At Neri was a large tree, on which the Abyssinians and others passing had carved their names, and amongst them I deciphered that of Azach Kalile, much to the interest of our Abyssinian guide, who could not read or write. In the riverside trees could be heard the croaking of Colobus monkeys—a sound we had also heard in the Omo forest belt.

In front of us was the precipitous side of the mountains, at the top of which we learnt was a station called Kurre, several thousand feet above us.

The camels were unwilling to eat, and it became evident that, not only were they played out, but had also eaten something poisonous, as this alone would account for their abstention from food and the unaccountable way in which they had all suddenly given out. We afterwards learnt that there were several plants known to the Abyssinians which are poisonous to camels. Although they say that these plants are not found on this side of the mountain, they may be in error, or there may be some other plants equally poisonous.

In any case it is a noticeable fact that none of the tribes from the Reshiat onwards possessed any camels, although they had other stock, and the country appeared suitable for these animals. All the other tribes, such as Turkana, Borana, and Rendile, own camels, and even the Samburr have a few for baggage purposes. As the Samburr have at one time freely intermarried with the Reshiat, it is curious that this people have no camels, if there is not some good reason against it.

It would have been useless to try to proceed even along the flat with loaded camels ; much less were they likely to be able to ascend the steep mountain-track in front of us. The only course open to me was to ascend to Kurre, and see if any help would there be forthcoming to get our loads up the hill.

I therefore decided to make the ascent the next day, taking with me Abdi and some of the men with my private loads, leaving Omari and the rest of the men with the camels and the bulk of the things.

CHAPTER XVII

A MOUNTAINOUS COUNTRY

FROM our camp on Neri stream we marched a few miles to the foot of Kurre Mountain, and then commenced a steep ascent. The path was at times very steep, while at other times it wound round the side of a razor-edged ridge, with a precipitous drop into the valley below. The path was fairly broad, being a mule-track made by the Abyssinians ; but if any animal were to fall over the edge it would certainly roll to the bottom—perhaps a thousand feet below.

Forty minutes' steep climb brought us to the top of the first series of hills, another forty minutes of winding up along the side of the narrow precipitous ridges, then a drop into a little valley, and we reached a clear stream called Balo.

High up on the summit of the mountain in front of us a large sycamore was pointed out as our goal. After a rest at Balo, another steep climb of an hour and a quarter brought us to this tree at the summit, and just over the brow was a big village of mixed Abyssinians and Bako. Probably the Bako were chiefly wives and children of the Abyssinian soldiers.

Although the climb had been steep and severe, the mountain air was so cool and fresh, and such a delightful change from the stifling, dust-laden, hot wind of the plain below, that fatigue was hardly felt.

The chief soldier in the village came out to greet me, and I managed to make him understand what I wished to say by pointing to words in my vocabularies. When my men arrived, he showed us a camping-ground, and brought me a small gourd of beautiful white honey.

This man was most pleasant during my stay at Kurre, and spent nearly all day with me, teaching me Amharic. However, he was not the most important man at Kurre, as presently three old men, who had been sent for on my arrival, rode up on mules, each with an attendant carrying his rifle. The chief of these was called Basha Gabri—a very cross-looking old man with a limp.

A *basha* is perhaps the equivalent of a captain or centurion. However, in the Abyssinian feudal system there is no fixed number of men under each rank, so perhaps the old English " esquire " would be a better description of his title.

Basha Gabri said that the Fitorari (Baron or Governor) of Bako must be immediately informed of my arrival, and that I must await the answer here.

As I was sitting here, two Arabs appeared, and one of these, whose name was Kassim, claimed consideration, on the score that he was a British subject. He really came from near Hodeida, but, as he had lived a year or two at Laheg, north of Aden, he considered himself quite British, as this Sultanate is under our protection.

I took him on as interpreter, and he accompanied me as far as Uba, and made himself most useful, as my Amharic was not of much use as yet, and Abdi knew only Galla. The other Arab, Said, lived in the village with the Abyssinians, whilst Kassim, who had married a Wallamu woman, lived apart, as he did not get on very well with them.

I tried to get the Abyssinians to send natives to fetch up my loads, but they refused, although very politely, to do anything until they had heard from the Fitorari.

The next day there was no answer from the Fitorari, and I was getting impatient at the delay; moreover, I had had a letter from Omari to say that one of the camels was dead, and several more dying. So I announced my intention of proceeding. Basha Gabri said that he could not allow me to proceed till he had heard from the Fitorari. As the old man had prevented my obtaining some of the local natives to go down for my loads, although they were quite willing, and was trying to obstruct me in various ways, I felt rather annoyed with him.

I therefore told him that I had Menelek's leave to proceed through his country, so it was not likely I was going to be stopped by a little man like himself. When I wanted to go on, I would go on, and when I wanted to stop, I would stop. He replied that he could not let me go on without leave from the Fitorari.

To this I replied that I was going on at a certain hour, and so, if he wanted me to stop, he would have to turn out all his soldiers. I felt perfectly certain that he would never risk the displeasure of his superior by doing this. To my surprise, my friend who had been teaching me Amharic, although very junior to the triumvirate of old men who were arranging my destinies, stoutly took my part, and said that I was perfectly right.

The old men were still sulking over this, when suddenly a letter arrived from the Fitorari saying that porters were to be sent to get my loads, and asking me to come to see him at Bako. The bearer of the letter also brought a sheep as a present.

Old Basha Gabri jumped up, and hobbled off as fast

as his game-leg would permit him to make arrangements, and presently returned with a gourd of honey as a present, saying that he felt ashamed at having given me nothing so far, but that his house was far away.

I soon got under way for Bako—a high mountain to our east, often covered with cloud. To the north of this is a huge flat-topped mountain, called Shangama, at the top of which is said to be another Abyssinian station. It must be considerably higher than Bako, as the top was hardly ever visible, whilst we frequently had a view of Bako.

I left Abdi behind to superintend the arrangements of fetching the loads up, and took Kassim with me, while Basha Gabri accompanied us part of the way. The old man tried to take us a long way round, but Kassim having told me which was the shortest route, I declined to take his advice. It afterwards transpired that he wanted to take us out of our way so as to pass his house. When we came to the upper waters of Neri, the same stream that we had crossed on the plains below, he said good-bye, as his jurisdiction ended here.

We then ascended, by steep and winding paths, to the summit of Bako Pass above us. Here we camped, with Bako's summit rising a thousand feet above us to the north, and other big mountains to our south. Just before reaching the summit, we came through a grove of very big coffee-trees.

Bako grows products of civilization, such as coffee and *kat* (an Arab stimulant), which are not found again until one reaches the heart of Abyssinia. Farther north, there is also said to be much coffee.

Now, the coffee-trees we saw were much more than ten years of age, whilst the Abyssinians have only occupied this territory for about that length of time. The Bako are much too primitive to grow the civilized products of *kat* and coffee, so to what old civilization are we to attribute these ? When we come to the Wallamu to the north-east, I will try to show that these people are, in my opinion, a highly civilized people, compared with the usual African native, especially when it is remembered that they were cut off, before the Abyssinian advent, from the exterior world.

As to the Bako, I have already described the way the men do their hair and the palm-leaf skirts worn by the women. The men make for themselves funny little caps out of the leaf of the wild banana, a fresh one every day ; while the women very often string a few strips of these leaves, freshly gathered, over their skirts.

The hats may be to protect the hair, but I cannot imagine what the women wear the strips for, as the lower parts of their persons are already well covered with palm-leaves. As the root of the wild banana is their staple food, perhaps it bears some religious interpretation.

The agricultural implements in Bako are about the most primitive I have ever seen. To remove the turf from the surface of the ground they use long, pointed poles. One sees a row of natives with one of these poles in each hand, driving them into the ground, and then levering up a sod. When the surface has been broken in this way, another agricultural implement is brought into play to further break up the ground. This is a little pick, made of two fire-hardened sticks, lashed side by side, and fastened to a third stick by way of a handle.

A curious thing about the Bako is that there are three tribes living amongst them, and subservient to them, resembling in this respect the Tumals, Midgans, and Yebirs of the Somali. Two of these tribes, the Gitamana and Fuga, are blacksmiths and leather-dressers, as are the Tumals and Yebirs. I could not ascertain what the third tribe, the Ghansa, did, as to all my inquiries I received the reply that they were just slaves or servants.

While we were pitching camp under Bako Mountain a pleasant-looking youth watched the proceedings with great interest, and then went away, and presently returned with a present of a chicken, milk, eggs, and grain. He was a Jima, a tribe living to the north of the route we took to Addis Ababa, and owned a little village of a few huts close by our camp.

During my stay at Bako, which was several days, he was most kind and attentive, and showed me the greatest hospitality, unlike the usual native hospitality, purely disinterested. As a rule, the native host, after making his first present, is ceaseless in his clamourings for presents. Many of the Abyssinians were very trying in this way, as, if they were not kept at a distance, there was a crowd round one's tent all day asking for everything they saw. This Jima youth, however, never asked for a single thing, and came several times a day to find out if there was anything I wanted.

A steep path ascended to the stronghold of Bako from close by our camp, and all day long a stream of soldiers, mounted or on foot, was to be seen crawling up and down the mountain like ants.

The Fitorari, I was told, was away for the day. Shortly after sunset a procession came down the mountain towards my camp, stopping a few hundred yards off, in the usual Abyssinian courteous manner, for permission to approach any nearer. On being told to approach, an old man came forward dressed in a *shamma* (or blanket) of red and white cotton, and wearing a sword, with a rhino-

horn hilt, silver inlaid. The Abyssinians always wear
their swords on the right side, and for this reason they
mount from what is to us the off side of an animal.

The old man, whose name was Basha Tazama, said
that the Fitorari had only just returned, and had sent
him to look after me, and he himself would come in the
morning. Two little basket-work stools were then brought
forward, and on being uncovered, a number of thin red
breads, as made by the Sudi, were disclosed. Two pots
of *tej* (honey-wine), a large calabash of honey, and a little
pot of red sauce, were also presented. The Basha then
said good-night, and went off to his house, which was
about a mile away under the hill.

Sadi was very curious to know what the red sauce was.
Thinking that it might be red pepper, I tried a very small
quantity, which did not taste particularly hot, so I said
that I did not know what it was. Sadi then had a try ;
he took a large spoonful, and after invoking the name of
Allah, popped it in his mouth. After much spluttering,
with streaming eyes, he pronounced it pure red pepper.
We found out afterwards that it was made of several
ingredients, but chiefly of a kind of *dhal*, or lentil flour,
mixed with butter and red pepper. As a sauce it was most
excellent when freshly made, and almost as good as *tobasco*.

Next day an enormous procession of servants and
soldiers, mounted and on foot, was seen coming down
the steep mountain-path. They drew up and dismounted
a couple of hundred yards from my tent, and on being
told to approach, Fitorari Mashasha came forward with
Basha Tazama. He was a tall, good-looking man, dressed
in a long flowing robe of black silk, with a soft felt hat.
He and the Basha sat in my tent, and he told me that I
was to ask the Basha for anything I wanted.

He himself and the Basha did not appear to be able to read or write, but both had smart, intelligent sons, about twelve years of age, who acted as their scribes. When I was hung up for a word I would look it up in my vocabulary, and point to it, and then they would explain to their fathers. However, at this time Kassim did most of the interpreting.

The Fitorari only stayed a short time, and then went away I said that I would call on him the next day, at which he expressed himself very pleased

As we were at Bako the heavy rains I had been fearing broke, and from now onwards it poured during the whole of our journey to Addis Ababa, rendering the ordinary valley routes impossible.

Bakari, the cook, did his best to stop the rain by Swahili magic, whilst Sadi invoked the name of Abu Bakr, but all to no purpose. The latter is a patron saint of travellers, and prayers to him are generally supposed to be efficacious. I asked Sadi what would happen supposing one man was on a journey, and prayed to Abu Bakr to stop the rain, and another man, sitting at home, prayed to Sheikh Abdul Kadr for rain for his crops. Sadi's answer was very simple ; the man would get rain for his crops, but at the edge of his fields the rain would stop, so as to permit the man on the journey to proceed in comfort.

The Swahili methods of stopping rain are as simple as they are ineffective, so I will give them for the benefit of the traveller. An axe is dipped for a moment into the fire, and then stuck up in a tree. An alternative method is to dip a long spoon in the ashes, and then stick it upright in the ground. Later on, when I called out at intervals to Bakari to stand up his spoon as the rain was coming on, he professed himself sceptical of its real virtue. However, such scepticism is only a temporary phase with natives, as no amount of failure will really convince them of the futility of charms and black magic.

Perhaps even at this very moment Bakari is holding forth to a credulous group of porters on the wonderful way in which he staved off rain for months in the country of the Wahabashi, and if they do not believe, they can go and ask the Bwana Komandari (as they called me).

It was very wretched for the mule having to stand tethered in the rain all night and day, till the old Basha, of his own accord, carried him off with the sais to live in his house.

The Abyssinian chief of a little village under Bako visited my camp from time to time, his arrival always being announced by a few very abusive words in Swahili, said in the politest manner imaginable These he had learnt from an East Coast Arab whom he had met, and he used to address my men, much to their amusement, with these words, as if he were bestowing the greatest compliment on them.

I went up to see the Fitorari on the day after his visit to me. As Bako Mountain is a typical *amba*, or Abyssinian mountain stronghold, I will describe it. The Abyssinians are a race of mountaineers, and each chief or governor looks out for some precipitous mountain or which to live with his people, where they will be safe in time of trouble.

A long, steep ascent by a winding mule-track brought us at last to a small hilly plateau near the top of the mountain. On this, at the summit of different hills, were dotted about little groups of huts, while horses, mules cattle, and goats grazed untended. In the flatter ground between the rises was cultivation. The only possible approach to this plateau for a hostile force was by the track we had ascended, or a second one equally steep and winding.

The rest of the mountain was too steep to be practicable for an enemy. At Bako there was but little cultivation, the greater part of the crops of the occupants being below the mountain. However, some of the *ambas*, having a broad expanse of open country on the top, are self-supporting, and so could sustain a siege indefinitely.

The Fitorari's residence I will not describe, as it was dirty and poor, and perhaps not typical of an Abyssinian governor's house. He gave me *tej* and *biris* (honey and water) to drink, but he himself did not take any, as it was Lent. The Abyssinian Lent lasts two months, and during this time they fast for most of the day, and do not indulge in certain things, such as milk. Fitorari Mashasha is the Governor of Bako, but he, in his turn, is under Dejaz Biru (an abbreviation of Dejazmach Biru), who is the Governor of the whole province, and lives at a place called Uba.

Every Saturday there is a market on the top of Bako. Merchants appear with calico, *shammas* (locally made blankets), sheep, cattle, honey, and other local products. In Abyssinia one is able to get more variety in the way of local food-supplies than in any other part of Africa I know of. On the way through the Rendile country nothing but sheep and bad camel-milk was obtainable, whilst in many other parts chicken and sweet potatoes are all that one can procure.

Bako was indeed a land of plenty after the very hard fare one had had coming through the low country. Basha Tazama's wife made butter and breads of a whiter-coloured flour for me ; the Jima youth brought me milk, chickens, eggs, sweet potatoes, and other kinds of bread, and the Fitorari sent honey and red-pepper sauce, whilst after the first rains the whole ground was covered with mushrooms.

I visited the Jima's house to see how the large flat breads are made, and his wife gave a special performance for my benefit. The red flour is stirred into a kind of liquid dough, which is poured carefully all over a large earthenware plate, heated over the fire, till it covers it completely. In a few seconds it is baked, and the bread is rolled off the plate. In size it is about one and a half to two feet across, and not thicker than a biscuit, quite soft, and with holes like a crumpet on the side uppermost on the plate.

I have never seen any native hut approaching in any way the clean and tidy appearance of this youth's hut. The floor was carefully swept, and consisted of well-smoothed and baked mud. Halfway round one wall was a raised seat of the same material, covered with tanned skins. One part of the hut was screened off as a sleeping apartment, while another corner was devoted to cooking. In different recesses round the walls the various utensils were stowed away, whilst others were hung up.

Basha Tazama's wife came to call on me one day, and wanted to know why I had not been to visit her. She was a most delightful old lady, and most friendly. She sat on the end of my bed and drank tea, and when she left I gave her a coloured handkerchief, and a looking-glass, and some medicine. She then mounted her mule, and rode off with an agility surprising in such an aged person.

This same looking-glass the Basha had seen lying on my table, and he had evinced a great interest in it. On

17

my offering to give it to him, he said : "What does an
old man like me want with a looking-glass ?"

However, old though he was, he had not quite put away
all vain thoughts, for every day when he came to see me
he used to take the glass and examine himself carefully in
it, smoothing his beard, and preening himself during the
whole of his stay. When he finally put down the glass,
I knew that it meant that he was going. He also had a
genial way of wanting to try my pipes, toothbrush, and
other toilet accessories.

Next time he came I asked after his wife, and he said
that he had not been on speaking terms with her since
she had paid me a visit. When I inquired as to the
reason of this, he said that I had given her some medicine,
and when she had got home he had asked for half of it,
but she had refused him, and eaten it all herself.

The Abyssinians are mad on medicines, and during
my stay at Bako I had a crowd clamouring for medicine
from morning to night. I had to start consulting hours,
and at other times put on sentries to keep my would-be
patients away. They were as a rule very ungrateful
patients ; of about a hundred people I attended to here
and at Uba, in only two cases did the recipients show any
gratitude. In both these cases they were women, and
they brought me a present of bread and flour afterwards.

One man brought his wife, a pretty Tigre girl, to be
attended. She had a nasty cut on her forehead, which had
inflamed, and affected her ear. I asked how it had happened, and he said that he had hit her on the head. I
told him : "You have injured your wife, and now you
bring her to me, a stranger, to cure ; it is your business to
cure her ; a man has no right to hit his wife like that."

He replied that it was customary for them to beat their

wives ; perhaps it was different in the country from which
I had come. To this I said that it was customary in many
countries to beat women, but never on the head. His
answer was that Satan had entered into his heart for a
moment, but now he was very sorry, and, moreover, he
had been severely punished, as he had no one to cook his
food for him, so I must do my best to cure her.

Sadi was always full of contempt for the really fearless
way the Abyssinian tried anything in the way of medicine
or food he saw or was given. At one place some of them
brought a tin of brown boot-grease to me, and asked what
it was. This they had got hold of somehow, and had been
tasting it with the idea that it was either some valuable
medicine or a sweetmeat. Sadi used to say : " I should
like to come to this country with a medicine which would
kill people if they smelt it, for all the Wahabashi would
rush to smell it at once."

I paid a return call at Basha Tazama's house, and was
received very hospitably. The Abyssinian, being a
Christian, is only allowed one wife, but he manages somehow to collect children from other sources. The old Basha
had his quiver very full, as there were quantities of
children of all ages, and he claimed the whole lot as his
offspring.

I had brought the old man a present of twill, and he at
once unrolled it, and measured it out several times in my
presence to see how much I had given him The proverb
about the gift horse seems not to have reached Abyssinia
yet, or, indeed, any other part of Africa. Not only is the
gift horse looked in the mouth, but it is generally also said
to be an old crock, whether that is the case or not.

However, at heart the Abyssinians—and especially
their womenfolk—have very friendly dispositions, and I

was especially struck with the very open handed way they treated the sais who had lived with them in company with the mule. From him they could expect no return for the kindnesses they heaped upon him.

When the evening repast was served, Mrs. Tazama and some of the girls personally waited on me, and spread butter and sauce for me with their fingers—acts I tried to accept in the kindly spirit in which they were meant.

The Abyssinian ladies' dress is not becoming. It consists merely of a sack-shaped dress of cotton hung from the shoulder, and sometimes tied round the waist with a shawl or girdle. When they go out, they wear over this a *shamma* and an Italian organ-grinder's hat. This headgear is also affected by the men.

The *shamma* is a product of Abyssinia. It is a blanket made of loosely spun cotton, grown locally, woven by a kind of Malay hitch. The dress is made of the same material, which is soft and warm. However, the cotton only remains white for a day or two, and so a clean white one is seldom seen, and everyone looks filthy dirty. Some of the *shammas* are made with a broad red stripe down the centre.

The wealthier men wear a black cloak of silk or bombazine, which looks smarter. The men affect Italian hats to a great extent. In wet weather a *bernus* is worn. This is a black cloak of wool, with a cowl for the head, and keeps the wearer beautifully dry and warm. This article is a product of Northern Abyssinia, and is not made at Bako or Uba. The *shamma* is, however, largely made in the vicinity of the latter place.

The better class wear a sword, often with silver inlaid sheath, while an attendant carries their rifle in front. Round the waist a bandolier of cartridges is always worn, and sometimes a revolver or pistol. Some of the older men still have the old Abyssinian shield, carefully done up in a cloth bag, carried by one of their attendants.

It is beneath anybody of any consequence to walk on foot for even a few yards, and to cover the shortest distances a mule is saddled. From my camp at Bako I could see everyone who ascended or descended the mountain, and never did I see anyone dismount to lead his mule up. Even after coming in from the longest journey they expected their mules to carry them up the steep ascent.

Owing to the hilly nature of the country, a mule is always used to ride, while a horse is supposed to be only an animal of war. Some of the trappings of different coloured morocco leather look very nice when new. The stirrups are small, and only intended to take the big-toe, as the Abyssinian always goes about barefooted.

In a precipitous and mountainous country like Abyssinia this is a great advantage, and the Abyssinian, so ready to accept most things European, shows his sense in avoiding boots and European clothing. The usual native is only too anxious to learn how to wear boots, with the result that he suffers great discomfort, and grows heavy-footed in place of being active. To accustom native troops to wear boots is a great mistake, as it lessens their marching powers and reduces their mobility. The most that should ever be allowed them is a pair of sandals, to be worn attached to the waist, and only put on in thorn or other very bad country.

After a long delay at Bako, finally my loads were brought in, some by my own porters, and others by some of the Bako natives, accompanied by Basha Gabri. To the latter I made a present, and the old humbug kissed my hand, and said that he was my servant, and would do anything for me. Of the camels, some had died under Kurre, and others after making the ascent, and the few that remained were too sick to proceed, so I gave them to some Abyssinians.

I had brought with me some Marie-Thérèse dollars, for use in travelling through Abyssinia. These were brand-new, and I thought would be appreciated more than old ones. However, the natives of this part looked on them with suspicion, as they were not old and dirty, like those they were accustomed to, and so would not accept them. I was fortunate enough to be able to dispose of a lot of my trade goods to some merchants, and so was able to reduce my loads, and obtain money for the journey. Other things I discarded, but I still had too many loads for my own porters to carry.

The Fitorari promised me some porters, but I had to wait several days before they appeared. Finally, they turned up, and the Fitorari came to say good-bye. I paid a last call on the Jima youth, and took him, amongst other things, a Swahili cloth for his wife, at which she was delighted, as they are Muhammadan.

He was one of the few natives I have met who have any sense of gratitude, for during my stay I mended his rifle for him. Instead of taking it away directly I had finished, and saying no more about it, he repeatedly thanked me, and said many times afterwards how glad he was to have it whole again. Finally, he accompanied me, on the first day of my journey, to Uba, and there said good-bye.

* This dollar, struck from an old die, used to be the universally accepted coin of Abyssinia and Arabia. Now Menelek strikes his own dollars, but many of the country folk still prefer the Marie Thérèse.

CHAPTER XVIII

UBA

THE Basha's wife had been to call on me again the day before I left, and made me promise to come and say good-bye on my way. So when the men had all started, I rode over to their house, which was not far out of the way. The old lady had made me up some little stores of flour and bread and red pepper for the journey.

The bread she put in a flat, round, leather-covered basket, such as almost every Abyssinian fastens to his saddle when he goes on a journey. This and several other instances of kindness convinced me that many of the Abyssinians are at heart exceptionally nice people, although their usual grasping demands and exasperating habits of procrastination are apt to make one overlook this.

Our way led first of all along fairly level country, between Bako Mountain on one side and several large hills on the other. Scattered about on the tops and sides of the hills were a few villages and groves of what appeared to be bananas. These are in reality the wild banana, cultivated for the sake of its roots. Out of these the natives make a kind of bread. I have never seen this eaten in any other place, although, growing wild, it is common over most of tropical Africa. From Kurre and Bako onwards this forms the staple food of the people, especially just before and at the beginning of the rains.

Presently we came to the edge of Bako Plateau—a great drop of two or three thousand feet. The sides of the hills were, as elsewhere in the Bako Mountains, exceptionally steep, although clothed in grass. This latter circumstance would make their ascent more difficult, as there is no foothold on the grassy, precipitous sides. Down this a rough mule-track, cut in the face of the hills, wound along the sides of spurs and ridges, till it reached the valley below, bounded on all sides by precipitous hills.

We camped at the foot of the hills, and I gave the porters who had been sent by the Fitorari each a present, in the hopes that they would stop with us ; but they all went off, saying that they had only been told to come one day.

Omari had been very trying all day. Kitabu had been doing the work of headman lately, as Omari had been behind with the camels. This was the first time I had had the porters without Omari, and it was most pleasant, as there were no squabbles and refusals to do the ordinary duties of camp, but they were all most exemplary in their behaviour.

Omari attempted to resume his duties as headman by counting the loads at Bako, and solemnly came to me and reported that there were sixteen less than there actually were. As I had counted them myself, I knew how many there were, and suggested that he should try again for practice, as a headman who could not tell one how many loads there were was fairly useless.

When he came in to camp, I asked him how many Bako porters had come with him, as he started with a little party after we had left. He said : " Four ; but one is carrying the load of the other one who left, and the other man who wasn't carrying a load joined us, and took the load of the other man whom I called on the way, but he is not here."

Then I asked : " How many men did you come into camp with ?" He replied : " I am telling you, bwana. The other man who didn't come," etc., etc. After about ten minutes of this, I called Sadi, and said to him : " Perhaps I have forgotten Swahili since I have been learning the language of the Wahabashi. Make Omari say slowly to you what he has just said to me, and see if you understand. If you don't understand, ask him how many Bako natives he came in to camp with, and, when you have heard, come and tell me. I am going into my tent to rest my brain."

Presently Sadi came and said : " I can't understand what he means, but we can count all the natives in the camp, and find out like that."

Omari is not a great mathematician. One day, when we had all our tanks full of water, and also the water of a lot of *hans* brought in by the Rendile, we were just about to start on a march. As we had no receptacle in which to put the water of the *hans*, and had to return them to the Rendile, it was necessary to give out all they contained before starting. This seemed a pity, as there was rather more water than we wanted for the moment. I gave the order to the men to fill all their water-bottles from the *hans*, and also to take so many for each camp. Omari, however, had a brilliant suggestion.

He said that if I gave out the water from the tanks to the men, I would then get the space in the tanks in which to pour the water of the *hans*, and so we should be able to take more with us. I replied that, whatever we did, we could only take each tank full of water, and they were all full now. Omari said that I did not understand. I agreed with him, and gave out all the water the men wanted from the *hans*, but at the end there were several *hans* full, which we did not know what to do with, as everyone had filled his water-bottle and drunk all he wanted.

Omari said : "Now you see what my plan was. If the men had filled their water-bottles and drunk from the water of the tanks, we would then have been able to pour all the water of the *hans* into the tanks, and have none left. Now it is wasted."

After we had finally settled the problem of the Bako natives, and all the porters were cooking food, I noticed that the agitated Omari had forgotten his rifle, and left it standing up against a tree some way from any of my porters' camps, but near where the Bako natives were squatting. I was very much annoyed at this, as it might have easily been stolen, and I had given orders that the men were never to let their rifles out of their sight, and to sleep on them at night.

I was on the point of calling Omari, when I thought that I would teach him a more practical lesson instead, so I fetched the rifle, and put it in my tent. Nothing more happened till the porters began to go to bed, and then I heard Omari's voice asking if anybody had seen his rifle. After a search for it, he went off to bed himself, without attempting to report his loss.

This is a most annoying trait of natives. They seldom come and say, "I have lost this," or "I have broken that." They wait for you to find it out for yourself, and then they say : "Oh, that ! that was lost long ago."

I always tell them that it is much better to come and tell me at once, and then I may be a little cross, or I may not ; but I am sure to be angry when I am not told.

With the ammunition given out there was constantly a round being lost here and there. If the man came and told me at once, I did not say anything about it, but if, at an inspection, I found that anyone had neglected to do this, I used to charge him for the value of the lost round.

Next morning an Abyssinian living near came to see me, and promised to try to get me some more porters to take the place of the Bako who had stopped to cook the food I gave them, and then gone off. However, he only managed to secure five men.

I called out to Omari to bring his rifle, as the Abyssinian wanted to see what it was like, and he pretended not to hear. I then told Sadi to call him. When he came and I asked for the rifle, he said he would go and fetch it. He did not come back, thinking that I should forget.

Finally, Sadi spoilt the joke, as he called him again, and then exploded with laughter. Omari then said that he had had his rifle a moment before, but now it had gone, and he thought that Sadi or someone must have taken it.

Most of the loads that had been brought by the Bako were now stranded, so I decided to leave Omari and a few men with them, and go on and try to get help from Uba.

We marched on two days up this valley. The five Bako men, after receiving a good gorge the first night, and a promise of a big reward, said that they would come on to Uba with me. However, our marches were too long for them, and the second day they left their loads and went off.

Near our camp, on the top of a little hill, lived two Senegalese, who had been brought here by a Russian expedition. They came down to see me, took my spare loads, and put them in their house, and then rode on to Uba to make arrangements for me. One of them, a

Barrambaras, spoke a little French, and was a most pleasant man. His name was Osman.

The word Barrambaras means a commander, something above the rank of Basha. In an old book on Abyssinia the first Abyssinian met by the author on arrival at the frontier happened to be a Barrambaras, and he translates this word as "guardian of the frontier." It is rather comic to see this mistake occur in several other books on Abyssinia, as it shows that the authors copy from the writings of others. When I asked if they only lived on the frontier, I was told that there were many in every big station, and that the road up to Addis Ababa was thick with them.

On proceeding from here, we came to the villages of the Uba. We met a man carrying two gourds of milk—one fresh and the other sour. I arranged for the purchase of the fresh gourd, Kassim acting as interpreter, as he knew the language well, from having a Wallamu wife.

After we had arranged the purchase, Kassim harangued the native, and then turned to me and said in Arabic that the man wished to give the other gourd to my servants. As the man had said nothing, I knew that Kassim was "trying it on," so I said : "Did the man say that, or did you say that ?"

Kassim looked rather foolish, and Sadi, who understood Arabic, frequently got a rise out of him afterwards by saying, "So-and-so wants to give you all his wealth, Kassim," or "Here is someone else trying to give you milk."

The Uba are a subsection of the Wallamu, and talk practically the same language. One of the most curious things about them is their variation in colour. They are either very dark or very fair, either blackish-brown or very pale *café-au-lait* coloured ; but few are seen who are intermediate between these two colorations.

Tribes differ enormously in colour, and amongst individuals there is generally considerable variation ; but then the majority of the tribe are a mean between the two extremes. With the Uba and Wallamu, however, there may be two children by the same father and mother, and whilst one is as dark as a Masai, the other is as pale as a town Arab or Egyptian, who has never been in the sun.

We climbed up the foot-hills of Uba Mountain, and there we met the Barrambaras and some men sent by the Dejazmach to attend to me. The last few miles of our way had led us through a big village of the Uba, and then on to a high shelf below Uba Mountain.

The village was peculiar in that it was divided up by roads into rectangular enclosures bordered by hedges and low stone walls. Stockades and hedges are often made among African tribes for purposes of defence, but it is most rare to see them used as boundaries for property. In fact, the only place where I have noticed this in uncivilized Africa is in Uganda.

Another thing that struck me as peculiar during the day's march was the sight of some roughly-made ploughs. I had thus seen in the course of two days the most primitive agricultural implements I had ever come across—those of the Bako—and the most civilized yet seen in Africa.

The Barrambaras and some of the Dejaz's men sat with me till tĕn o'clock at night, although I made several attempts to get rid of them. Meanwhile, their attendants were shouting from hill-top to hill-top, and exhorting the natives to bring in supplies. They refused to budge till all the supplies came in, saying that if they did not turn up all right the Dejaz would be very angry. At last all the food was collected by contributions from different villages, and a sheep, some chickens, milk, and various red-coloured breads, were brought in, and they returned to the *amba* of Uba.

Next day a stiff climb of about three miles brought me to a level plateau on the top of the mountain, on which were situated several villages of Abyssinians, and on the summit of one flat-topped rise was the house and precincts of the Dejaz.

Near the top of the ascent a group of mounted Abyssinians with a hundred or more soldiers were ready to meet me, and I thought that it must be the Dejaz. They dismounted and came forward, and I was told by the Barrambaras Osman that they were only a few Bashas and Barrambaras.

The first thing I noticed on breasting the summit was an enormous white tent, which many men had just finished pitching, and it was to gain time to get this ready for me that I had been made to camp under the *amba* the night before.

I was ushered into this, where two chairs and a table had been placed ready, and a caraffe of very clear and excellent *tej** was brought. I was also told that a house near had been placed at my disposal.

A genial, fat, bald-headed merchant from Ankoba did the honours, and I found out afterwards that he had turned out of the house, and was living in a small tent with his whole family, so as to let me have it.

It was now Easter, which is observed as a big feast by the Abyssinians, and everybody was very cheery on *tej* and *araking*—the latter a sort of gin. In the afternoon a horn was blown from the Dejaz's quarters, and

* Hydromel or honey-wine.

presently we could see soldiers and mules collecting from every direction. After about two hours of preparation, several hundred men, mounted and on foot, were seen approaching our camp.

The bigger the man, the greater retinue he moves about with, and even a Basha will often collect about half a hundred followers before he moves from home. I used to be the object of great sympathy to everyone I met in the road when I was seen to be walking alone, or with one attendant, in my very battered and ragged clothes, torn by the thorn of the Elges and the low country. Even strangers on the road would stop me and say that it was not fitting for me to be seen alone. When I climbed a steep hill on foot with a horse led behind me, and some of my sick men on mules, their astonishment was unbounded, and they certainly thought that I must be mad.

The Dejaz brought with him an interpreter called Kalkai, who could speak French well. He was very interested to hear by what route I had arrived in the country, and asked me many questions about the low country. He only stopped a short time, and then left. Presently Kalkai came back, and said that the Dejaz had sent him to talk to me, as he saw that I was alone, and had no one who could talk my language. He also begged me to ask for anything I wanted.

Barrambaras Osman and the Dejaz both expressed themselves most anxious to get me the loads left behind as quickly as possible, and I am sure that, according to their lights, they did their best.

However, interminable delay is inseparable from Abyssinian methods, and so I had to wait at Uba a long time for my loads, and also to make arrangements to proceed. To one thing I made up my mind, and that was that when I could proceed I would take no more than my own people could carry, however many things it meant abandoning, as I was anxious to be absolutely independent again of help from the Abyssinians.

Nevertheless, during my enforced stay at Uba I spent a very pleasant time. The Dejaz's amanuensis and several others were only too eager to help me learn the language, while even the Dejaz himself used to teach me words, and he also lent me an Amharic Bible to read.

The first night at Uba I somewhat rashly decided to take up my quarters in the house, as the mountain-top was chilly, and there was generally a thick mist. The idea of sitting snug and warm over a fire in the well-built little hut appealed to me. I had not been there very long, however, before I began to feel a tickling about the legs, and then an itching, so I made a hurried exit, and transferred my quarters to the tent. This was very spacious, and entirely home-made from ordinary *Amerikani* calico.

I did not want to hurt the feelings of the owner of the house, and so I sent word to him that I had no idea that he had turned out of it on my account, and insisted that he should return at once. Had I told him that there were any other inhabitants in it besides himself and his family, he would probably have thought that I was romancing.

The Dejaz sent me a present of an ox and different kinds of food, and also, to my surprise, some excellent tinned provisions that were very acceptable, as I had had to throw away most of my stores.

I must say a word now about the politeness of the Abyssinians, a fact which impressed me very much, and for which I was not prepared amongst a comparatively speaking uncivilized people. There is no nation I have ever met, not even the French, who can be compared with the Abyssinians in this respect. Many of them are exorbitant in their demands and dilatory in their methods, but they are so courteous in their exactions and procrastinations that it is difficult to take offence.

The " small boy " is the rudest product of civilization, and one can easily imagine how an Abyssinian walking about in his native dress in London or Paris would be the victim of all sorts of gibes and jeers from the street urchins. He would, indeed, be lucky if he had only these to put up with, and was not bombarded by stones, cabbages, mud, or anything else that came handy. To compare Abyssinia with another self-governing, semi-civilized race, a European in Arabia would be followed about by a crowd of small boys, who would surround his camp, and sing vulgar verses about him. Yet I was able to walk through the whole length of Abyssinia in a costume which, in my own country, even, would have caused some comment, and I have never heard a single rude thing said about me by any Abyssinian small boy. On the contrary, every child greets a stranger and his own elders in a courteous and respectful manner, which might well be imitated by their white brethren.

As regards their form of address, they perhaps carry politeness and punctiliousness to too great an extreme. One sees two men meeting each other, and apparently holding a long conversation, and then each proceeds on his way. In reality they have said nothing but the equivalent of " How do you do ?" but something after this manner :

" Is your afternoon good ?"

" Yes, thank God. And is yours, my brother ?"

" Yes, thank God. And have you spent the fore-noon well ?"

" Yes, thank God, I have spent the forenoon well. And you, have you also spent the forenoon well ?"

" Yes, thank God ; and have you passed the night well ?"

" Yes, thank God ; and have you ?"

" Yes, thank God ; and have you safely arrived here ?"

" Yes, thank God."

" And have you had a good journey ?"

" Yes, thank God. And you, have you spent the time well since our last interview ?"

" Yes, thank God, I have ; and have you also ?"

" Yes, thank God ; and are you in good health ?"

" Yes, thank God. And are you also well ?"

" Yes, thank God."

" May you have a safe road."

" Thank God. Good-bye."

" Good-bye."

" Amen."

The day after the Dejaz had been to see me I went up to visit him. He received me in a large barn-shaped building, one end of which was screened off by a large curtain forming a little reception-room, whilst the rest was open to his attendants and hangers-on.

He said that he had been told how I had lost my dog, and how I had fired at the crocodile. This latter seemed to have produced a great effect on my Abyssinian guide from Karo to Kurre, as I was constantly being asked about it. Those living in these parts had never seen or heard of a repeating pistol, and so thought it a most wonderful performance to fire so quickly. He asked me if the dog had been a very valuable one, and I said :

THE DEJAZ'S PRESENT

This is the horse given me by Dejaz Biru. I fitted the native saddle with my own stirrups, so as to be able to ride off on him when he was given me. The Abyssinian stirrups are made to take the big toe only. The man holding him is an Abyssinian soldier in characteristic dress, with a "shamma" over his shoulders.

No, it was not that, but it was that I had lost my only companion.

For long after Narok's tragic end I used to wake up at night and listen for her pushing in under my tent-flies. She used to have the most friendly way of always rubbing her nose against my hand to tell me that she had come in, before lying down. I would wonder where she was, and then would suddenly remember her as I had last seen her. Then I would think that, if I had run faster or started sooner, I might have saved her.

The Dejaz said : " You must let me give you another companion, as I have a puppy here of a European breed." It would have been of no use to carry a small puppy with me, and, anyhow, I had only a few weeks' trek before me to the coast, so I declined his offer, thanking him very much for what was a very kindly thought.

He then took me round his houses, and showed me his dogs and a baby giraffe, which ran towards us and fed out of the hand. A horse was then brought out, and the Dejaz said he was going to give it to me when I left, but that, as I had nowhere in my camp to put it, he would keep it till then in his stables.

Another day the Dejaz came down to see me in the evening, and talked for a bit. It then began to thunder, and he looked out at the black clouds gathering, and said he had hoped to stop to dinner with me, but he did not want to be caught by the rain. I immediately sent out to tell my cook to get ready some food, and told Sadi to do the best he could ; but it appeared that the Dejaz had brought his own dinner with him, as his attendants rushed in and produced a rice stew and some bread, and we made a hurried repast, the Dejaz asking for news of the rain between every two mouthfuls.

The day after he asked me up to lunch, and gave me a really excellent meal. He entertained me in a circular hut behind his audience-room. On the floor were strewn freshly-cut, green rushes by way of a carpet.

Barrambaras Osman sent me a letter in Amharic to tell me that my loads had arrived at his house, and would shortly be forwarded. The Abyssinian letter is a slip of paper with close, but regular, writing. Every man of importance has a large seal or die, on which his name is written. This is inked over and stamped at the foot of the letter close under the writing. They are very economical about paper, and when the letter is finished any paper that is not written on is carefully torn off, and the letter is then carefully folded up into a pellet, and sent to its destination.

The writing is generally a laborious proceeding requiring great mental strain and frequent wipings of the pen on the hair, which forms a handy and serviceable pen-wiper, and, moreover, being black, does not show the ink-stains.

At length Abdi and the last of the loads arrived at Uba, but they brought the news that Yusufu, who had been one of the men left with Abdi, had suddenly been taken ill with colic. He had been taken into the house of an Abyssinian, who had treated him with every kindness, but after two days of illness, the poor little fellow started away on his last great trek, and was buried by Abdi and Tumbo. He was one of the most cheerful and willing of my men.

The cold and wet of the highlands was very trying to the men after the great heat of the plains below, and during the whole of the journey to Addis Ababa there was always one or two of them ill.

I was fortunate enough to be able to buy several mules at Uba, which would serve to carry food for the men. I then went carefully through my loads of trade goods, and threw away all the things unlikely to be of any further use —all my beads, half my medicines, half my axes, my water-tanks, and various other things. At last only sufficient things remained to be carried by my men, and we were once more, to my delight, absolutely independent of help from the Abyssinians.

The Dejaz presented me not only with the horse, but also a mule to ride myself. On leaving, I was very much exercised in my mind as to what I should give him as a souvenir of all his kindness and generosity. Such usual presents as *maradufu*, a rifle and ammunition, I gave him, but of all such things he had plenty, and, moreover, being very well off, could get as much as he liked from Addis Ababa.

He had consulted me frequently concerning his ailments, but of medicines he had sufficient to stock a chemist's shop, although he did not know which to use. What was I to give him, then, besides the ordinary commonplace presents given by every traveller in Abyssinia ? At last an idea struck me : I had the skin of the lion shot at Horr. This is an article highly prized by Abyssinians, whereas I had plenty at home, and, moreover, this one was hardly likely to survive a journey through Abyssinia in the wet season without getting spoilt.

So I sent Abdi up with the skin, and the Dejaz appeared very gratified that I should give him such a present.

Amongst my loads was the massive head of the buffalo, which was a man's load—about sixty pounds. I had often thought that I ought to discard this, but I could not bring myself to part with it, and so I discarded any food-stores still left to me, which were few, and only kept tea, salt, and pepper, sufficient to take me to Addis Ababa, and a few of the tins given me by the Dejaz, whilst the remainder I consumed or gave away to the men.

Abdi had picked up two Somali pals on the way. They were living with Barrambaras Osman, and they and he both came into Uba the night before I left. Osman sold me a mule, which was afterwards always known as Barrambaras, and proved to be a most exceptional animal for a mule. He was always sweet-tempered and friendly, and had many other peculiar qualities.

Abdi's Somali pals came to see me, and one of them said that he had been with Abdul Hassan, the Somaliland Mullah, during the first stages of his career. He said he had been present at the attack of the Mullah's forces on the Abyssinian post of Jigjiga.

I asked him whether they still believed in the Mullah's statement that hostile bullets would turn to water. He said that this was quite true at first, or, at any rate, their enemies' rifles would not fire when they first attacked Jigjiga. The Mullah told them not to give the alarm by firing their rifles, but to enter in silence. They entered the fort, and got amongst the huts, and not a. single Abyssinian was able to fire his rifle till the spell was broken by an Arab, a British subject, who fired off his rifle, and then all the Abyssinians were able to fire, and drove them out of the fort with great loss.

Soon after this he got tired of Abdul Hassan, and ran away from him, taking with him one rifle and four horses belonging to the prophet.

Abdi was very full of his Somali pals, and what fine people the Somalis were at first, but he got very bored with them after a short while. He said that he was a

ABYSSINIAN AND HORSE

The photograph shows the Abyssinian saddle and the trappings, which are studded with brass, and look like a poor edition of the decorations of the ordinary English plough horse.

Somali had met other Somalis in a strange country,
and ehoved him to make them a present. So he
ᵛ several dollars each, but instead of thanking
- ; very generous action, they said : " Now ycu
m ome calico for us, and if you cannot get some
cali must give us another dollar each."
Ab me to me and said : " I don't know what the
people ᶜ his country take us for. I have never met their
like for asking for presents. I think that they must
imagine that we have passed through a country where we
have been picking up money from the ground, and now
want to get rid of it."

Finally, all arrangements were completed ; food for
the men had been partly purchased and partly presented
to me by the Dejaz, and we once more took the road.

My men now presented the most comic appearance, as
I had bought them all *shammas*, to replace their torn and
worn blankets. These, and trousers made of calico,
which ⅼ had given them, surmounted by head-dresses of
zebra's mane and battered fezes, and the lusty way they
swung along with their loads, caused everyone in the
road to stop and stare at these quaint objects.

I rode up to the Dejaz, and sat with him for half an
hour or so, and then he mounted his mule, and, with a
large retinue, accompanied me for part of the way.

The road wound along the top of a razor-edged spur,
and so we had to ride in single file. After proceeding
about a mile, I begged him not to come any farther. So
he shook hands, and, after thanking him again for his
mar ⲅ kindnesses, I rode off after my men, who had precede ⅼ me, while the Dejaz stood and waved his hat, and
theɪ turned round, and, accompanied by his retinue,
returned to Uba.

CHAPTER XIX

CROSSING THE MOLSHA

KASSIM had gone home from Uba. I was sorry to lose his services, but I now knew enough of the language to be able to get on fairly well with an Abyssinian guide. The Dejaz's amanuensis accompanied us during the first day out from Uba, and led us along a ridge leading north-east. We only went on a few miles, and then camped on the top of a narrow neck of this thin, razor-edged range, with a precipitous drop on either hand.

A Barrambaras lived close by our camp, and he had been deputed by the Dejaz to get provisions for us. He came and sat in my tent till a late hour at night, while the usual shouting from hill-tops took place, and, finally, a quantity of food was brought. Although we had not come far, it was a great thing to have made a start, and still more satisfactory to feel that we were perfectly independent again.

The Dejaz's writer had a Mannlicher rifle, and was very anxious for me to sell him all my ammunition. I gave him a little, and said I could not spare any more, as I wanted it for myself. He continued to importune me, saying that I could not possibly want any ammunition on the way to Addis Ababa, and when I arrived there, I could buy as much as I liked at ten for a dollar. To this I replied that I did not want Addis Ababa ammunition, as it was sure to be bad. He assured me that it was of the best, and showed me that which he was wearing in his bandolier.

Wishing to close the discussion, I said that I would prove to him that his Addis Ababa ammunition was not so good as mine. We would each take our rifles and our ammunition, and fire at a mark, and see whose bullet went straightest. I knew that I should be easily able to defeat him, as the Abyssinians are, from our point of view, ridiculously poor marksmen.

A gourd was put up on the top of a rock, and I was requested to fire first. If one makes a clean hit, natives, seeing no apparent movement of the target, are always good enough to say that one has missed, and may even give one instructions as how to shoot the next shot. When the object is subsequently examined, and a little hole is found drilled through it, as likely as not they think it some fake, especially if the hole appears smaller than the bullet. What appeals to them is visible effect when a shot is fired.

Knowing this, I aimed below the gourd, and was lucky enough to hit the rock just in front of it. The splinters sent the gourd flying, and so scored one to me.

The writer next fired. I was prepared for a miss on his part, but not for what actually occurred. When he pressed the trigger, his rifle gave forth a tired hiss, and a subsequent examination proved that the bullet had not sufficient pressure behind it to cause it to travel more than halfway up the barrel. We then adjourned to camp, and I had to extract it with my clearing-rod.

While at Bako, a Gerezmach (General or Brigadier, under the rank of Fitorari) had come often to my camp and extolled his prowess as a hunter. It appeared that it was beneath him to shoot just an elephant or two at a time, for whenever he met elephants, he killed from twenty to a hundred. I got so bored with his stories and with the thought that he mistook me for such a fool as to believe them that I said to him that he must not only be a wonderful marksman, but most marvellously rapid. I should never forgive myself if I left without having had an opportunity of observing his skill with the rifle.

Abdi took a spiteful delight in cornering him, as the Gerezmach had assumed that no one but an Abyssinian had ever been able to tackle dangerous game. Finally, the old man was induced to give us an exhibition. A mark was put up, and he scored a few very bad wides, and then said that his rifle was bad.

From our camp on the neck the writer returned, and the Barrambaras provided us with two guides to take us to Dalbo—one a tall Arusi Galla, and the other a short native of Uba, called Dasita.

One of the least conspicuous, but most important, personages of a caravan, as concerning the comfort of the white man, is the cook's boy. He carries the load of cooking-pots, and on arrival in camp finds firewood, and stones on which to rest the pots. After a week or two of trek he often has learnt all the cook knows—which is never very much—and the latter sometimes assumes airs, and cannot do this, that, and the other, till at last the cook's boy does everything under the superintendence of the *chef*.

Although his job is a staff billet, and he thus receives an honorarium slightly in excess of the mere porter, this individual is apt, after a time—often not without just cause—to think that he is being put upon. It is seldom that a cook and his boy go through a long trek without friction, and more generally, there are at periods serious disagreements between the two.

I had been exceptionally lucky in my cook's boy, as this office had been filled by a sturdy and good-tempered little youth called Maguru-Kwenda (literally "legs go," meaning "best foot forward," or "twinkle-toes"). His name was no misnomer, as he was always in front of the caravan, and the first to arrive in camp, so there was never long to wait for food after getting in. He was a Kikuyu by birth, but had lived on the coast, and then taken to the life of a professional porter.

On the day we left our camp on the neck, everything was packed up ready to go, when it was found that Maguru-Kwenda was missing. The cook told me that he had gone out at dawn to look for some firewood, and had not returned.

Men were sent out in all directions to look for him, and I feared that some mischance had befallen him. Either in the mists of the early morning he had fallen over one of the steep precipices that abounded on either side, or that he had had a fit, and was lying unconscious somewhere near.

A long search produced no result, so I interrogated the cook carefully. It then transpired that he and the cook had fallen out, and Maguru-Kwenda had walked off in a huff—a common trait in the generally cheerful, but rather peculiar, disposition of the Kikuyu. I reprimanded the cook for not telling me the truth at once, and so keeping the whole caravan waiting. As a punishment, I made him carry Maguru-Kwenda's load during that day's march.

We started away, and, after going half a mile or so, I called Abdi and Tengeneza, and said to them : "The

heart of Maguru-Kwenda is sore, because of the words
of Bakari, and so he will sit alone amongst the rocks,
because of the badness of his spirit. When noon comes,
the pain of hunger will seize him, and he will forget his
vexation, and come forth. He will come to our camp,
and, when he finds that we have left, he may go to some
village. If the people there give him food, he will forget
his hunger, and sit there a while, till, perhaps, it may be
too late to rejoin us. Therefore, you two go stealthily
back, and conceal yourselves near our old camp, and
watch for his coming."

After proceeding a short way, our path made a steep
descent to the valley to our east. Kalkai, the Dejaz's
interpreter, had a house farther along the ridge on which
we had travelled from Uba. He had sent a man the night
before with a present of honey from himself and a loaf
of sugar from the son of the Gin (or Genni). The Genni
is the Queen, or chieftainess, of Goffa. She was now
on a visit to Addis Ababa, and her son was stopping with
Kalkai.

I knew that it was sugar he sent, because there was a
label on it to the effect that it was sugar especially made
for the Abyssinian trade. If it had not been for this, I
should have thought that it was a block of stone.

Both of them asked me to call in on my way, so, when
the path began to descend, I left the caravan, and kept
along the ridge. First, however, I selected a site for
camp from afar, as the valley was laid out below us, like
a map. There was a horseshoe of thorn-trees to be seen
up the valley, and, having ascertained that our path
passed near, I chose that spot.

The Barrambaras of the night before accompanied us
as far as the top of the descent, and when he said good-

bye, he immediately sat down on a rock, and began to hear a case between two Esa Somalis who were serving here with the Abyssinian soldiers. While the Abyssinian sat stolid and unmoved on his improvised throne of justice, the two Somalis grew vehement and excited. They each spoke in turn, and shouted, screamed, and gesticulated, and danced at each other in the most ridiculous way. Every point or hit the orator made, or imagined he was making, was accompanied by a kind of overhand bowling at his adversary. The imaginary ball was delivered at the other's head at the same time as the barbed words were launched at him.

I proceeded along the ridge to Kalkai's house, and on the way met a pleasant-looking youth, who said that he would come to Dalbo with me and look after the mules on the way. He ran off home to get a few belongings for the journey, and I did not expect to see him again, but he turned up all right, and came as far as Addis Ababa. His name was Alamu, and he turned out very useful.

As I made my way by a rough track along the summit of the ridge, I could see the long range of Goffa to the north-west, behind which, I was told, flowed the Omo River. The district of Goffa, ruled by the Genni, whose name is Wezoro Akalesa, is, from all accounts, a flourishing dependency of Abyssinia. A great quantity of coffee is grown there, and when our route joined with the Goffa-Addis Ababa track, we met caravans of fifty or a hundred mules at a time conveying this product up to Addis Ababa.

On arrival at Kalkai's house, I was introduced to the Genni's son—a tall, fat youth, to whom Kalkai referred as *Le Roi*. Kalkai's house was a large, circular hut, consisting of a central portion, surrounded by an outer

wall. Between the inner and outer walls were com-
partments used as store-rooms and stables.

The inside portion was divided into two parts by a
dirty curtain. One of these parts was arranged as a
sitting-room, and skins and cushions were thrown about
to sit on, while the other half was for the cooking and
servants. As the living-room. is surrounded by stables
for mules, goats, and cattle, divided from it only by an
open-work wall, aroma and insect-life pervade the inner
room.

Kalkai gave me a very good meal, consisting of *tej*,
tef (a white bread), and a splendid sauce of chillies and
minced meat, followed by coffee. The thin, large, flat
breads are piled up on a basket-work table, the sauce is
poured on to the centre of the top bread, and the party
then sit round and feed out of the same dish. At first
I had considerable difficulty in scooping up any of the
mince and chillies with my flat pieces, broken off from the
edges of the pile of soft breads.

I watched my companions closely, and presently saw
how it was done. The little pieces of bread were thrown
on the top of the mince-meat, and when they were
pinched with the fingers, they enclosed some of it, without the fingers having to come in contact with the meat
or sauce.

Abdi and Tengeneza arrived in time to finish up the
remains of the repast, bringing with them Maguru-
Kwenda, looking very sheepish and ashamed of himself.
Abdi said : " As you said, Bwana, so it came to pass. We
waited near our camp, and about noon Maguru-Kwenda
came forth."

He was so ashamed of himself that it was quite unnecessary to punish him for the delay he had caused us.

KALKAI AND THE GOFFA LIJ

Kalkai, on the extreme right, was at one time interpreter to Count Leontieff. The large man on the mule in the centre is the son of the Ginni (Queen) of the province of Goffa. This province is noted for its coffee.

He retired into a corner, with his back to us, to eat his food, while I chaffed him about his running away. I told him that I had been trying to sell him as a slave to the Abyssinians, but, as they did not think he was worth more than one chicken, I had decided not to sell him, but to take him on with me.

Kalkai said that we must not start too early next day, as they were coming to see us off. We descended the hill, and found our camp in the spot I had chosen at the bottom of the valley.

Very heavy rain fell during the night and early morning, so we were glad of an excuse to wait till it cleared up. When everything was packed up ready to start, Kalkai and the Genni's son appeared, and accompanied us a little distance on our way.

The low-valley route to Dalbo is the quickest and easiest in dry weather, but now it was nothing but a morass, and it took us all the remainder of the day to get about ten miles. The road carefully followed the lowest part of the valley, where the swamp was up to our knees for the greater part of the time. By the thick green grass it could be seen that water was accustomed to lie here, whilst a few hundred yards to our right there was short grass and fairly open country. As there was but little water there I left the track, and went across country parallel to the road.

Our guides, like many other natives, were averse to following any other route except that which they had been always accustomed to. They said that I should get lost if I did not follow the road, and advanced various other specious reasons why we should walk in the swamp.

Next morning early we reached the Molsha River, which cut across our path, and flowed through a gap in the ridge to our left to join the Omo. It was in full flood, and flowing at a tremendous pace. On both banks there were camps pitched of caravans held up by the river. On our bank there was a large caravan carrying coffee from Goffa, bound for Addis Ababa.

At the ford the water was only five feet deep at the deepest part, but it was impossible to cross owing to the tremendous pace at which the river was flowing.

At this place Maguru-Kwenda came out in quite a new light, as it appeared that he was a strong and powerful swimmer. Few of the up-country natives as a rule are able to swim, but he had lived on the coast for a number of years, probably having been taken down originally as a slave. Majaliwa was also a good swimmer, and so we three tried different places in the river to endeavour to find a better ford.

It was impossible to stand up at all in the water except quite close to the bank, where it was shallow, and so we had to abandon all hope of crossing that day. Next day, finding the water had gone down a little, I set out downstream, and found a place where the river was much broader, and also flowing in two channels, a small and a big one, separated by a little island. Here the water was not much higher than the waist, but it was doubtful if we could cross, as the river had a way of suddenly sweeping one off one's feet and downstream, perhaps into a deeper part.

However, we made an effort to cross, and succeeded in reaching the island. Some of the men who had posed as braves so far proved to be most hopeless funks in the water, and had to be pushed and jostled across by their companions. To cross the big arm of the river I had prepared poles and ropes, it being my intention to have a line of men supporting themselves against the current with poles stuck into the bottom, and holding the ropes to help those with the loads.

We tried several times to establish this line, but each time a confused mass of men, and ropes, and poles was swept down, and we had to laboriously cart all the paraphernalia up again. Another thing which added to the difficulty was the branches and bits of trees being carried down by the stream, and one had to be constantly on the look-out to avoid them, as it would have been most dangerous to get entangled in these masses of branches, which were often revolving as they went. Finally we had to abandon the attempt, and return crestfallen to camp.

The Goffa caravan, being natives, had stuck religiously to the ford without trying to look for another place. They had attempted to get a few of their animals across ; a horse, a mule, and a donkey had been swept down some way, but eventually had been dragged out, the horse unconscious.

There was no rain during the next night, and in the morning I went to look at my ford, and found it a little better. I returned with glowing accounts of the ease with which I had crossed and recrossed, and so all the men set off with shouts and singing.

The élan with which they started carried all but a few of the faintest-hearted across the first arm, and Maguru-Kwenda and two more of the boldest spirits actually started across the big part without waiting for assistance.

I had intended to ground all the loads on the island, and then take them across with three men to each load, so as to minimize the danger of loss. However, when I saw them start away I decided to risk the loss of a load, as, if one or two got across, it would show that it could be done, and give confidence to the others. These three were soon followed by Tumbo, Kitabu, and a few others,

19

who rushed into the water with shouts, and by the time these had reached the worst bit the redoubtable Maguru-Kwenda had already deposited his load on a spit of land on the other side, and come back to help them.

Seeing this, others followed, and the first ones returned to take the loads of those who would not venture across. The sais, although he could not swim, seized a load, and plunged across with it, to show that a Masai was as good a man as anyone else. He had reached a little more than halfway when he began to be carried downstream, and nearly lost his load. Fortunately I saw what was happening in time, and, rushing after him, held out a long bamboo, which enabled him to steady himself.

In this way all the loads were got safely across, the only mishap being that one porter, mistaking a big water-lizard for a crocodile, dropped his load in the water and fled, but, being in shallow water near the bank, it was rescued. Then those men who still hung back were pushed and jostled across by their comrades, and well chaffed, and some of them ducked for their timid behaviour.

It now only remained to get the animals across, so they were taken well upstream, and the horse was then shoved in, the sais taking his head and Abdi his tail. When the current took him he allowed himself to be carried down, and then tried to turn back to the bank. I had posted myself downstream of him, and, splashing water into his face, turned him into mid-stream. The Abyssinian mules followed the horse, and all arrived safely on the tail of the spit of land opposite.

At last there only remained our Nairobi mule on the far bank, waiting for someone to take him, and as he was unaccustomed to water, I expected some difficulty with him. However, he entered without protest, and then, shaking his halter out of the guide's hand, plunged across the river with so much vigour that, amidst the cheers of the porters, he made a point on the spit much higher up the stream than any of the others had been able to reach.

Omari said : "I see that out of all these animals our Nairobi mule is the only man." The porters never took much interest in the animals, and they and Omari could never tell one camel from another, even after two months' trek with them. Now they took no interest in the other mules, but their hearts had gone out to Nairobi, who had suffered hunger and thirst, heat and cold, with them.

Omari said : "If only Nairobi could talk, what tales he would be able to tell these other Abyssinian mules!" I am afraid that I was less constant in my affections, as, having lost my old friends, Ndume, the big male camel, and Mwana, the little white one, I had now made new friends, and amongst the mules Barambarras was my favourite.

We rested a little on the spit, and then investigated further. Between us and the high bank was a broad belt of mud and reeds. We had to cut our way through these, and then proceeded, going at times up to our knees in mud. When we reached the bank, we sat down and washed off the thick caked mud.

In front of us was the valley route to Dalbo, but the swamps we had experienced at the other side of the Molsha decided me in favour of the hill route, so we turned off to the left, and climbed the steep side of Kucha Mountain, a continuation of the ridge we had taken from Uba, but separated from it by a deep gorge through which ran the Molsha. After an hour's hard climb we found a suitable camp on the shoulder of the mountain, and were glad to get out of the feverish valley into the fine mountain air again.

CHAPTER XX

THE WALLAMU

THE valley beneath is uninhabited, whereas the Kucha ridge is dotted with the villages of the Kucha, a people resembling the Wallamu. As the ground which can be cultivated only consists of small patches on shoulders and shelves on the steep face of the mountain, there are no big villages. As a rule, only a few beehive-shaped huts are clustered together on such places, and sometimes the level ground available only suffices for a single hut.

Round the huts are clustered plantations of the wild banana and bamboo; the latter they grow, as they utilize the stems for building purposes. On the mountain-side are little terraces, on which are planted a few crops, and the large yam known to the Kikuyu as *kikwa*. The terraces are built up with a stone wall at the lower end to prevent the soil being washed off the surface.

From the numbers of these stone walls overgrown with grass seen on the Kucha and Uba Mountains, it would appear that in former times a much larger population must have inhabited these places.

The huts are generally pleasantly situated on little level spots, while in the little dips there are often arrow-root and other plants, irrigated by miniature channels.

We ascended to the summit of the ridge, and then followed a path leading along the crest. The track was fairly good, but part of it was of soft bare rock, and grew very slippery after rain. I could get no flour for the porters here, and even maize and millet were hard to obtain, except in very small quantities, as the inhabitants were living chiefly on the root of the wild banana.

The Kucha hold markets in many different spots on different days, but there is but little to be obtained at these, except an occasional chicken or roll of butter.

The Kucha ladies dress in robes of locally-woven cotton, tied with a cord round the waist, and often kept over the shoulders by the ends being knotted round the chest. They present a very bulky appearance when going to and from market, as numbers of small packages are carried by being slipped in under their robes next their skin. The blanket-like dress is then drawn round them, and knotted round the chest, whilst the cord or cloth fastened round the waist prevents them from slipping down.

I met a party of these ladies coming from market, carrying parasols made from the broad leaves of the banana, and asked if they had any butter to sell. One of them immediately undid her robe, and produced a little roll, done up in the fibrous bark of the banana, which had melted with the heat of her body, so I refused to buy it.

It rained every night we were on trek, and in the morning there were dense mists, so the porters and animals had a wretched time on the slippery roads. Nevertheless, the men were very cheery about it, although they frequently slid and fell.

As the porters came into camp, it could be seen at a glance who had been unfortunate in this way, as their backs would be plastered with red mud.

Gobana, the *Negus* (King) of Kucha, sent in to say that he was coming to see me, but I could not wait for him, so trekked on. Finding me gone, he sent after me a large tray containing about a hundred eggs as a present. I sent back a present of a tin-plate and bowl, and immediately ordered an omelet to be made. By the time two good eggs had been found for this purpose more than half the eggs had been expended.

The word *Negus* is generally translated by "King," as it is supposed to mean "the ruler of a tribe or country," whilst Menelek is called Negus Nagast (the King of Kings). When, however, the "King's" subjects only number a few thousand, it is rather a ridiculous word to use.

After three days' trek along Kucha the range curved round to the north, while we, continuing in a northeasterly direction, descended the mountain, and came to the Deme River. It is here that Menelek's own military domain commences, the provinces we had already passed through being ruled by various governors under him.

We had been told that the Deme River would be unfordable, but when we arrived on the bank we found that the ford was not very deep. We crossed the river, and camped on the far bank, and almost immediately a storm broke, accompanied by heavy rain preluded by hail. Not an hour after the storm broke the river had risen several feet, and I felt thankful we had got across it instead of camping in a better site pointed out to us on the other bank.

In front of us the country rose to the broken plateau of the Wallamu, ascended at a place called Kella. There are no inhabitants in the low country near the Deme' but directly the plateau is reached the country is thickly inhabited, and it is in places difficult to find a nice open camping-ground. There is a considerable amount of country under cultivation, but we found the people, at the time we passed, mainly subsisting on the banana-root, as had been the case with everyone we had met from Bako onwards.

We camped close by some huts in the only space available. A nice old man came out, and brought me some milk. He had a stiff arm from a leopard-bite. The animal had broken into his hut at night to seize a goat, and he had killed it with a spear. The people about here were very pleasant indeed, and hospitably inclined towards strangers.

Many of them came to solicit medical advice and obtain medicines, as the Abyssinians had done, but with this difference: none of the Wallamu came empty-handed, but each brought a little present as a medical fee paid in advance.

The ailments I had to treat were most varied, and the patients were very secret about them, taking me aside and conferring in whispers, whilst their friends tried to hide behind trees and listen to the conversation. One man brought two chickens and some firewood, which he presented to me, and then, taking me on one side, said that he wanted a child, but could not obtain one.

Faith almost always effects a cure with natives, and, in any case, I did not wish to be defeated in anything I was asked to do; so I gave him some innocuous medicine, and prescribed a diet. I explained that all my best child-begetting medicines had been abandoned on the way, but that if he prayed to Allah fervently enough, and followed my instructions, he would soon become a proud father. As I did not care to accept the presents for such pure quackery, I gave him a present in return. This he did not wish to accept, but when I insisted, he went home, and presently returned with some eggs.

This will show what nice hospitable people the Wallamu are, as most natives take everything they can get, and then ask for more. However, near their head villages and big markets at Dalbo I found them very different.

The Wallamu have a money of their own called *mărcho*. This money is not easily carried in the pocket, as it consists of long thin bars of roughly smelted iron about two and a half feet long, the last nine inches or so being turned up at an angle to the rest.

About ten of these go to a dollar. The end turned up is generally slightly rounded at the edges, like the rim of a bicycle. The other end, or long handle, is shaped much like the blade of a spear, being pointed, but not sharp, and thicker in the centre than at the edges. The *mărcho* is distinctly money, as it is used for no other purpose but buying and selling. Men can be seen walking to and from the markets with a bundle over their shoulder, neatly tied together with fibre.

The quality of a *mărcho* must be apprised before it is accepted as payment. It is not either bad or good, like money, but it has different values according to how good or bad it is. This is ascertained by taking the end in one hand, with the thumb on the top, and flicking it several times in the air. A *mărcho* is never accepted before this is done several times over.

I could never see what it was that was liked or disliked in a *mărcho*. I thought at first that one that trembled as it was flicked was a good one, but I was told that this was no guide, and that it was the weight by which it was judged. However, this also was not quite the case, as some manifestly heavier than others were assessed as good and others bad.

Finally, I made up my mind that they really had no means of telling, and that they only pretended that they

could apprise the value so exactly. So I collected ten
mărchos, and gave them to a man, and told him to choose
the best and the worst; and when he had done this,
I marked them, and told him to put the rest in two piles,
the best together and the worst together. He put five
on one side and three on the other. I then mixed them
up and called another man who had not witnessed the
performance, and made him do the same. To my surprise,
he selected exactly the same ones, except that he considered one of the best five bad enough to put with the
other three.

Near my camp there was a great function in progress.
A widow lady, I was told, had bought much millet beer,
and was giving a dance at which she was to select a
husband for her daughter. There was a band of drums
and long horns made out of bamboo, with a topi's horn
fixed on the end. This is almost exactly like the horns
seen in Uganda, except that the bamboo part is surmounted there by a hartebeest horn.

The drums of the Uba and Wallamu are peculiar for
two reasons : firstly, there are two drums in different
keys played alternately, and secondly, they are played
with sticks or withies. The drums are beaten with the
flat of the stick. Nearly all the African natives I have
met play their drums with the hand.

When I arrived on the scene, a crowd of horn-players
levelled their horns at me, and advanced playing lustily.
They surrounded me with a forest of instruments held
only a few feet off my ears, perhaps thinking that I had
some difficulty in hearing the music.

The hostess herself, who was rather drunk, was mounted
on a gaudily-trapped mule, and was led very slowly
backwards and forwards by a host of attendants. She
wore on her head what appeared to be a sort of crown

of silver spikes and ornaments. When she mounted, a blanket was held up to screen her from the public gaze, till she had settled herself in the saddle, and arranged her draperies so as to conform to decency.

The Wallamu appear to have reached a very advanced state of civilization for an African tribe, until just lately, entirely cut off from the outer world. Since the Abyssinians have taken their country they have been brought more or less into touch with the civilization of the latter, but they probably have not advanced—more likely they have receded a little since that date.

I will enumerate the points that struck me most about their civilization. They are a big tribe, and, with the exception of the Uba and the Kucha, subsections of the tribe, were gathered together under one ruler or King— viz., Tona. Their huts are larger, more roomy, and better built than the average African hut, such as those of the Bantu. They possess money and hold markets (great steps in civilization and commerce).

They grow cotton and wear cloth. They use the plough, of a very rough pattern it is true, but still a great advance on the hoe, an implement which is used over the greater part of the continent. Property is divided by fences and walls.

Amongst the many tribes I had visited in Eastern and Central Africa, I had never seen natives kiss each other, only excepting some on the coast, who had learnt this habit from Arabs. In my trek northwards these people, including the Kucha, were the first natives I saw who indulged in this practice. I omit the Abyssinians, who do a lot of kissing, as they do not properly belong to the country to the south, but are only occupying posts there.

This habit, then, is a sign of an advanced civilization,

as it is otherwise only indulged in by Abyssinians and Arabs. Very possibly the area over which this custom prevails delimits roughly the extent of country covered by an old civilization.

In many ways the Wallamu remind one of the Baganda. Both have a money and cloth of their own—these being cowries and bark cloth with the latter people—and both enclose land, while I have pointed out the similarity in the horns used. By some it is thought that the Baganda have received an admixture of blood from the north, and if this is the case, this may account for the similarity of these peoples.

However, in type of features the Wallamu are very different, as they are of regular Hamitic features, and on the whole much fairer than the Abyssinians.

Amongst the Wallamu is seen a curious kind of guitar that is used by some Arabs of South Arabia, such as at Shahr, and also by the Kisii and Kavirondo in British East Africa. It is made of a wooden drum or bowl, over which is stretched a piece of cowhide. A triangular wooden handle is attached to this, bearing five or six strings, which pass across a bridge on the cowhide top.

The next camp we made in the Wallamu country was near the house of a very hospitable native. I went into his house to see how the banana-root bread was made. The root is a mass of fibres, bearing little lumps of a white substance.

These are boiled, soaked, and pounded. All the longest fibres are then pulled out, and the remainder kneaded into a lump. This is then chopped up fine with a knife, so as to cut up small all the fibres remaining, kneaded again in the form of a muffin, wrapped up in a banana-leaf, and thrust into hot embers to cook, or on to an earthenware plate over the fire.

The hut was spacious and lofty, but was not sub-divided inside. A bar was put across one side of it, and behind this the cows of the owner were herded at night or at milking-time. He said that he would not allow an Abyssinian in his house, but that he liked the white men, and wished that they ruled their country. As I was camped beside his house, he would have liked to have given me some big present, such as a sheep, but he was poor, and had none, so would I accept some milk? He also housed the horse, as it had suffered much from the wet on the way.

The mules were miserable at being tethered without the horse. A mule has a most extraordinary objection to ever doing anything or going anywhere on its own initiative. On a journey they must always follow some-thing, or they will not make a good march. Some mules are especially bad in this way, and will not lead the way, however much they are beaten or urged on.

A mule will, as a rule, follow a horse almost anywhere, and seldom shies or takes fright. It has no fear of anything it has seen another animal pass, but if it is in front, it is subject to fits of panic. The Abyssinians generally have a servant running before them carrying their rifle, and their mules are trained to follow such a one.

When Omari saw how miserable our mules were with-out the horse, he said to me : " Now I believe the words you told me that, ' where there are mules and one horse, the horse becomes their Sultan.' "

Our guides wished to return from this camp, so I paid them off. Dasita, the little Uba man, then said that he would come on to Dalbo with us, which was not many miles ahead. My men had been out trying to buy flour with *mărcho*, and in the evening they brought back those that were left, and they were put down on the ground near to where Dasita was sitting. Omari picked them up again, but forgot one, which he left lying on the ground. Dasita was busy sewing his *shamma*, which was torn, but when he saw the *mărcho*, he began sidling nearer to it. As one of these had disappeared the day before in a mysterious manner, I thought that he would be worth watching, so I told Abdi, who was standing by, to see what he did.

Presently he carelessly let the end of his *shamma* fall over the *mărcho* lying near him. Abdi said : " Shall I take it away from him ?" But I replied : " No ; see what he will do." All the men could understand the conversation, but as Dasita did not know Swahili, he was not aware that he was the object of so much interest.

Omari thought that he would have a little joke of his own, so called him to draw his rations for the day. After a certain amount of fumbling with his clothes, Dasita got up and fetched his food, and returned again. As he had not left the *mărcho* on the ground, we knew that it must be somewhere inside his *shamma*, a garment well adapted to these conjuring tricks.

I asked Abdi what he would probably do next, and he said that he would wait until he was alone, and then go off ; so I told Abdi and the men to make themselves scarce while I went into my tent. Presently I saw Dasita hurrying towards the villages, so I told Abdi to call him back. When he came I said : " Ask him where that *mărcho* is."

Dasita swore by all his gods that he knew nothing about it, and that it was a vile imputation that he had had anything to do with its disappearance. So vehement did he become that he began flinging his arms about in an excitable way, and the *mărcho*, which had been held under his arm, began to slip down till its point appeared below his *shamma*. Unaware of this, he continued to protest with great verbosity, till about a foot of the *mărcho* came into view. At this Abdi and the crowd of porters who had collected could control themselves no longer, and we all burst out laughing.

Dasita looked down, and saw the tell-tale *mărcho* appearing to refute his protestations of innocence. I then said to him : " You know the penalty for theft in this country. Abdi, bring an axe."

The penalty for theft in extreme cases is, amongst the Abyssinians, the amputation of a hand. At this the unfortunate Dasita was terrified, and dropped the *mărcho* and a few other things he had picked up, and fled away Abdi asked if they should run after him, but I replied " No ; let him go."

It had often been my most cherished wish to catch a sneak-thief red-handed. Now that my wish was granted, the whole thing was so comic that I could not even bring myself to beat the man.

Some Wallamu who were present said that amongst them the punishment for theft was imprisonment in a hut for four months, with a minimum of food and water. The porters disapproved loudly of the dishonesty of the people of this country, as they always do when anybody has been found out, probably those who had lately pilfered from my stores being loudest in disapprobation.

Abdi grew reminiscent on the subject of theft. He said that not long ago he had told one of the porters to sew up one of the sacks of beads, and, looking back over his shoulder, he saw him transfer something to his pocket. He said nothing at the time, but later asked the man to bring his own load of private belongings to be inspected. The man pretended that he did not understand, and fetched Abdi's instead. Abdi then went himself, and looked into the man's load, and found some beads. As it was but a small matter, he very rightly had not told me, but made the man put them back.

When I told Abdi that I had suspected Dasita the day before, he quoted a Swahili proverb, "Who has tasted honey will always return to the honey-pot," which in this sense meant, "Give a dog sufficient rope, and he will hang himself."

Next day we proceeded on our way to Dalbo. We saw an Abyssinian stockaded post on the top of a hill to our left, and then reached a big village to the south of Dalbo Hill. At the foot of this hill used to be the residence of Tona, the "King" of the Wallamu, who has for the last seven years been detained by the Abyssinians in Shoa.

The country is thickly populated, and all the roads were crowded with people going to or coming from the market, as it was market-day. I have never seen such dense crowds of natives anywhere in rural Africa, for there were literally streams on every road and path.

Seeing all these people coming and going, one would imagine that a tremendous amount of produce was pouring in and out of the market, but this was not the case, as the majority only carried one or two little packets. Perhaps one would have two rolls of butter, while another carried two or three pieces of banana-root bread. These, done up in copious banana-leaves, would assume the aspect of a big load.

There is a telephone at Dalbo which was originally put up by the French, but is now in the hands of the Abyssinians. I tried to communicate with Addis Ababa through this, but was not able to do so. We then proceeded, and camped near the market-place, about five miles farther on.

CHAPTER XXI

ON THE ROAD TO ADDIS ABABA

In the market-place was a seething mass of humanity shouting and haranguing. Perhaps there were ten thousand or more. Yet amongst all these I was barely able to get enough food for my men for one day, as the chief article offered for consumption was banana-root bread, which they did not eat.

Such hundreds of sightseers crowded round to gaze at our camp that we had to put a rope round as a barrier, and post men with sticks to keep them behind it.

Amongst the people here were some suffering from those terrible leprous diseases known to the Swahili as *mti* and *mkoma*. Large villages are packed closely together here, and this probably conduces to ill-health. The people also were not so pleasant as those in the more rural parts we had just passed through. These were more like townsmen, and compared very badly with the simple, hospitable countrymen we had left behind.

I was very anxious to see the market, and how they conducted their business, so I paid it a visit in the afternoon. I was not able to see it quite under normal conditions, as the whole market, directly I arrived, left off buying and selling to follow me round, and see what I was going to do. One quarter of it was devoted to live-stock, and oxen were being slaughtered on the spot, and the meat cut up and sold. Sheep were offered for sale, as were also fowls.

In another part were foreign goods exposed for sale, such as *abu jadid* (calico), cartridges, looking-glasses, and knives. Close to these were the leather-dressers, selling ropes of tanned hide and bandoliers of morocco leather. There were rows and rows of people, chiefly women, each having only a few pieces of bread to sell.

In one corner of the market I came across a man squatting behind three gourds of honey, and beside him was a little stick. The use of this stick was to shove down into the honey, and on withdrawal the intending purchaser can see by the honey adhering to it the quality at the bottom.

I was anxious to obtain some good honey, so I inspected these. The honey-vendor put his stick in one gourd, showed me the honey sticking to it, licked the stick clean with his tongue, and thrust it into the second gourd, and then, having cleaned the stick again, put it down ready for the next customer, while waiting expectantly for my order. By the number of little holes in the top of the honey I noticed that this process had been repeated many times during the day. I did not buy any of his honey.

Next morning we started off again, but it was a very bad morning. First of all I found that my gun-case, with the gun inside, had been stolen, perhaps when I and most of the men were at the market, and no one was watching my tent. Next, a mule was very ill, having a swelling on his face which we attributed to snake-bite. Thirdly, the paths were muddy and slippery from the rain of last night, and it was still drizzling.

We started away, squelching through the mud till we came to a nullah, at the bottom of which was a little

20

stream, the margin of which was deep in mud. As we were picking our way in the drizzle down the steep and slippery descent a party who were encamped on the high bank above came out, and made fun of us as we passed.

I am afraid that I was in a shocking bad temper that morning, and when a chorus of about twenty men started slinging abuse at me I was bursting with rage. However, I said nothing, and we reached the morass at the bottom, crossed this, and climbed a steep bank at the other side. Here the poor mule, who had been following the other mules, lay down on the ground, evidently about to die.

From where we were we could see that the party encamped on the other side of the stream had returned to their tents, as it was still raining. I told the men to put down their loads, and, choosing ten stalwart men, said to them : " Come along now. Let us go and teach these Wahabashi a lesson."

We retraced our steps to the bottom, and then crept round under cover of the bank till we were opposite the spot on which their tents were pitched. I did not wish to approach in view from a distance, as, being all armed, they might have threatened us with their rifles before we reached them, in which case it would have been difficult to know what to do.

When we had advanced under cover to within twenty yards of the tents, I said to the men : " Beat them, but do not damage them. Now come on."

We rushed on to the tents, and began pulling them down on top of their owners. As they came out my men fell on them, and beat them lustily. Others came out of some of the other tents when they heard the row, and there was for a few moments a brisk mêlée.

One man, whom I recognized as one who had been most

offensive as we passed in the road before, flew out of a tent, and came cursing and swearing towards me. I received him with a half-arm in the short ribs, which sent him spinning backwards on to his tent, and it collapsed, with him on the top of it.

Meanwhile the rest were flying away as hard as they could go, leaving their camp deserted. Their tents were stocked with goods, saddles, bales of calico, etc., as they were some merchants and their attendants who had come down for the market. Fearing that my men might take the opportunity of purloining some of their goods, I called them together. Then I told Abdi to find out if the prostrate figure on the ground understood Borana.

As he sat up spluttering on his fallen tent, it was ascertained that he could. So I said to Abdi : " Tell him that they are poor ignorant savages who do not know what a white man is. Now they see one for the first time they think that they can abuse him. God has been very kind to them, for they have happened to meet a white man renowned for his good temper. Nevertheless, if they should meet with another, let them take heed, for he may be a fierce and violent man instead of gentle as I am."

In justice to the Abyssinians and other natives of the country I must say that we were always treated in the most courteous manner by the former, and generally hospitably received by the latter. The men we met this day were not Abyssinians, but I am not sure what tribe they belonged to, possibly Garaugi or Galla.

We then returned to our loads, and found the mule was just dying, and shortly afterwards he expired. After waiting a little, we proceeded once more. Whilst halting we were overtaken by a party of Abyssinians, and in their midst was Dasita, our erstwhile guide, being taken as a prisoner. We were told that he was a deserter from the army of Queen Taitu, and that he had been recognized and caught near Dalbo, and was now being taken up to Addis Ababa.

Alamu, the boy I had engaged to look after the mules after leaving Uba, said that it was an act of Providence. He had stolen from me after I had treated him well, and now, although I had let him off, he was punished for his offence.

That night we camped in a belt of junipers which we had seen from afar, and here found plenty of firewood—a thing that had been scarce in Wallamu.

We were now just outside the Wallamu country, and in a district called Badachu, the people of which are much the same as the Kambatta, and these latter are a sort of mixture of the Garaugi and Wallamu.

The Garaugi men wear much the same dress as the Abyssinians, but the women dress in ox-skins like the Masai, and have much the same barbaric brass ornaments pendant on each shoulder. With them, however, the brass is attached to locks of plaited hair, while with the Masai it is attached to the enlarged ear-lobe. So great was the resemblance that when a Garaugi woman passed carrying firewood, she was received with cheers from the porters, who said : " Here comes a Masai *koko* " (matron).

Chickens were cheaper here than in any place I have yet visited, being six for a *mărcho*, or sixty for a dollar (two shillings).

Natives' ideas of natural history are often rather quaint. While here we saw a party of slave-raiding ants returning from a foray on a termite nest, each one carrying one in its mandibles. Tengeneza's idea was that the slave-raiders could not breed, but used to take young

A GARAUGE STONEHENGE

I could obtain no explanation of these stones from the natives. Evidently they are very old, and used at one time to form a circle.

A GARAUGE UMBRELLA

This photograph depicts a Garauge lady, followed by her servant, crossing a stream. The umbrella is made of banana leaves, fastened on to a wicker-work frame.

white ants, and bring them back to their nests, and there transform them into other ants by smearing them over with mud.

The next few days were without incident. The country was very broken, and the constant rain made the roads and especially the ascents and descents very slippery, and bad for the men.

Poor old Nairobi had been carrying either a load or a sick man all the way, but now he was at last able to have a rest, and go without anything on his back.

When I announced that Nairobi was at liberty to follow the other mules unloaded, Omari said : " All the men will be glad to hear about our mule, for their hearts are sore every day when they see him going with a load. Had he been a slave, he would by now have gained his freedom." When Nairobi was seen trotting along by himself after the others, or running off to graze, and then galloping after the caravan, all the porters shouted : " There goes the manly one. He is a man, and no mistake."

He was wonderfully tough and hardy, and after a few days of liberty, he got so wild and above himself that I had to give him a load again for a few days. The Dejaz's mule, which I rode, was what Tengeneza called " A perfect professor of kicking." He was not so big as Nairobi, but very strong, and very free with his hind-legs. He would carry me down the steepest and most slippery paths, and refuse to stop to let me get off, so long as there was anything in front to follow.

Sometimes, going down some precipitous and slippery, rocky path, I would think that he must fall on his nose with my weight. He would slide and slither down, always keeping his balance, and sometimes in the middle of a slide he would suddenly pull up, in a seemingly impossible place, and let out with his hind-legs, just to keep himself in practice for kicking, and then proceed in the most ordinary way.

The Swahilis have a proverb, "Do not show kindness to a dog, for it is not sensible of kindness;" and this applies exactly to the ordinary mule. It is no good trying to make a pet of this very useful but cross-grained brute, excepting such a one as 'Barrambaras, for they are always uncertain. I used to give them salt at intervals, and they used to bite and kick me for my pains.

Barrambaras, however, was the most exceptional mule, as he never gave us a day's trouble, and was always sweet-tempered. He never bit, and one could hold his tail, and let him pull one about without any fear of a kick. He used to poke his nose into my tent to get some salt or a piece of bread, and was most sociable with human beings. With the other mules he was different, as he did not want their company.

This was one of the points I liked best about him, as it showed that he alone amongst all the mules had any independence of character. He always used to go off grazing by himself, and if the others followed him he would leave them, and go elsewhere. He never gave any trouble when it was time to tether the animals at night, or load them in the morning, as he always came quietly and never tried to run away or throw his load.

After passing through the country of Kambatta, we came to Lemmo—an Abyssinian station on the top of a flat-topped hill.

Shortly after our arrival, it began to pour with rain, as usual, and as there were many empty huts about, many of the inhabitants having gone off to a new station, I asked some of the men who visited camp if I could use some of them for the horse and mules. They said, "Yes," and pointed to several standing near camp.

Just then a violent rainstorm started, and the visitors to camp fled back to their stockaded enclosure. As they had said that we could use the empty huts, I told Abdi to put the horse and the mules in the one standing nearest to us.

Presently the sais came rushing to me, and said that an old man had come in with a stick and turned out all the animals, saying that the hut belonged to him. He did not use the hut himself, but he would not let us use it. The reason he gave for this was that he had come up to our camp and been turned away.

Since my gun had been stolen I had been very chary about letting people come into camp, as a great crowd of spectators always collected, and so I posted men to keep them away.

This old man, who was lame, having been turned away by one of my men, was quite within his rights to refuse to let our animals come into his house. As I told the sais, his argument would be that he had come up only to look at our camp, and been turned away, and now we wanted to use his house, so he turned us away.

I sent the sais for Abdi, telling him to bring the old man to me, that I might try to pacify him. A little later, Abdi came and said that it was all right now. The old man had turned himself and the sais and all the animals out to establish his right to the house. After that he had himself driven them all in again, and gone off and fetched barley and hay for them, and fed them with his own hands.

This little episode brought home to me how easy it is to misunderstand the natives of a country through which one passes, especially if one's men and interpreters do not tell one everything. Had I not heard that this old man had been driven away from our camp, and that he had nothing to do with the men who told us we could use the hut, I should have gone away with a very bad opinion of him.

As it was, I realized that he had behaved very well to us, as he had pointed out in his own way that he had a grievance against us, but that he would not only overlook it, but would heap coals of fire on our heads.

Next day I thanked him very much for his kindness, and apologized for the behaviour of my men in driving him away from camp. The misunderstanding having been cleared up, we parted the best of friends, whereas I might easily have carried away a very wrong impression of his behaviour, and left a bad impression of myself behind.

I went up to see the stockaded Abyssinian post, which was half-empty, as they have commenced a new military post to take its place, called "Abata's new encampment"—Abata being the Dejazmach of this district. The people that remain are only natives or settlers, and are under a Shum, or civil chief.

The Shum came to greet me, apologizing that he had not been to see me, as the weather was bad, and he was an old man. I was ushered into a hut, where there were several people, whilst others came in. Presently the Shum drove everyone outside, whilst he and another held up a *shamma* in front of me as a screen, and he then produced from under his cloak a gourd of milk. These precautions were to prevent being bewitched or poisoned by the milk.

Abyssinians believe that strangers are able to cause them illness by looking at them eating   Also, meat which has been exposed to the public gaze is supposed to be a very dangerous thing to eat. No Abyssinian of any standing will eat such meat or feed in public.

When I had finished drinking the milk, the others were allowed to come back. The Shum himself could not write, but there was another man present who could, and he went through the vocabularies I had made out on my journey, and suggested new words to write down.

Several of them sat close against me in the most friendly way, and said : " Has he got such and such a word ? Write it down for him."

One of them said : " Has he got *kuncha* down ?" I replied : " No. What is *kuncha* ?" " Oh, write it down for him ; he ought to have *kuncha*. Show him what *kuncha* is." My instructor forthwith opened a fold of his *shamma*, and out hopped about twenty fleas. He casually remarked : " These are *kuncha*. I will write it down for you."

At this I said I was afraid I must be going, to which they replied : " You have not got *kimal* yet. Let me write that for you. Show him a *kimal*." All those present began hunting in their clothes, and a very brief search sufficed to produce a few brace of *kimal*—an insect I trust my reader has not yet been introduced to.

At this I bid a hurried farewell, and departed. A subsequent examination of my clothes afforded me further opportunities of studying the natural history of the *kuncha* and the *kimal*.

Naked savages do not go in for such luxuries as these, and for this reason I think that natives should be discouraged from wearing clothes as much as possible, instead of, as is the case now, being taught that it is the proper thing to do. The great majority of the inland tribes never wash, and if they wear clothes, they never take them off, night or day, till they drop off. Yet there

are many white men who think that a state of more or
less cleanly nudity is horrible and unnatural.

After leaving Wallamu, where both sexes are dressed
in cotton clothes, we had come to a zone, reaching from
there almost to Addis Ababa, in which all the women
wear skins like the tribes to the south, such as Masai and
Samburr. These tribes are different subsections of the
Kambatta, Garaugi, and Galla. Their men-folk, however, copy the Abyssinian dress, but I imagine that not
so very long ago the males were nude, or semi-nude, like
those of the southern tribes.

I think that their present dress must have been adopted
but recently, or else the women would also wear the same
kind of dress. Some of the women of Lemmo and the
countries between here and the River Hawash were remarkably good-looking. Their hair was not shaved after
the unsightly manner of the Masai or Kikuyu, but grew
luxuriantly, and was well combed. African women
have, as a rule, but poor hair, but these had long and fine
hair, like Arab women. Their features were good, and
their figures slim and well made.

From the top of Lemmo the lake to our left could be
seen—Zwai or Dambal. We descended from Lemmo,
and in two days came to a well-cultivated low country,
called Urbarag. The descent to this was steep, and cut
deep with old cattle-tracks, showing that at one time
these people must have had much cattle, whereas now
they have but few.

The horse had been sickening for some time. He had
never been of much use, except as a guide for the mules
to follow, and he had suffered from the cold and damp.
It was useless to take him on, so I gave him to a native I
met here.

At Urbarag we camped by the church, and directly we arrived, the women turned up with food and firewood to sell, which saved a lot of trouble, as we had generally to send parties round to purchase these necessaries. *Mărcho* were now no longer used, and we bought things with Abyssinian money.

However, the people are very peculiar about this, as in one place they would only take half-dollars ; in another they would reject half-dollars, and only accept quarters. The change for a dollar also differed in every place we came to. At one we might get twelve *mahallak* for a dollar, while at others only eight. Sometimes it would be three-quarters and a *mahallak* for a dollar.

Next morning, while we were packing up to leave Urbarag, a crowd of people came to pick up any scraps or remains of firewood or other things we might leave behind. One youth was observed unostentatiously to leave the rest, and start strolling away.

When my attention was called to this, I thought that he must have some very good reason for abandoning the chance of picking up some of our leavings, so I sent a man after him, to see if he had helped himself to anything. Under his *shamma* was discovered a chicken belonging to one of the porters, which he had stolen, so I had him brought back and beaten.

From Urbarag we marched to a place called Warabe, and camped here in a pleasant situation on the high bank of a stream, but protected from the wind by a wall of rock behind us. One of the porters was taken very ill on the way here, and so we had to wait several days nursing him. He very nearly died, but was pulled round with my last drops of brandy, and after a few days he was well enough to be put on the mule, and we were able once more to take the road.

CHAPTER XXII

WE REACH ADDIS ABABA

WHILE we were encamped at Warabe, the Governor of the Siddamu Province passed us, returning home from Addis Ababa.

His name is Nagradras Gashautanna. He was accompanied by a tremendous retinue—perhaps five hundred or a thousand armed men, quite a hundred of whom were mounted.

The trappings of the mules, most of them brand-new, adorned with morocco leather and brass ornaments, looked very gorgeous from a little distance. Like all barbaric ornaments, however, they do not bear very close examination, for then they look cheap and tawdry.

A long line of baggage-mules followed the caravan, carrying his belongings, which chiefly consisted of cheap tin-trunks, as sold by Indian traders, and old packing-cases stuffed with odds and ends done up in filthy rags.

Our caravan was here augmented by another Somali, also called Abdi, who had been down into the Borana country, and also by a man who offered to hire his donkey to us as far as Addis Ababa.

As we had lost a mule and a horse, and there were always one or two sick porters to mount on mules, I was very glad to get this additional animal. Very useful it proved, too. It was but a small donkey, but it carried a full mule's load, and as often as not led the way. Our mules were rather played out by now with the muddy and hilly roads, and so I was glad to be able to reduce their loads.

Everybody we met always evinced great curiosity about my men, and wondered where they had come from. It was useless to say that they were Wanyamwezi, or came from East Africa, as they had never heard of either, so I always used to say that we came from the country of Zanzibar—a place some of them knew by name.

This was really quite correct, as the greater part of East Africa used at one time to belong to Zanzibar, and the Zinj of the ancients, from which the latter name (pronounced " Zingibar " by the Arabs) is derived, included East Africa.

One Abyssinian asked me if I knew a certain Abyssinian who had gone to the country of Zanzibar, and was now a man of very great importance there. I replied that it was a very big place, and I did not know everyone that lived there. To this he said : " But you must know this man, for he is a very great man—a sort of Sultan—and he has only one hand."

I said : " Long ago I had a Somali servant who had been to your country ; do you know him ? "

He answered : " A Somali is only a dog ; how should I know him ? But an Abyssinian is different ; moreover, this one has great honour in your country."

I asked Sadi if he had ever heard of him, and he said : " What ! with one hand ? Yes ; I know him, and will tell you about him. There is not a bigger thief in the whole of East Africa. He used to live at Mombasa, and his first effort was to steal a sheep, but he was caught, and imprisoned for four months. When he came out, he stole a chicken, and after that he broke into a house.

" After that, he walked into the Custom-house and shouldered a tin of kerosene, and tried to walk out with it ; but, as it had not the Customs mark on it, he was caught at the gate and put in prison again. When he was let out after this, he had grown tired of Mombasa, as he was too well known, and so he transferred the scene of his activities up-country."

So I replied to the Abyssinian : " I made a mistake about your friend. He is a very well known man in the largest town in our country, called Mombasa, and when he was last there, he was living in the biggest house in the place " (the fort).

The old Abdi and the new Abdi were now responsible for loading and looking after the mules, with the help of the sais and the Uba native, Alamu, who had accompanied us all this way. However, their loads were always slipping off, causing constant delays on the road.

Our wonderful donkey, on the other hand, was loaded by its Garaugi master, and never did its load slip during a whole day's march, although he appeared to take no trouble with it. I could not resist chaffing Abdi about this, as Somalis always think themselves superior to everybody. I said : " Here are you two full-blooded Somalis doing up your loads all day long, whilst this native, with his little donkey, never has to look to his load again after starting."

Abdi was, as I have said before, a very nice Somali, and not a bit conceited, so he only replied : " Yes ; I don't know how it is, or what he does. If he left his donkey alone with us for a moment whilst he went off, that donkey's load would at once slip off."

On reaching the summit of the mountains at a place called Silte, we had a view of a remarkable mountain in front of us. This was Zukwala—a steep-sided, square-topped mountain, of much the same shape as the mountains remarked from Karo, on the Omo. On its side is a shrine called Tabot Abo, which is considered by the Abyssinians as a very sacred spot.

At Silte I was fortunate in obtaining a large supply of flour for the men and a certain amount of firewood. Firewood had been scarce or unobtainable since Kambatta, and had had to be obtained by purchase from the villages.

For myself there was nothing to eat but porridge made of red flour, till a very pleasant Galla called Roba (Rain) came to call on me, bringing a present of a sheep, honey, milk, and bread.

Next we arrived in the district of Maska, the inhabitants of which are Christians, whereas the majority of the Garaugi are Muhammadan or pagan.

At this camp I had a curious dream. I dreamt that I found myself on a railway-line, and following this, met with an unknown kind of buck, which I shot at with a revolver, and which Narok then pulled down. Going on farther I met an elephant, with one tusk only, but of enormous size. Having no rifle, I rushed back along the line to a village to look for my rifle, and met Tengeneza. We both searched frantically for one, but could not find any of mine. Tengeneza then searched in the huts, and produced an Abyssinian rifle, a *fusil gras*, very rusty, and with but two rounds of ammunition. With this I rushed back down the line, and found the elephant still there, but was unable to make the rifle go off, and then I awoke.

The explanation of the dream was simple enough, as I had seen a large tusk being carried along that day, and had also been talking about the railway which I had been told had reached Addis Ababa now. Such is the reliability of native information, for it really had only reached Dirre Daua.

However, I thought that I would give Sadi a chance of displaying his powers, as he had a great reputation for the interpreting of dreams. Once before whilst I was on trek, a native in Nairobi dreamed that I had shot, amongst many black animals, one white animal.

This Sadi interpreted by saying that I had shot a lion, which was quite correct, although he could not possibly have heard the news so quickly. In this case, however, Sadi only offered the very dull interpretation that I had made up my mind to do something, and that afterwards I had not done it.

Our start was delayed, as two of the mules had broken loose during the night, and were with difficulty caught again.

Soon after we started we met a man on a grey mule. He offered it for sale, and as the price was reasonable, I paid him the money, and then we set out to look for some people of the neighbourhood before whom to declare the purchase. This is always customary in Abyssinia, as an animal is then known to have changed hands, and the new owner cannot be accused of stealing it.

We left the road, and visited a village where there was a great concourse of people sitting round a hut, much too busy to give more than a passing attention to our affairs.

It appeared that there had been a number of thefts of cattle in the neighbourhood, and so a magician had been called in to declare by divination who was the thief.

Just after we arrived, the ceremony ceased, and the locality in which the thief was to be found having been discovered by the magician, the whole assembly arose and rushed for their mules, held by attendants near by. Throwing themselves on their backs, they galloped off in great haste to catch the thief before he could change his quarters.

I then went back to the road, leading the new mule, and soon overtook my men. In the path we met a native coming the other way, who stopped me, and said that a lot of animals were being sent down to meet me from Addis Ababa.

I did not know what to make of this, but Sadi said that he was certain that the news of our safe arrival in Abyssinia had been heard, and that our friends were talking about us, either in East Africa or England, as he had felt a twitching of the eyelids for the last few days. This is the Swahili substitute for ears tingling.

Thereupon I said to Sadi : " This is the explanation of my dream. I went out and obtained a small animal, the buck, but did not get the large one, the elephant. This mule is the small animal I got, and those animals we have heard about are the large animal I did not get."

I preceded the caravan in the afternoon, and selected a good camping-ground beside a stream. Shortly afterwards a large caravan of mules carrying coffee arrived, and the drivers started unloading them where I was sitting, on the exact spot I had myself chosen. As I had arrived first, and occupied the place, I felt that I was entitled to first choice, and certainly I did not want to camp rubbing shoulders with another caravan, so I drove away the mules, and told the men they must go elsewhere.

They replied that they could not do this, as they had already unloaded some of the mules, and could not shift the loads. Just then the first of my porters came in, and so I told them to take away the loads that were on our camping-ground. These loads were about a hundred pounds in weight, but my brawny porters picked them up with ease, and, running off, deposited them at a distance.

The owner of the caravan came up furious, and said that he claimed the spot in the name of Menelek, whose merchant he was. I replied that he must show me Menelek's letter first. This he could not do, so I had him ejected.

Sadi said : " This all comes of breaking a gourd ; it is very unlucky to do so, and always means a quarrel. At Dalbo some of the porters broke a gourd, although I told them not to, and afterwards we had that fight in the road. To-day we dropped and smashed that gourd on the way."

That night some of the men and Sadi got hold of some *araking*, a spirit much stronger than any they were accustomed to in their own country, and consequently got very drunk. After becoming very abusive to each other, sleep finally overpowered all but Sadi, who crept into his tent thinking that he was a lion, and spent most of the night in roaring.

Next day I said to them : " Perhaps you did not know how strong the spirit of this country was. Now you know there will be no excuse for you, so remember that in future everyone that gets drunk also gets a dozen lashes. I have no use for men that get drunk, as they make themselves objectionable to their companions, and cannot carry their loads."

Next day we ascended the Maraku Hills, which are covered with plantations of wild bananas, and on the day following we descended the other side, and arrived in a country of thorn-trees, where at last we could obtain firewood again.

This day we passed some Galla villages. I passed these, and then waited for the men to catch me up, as they were behind. When they arrived, after an immense delay, I was told that they had got up a fight with some Gallas, and had been beaten by them.

It appeared that the man called Kobe (Tortoise) had arrived at the villages, and wanted to buy some millet-beer. Having no change, he, with that strange simplicity which characterized my men, called a woman, and, giving her a dollar, told her to run off and get change.

After waiting about an hour, it dawned on the Tortoise that he had become a victim of the confidence trick. At this he was very angry, and complained to Abdi, who had just come up with the mules. Abdi said : " You can do nothing now unless you know which house she has gone into." Kobe pointed out a house, and Abdi went in, but the woman was not there, and, of course, everybody denied all knowledge of her.

Both Omari and Abdi told him that he had been a fool, and lost his money, and that now there was nothing to do but he must pick up his load, and go on at once, as all the porters were waiting for him. He refused to go on, and said that he would not leave the place till he had had a fight about it. At this Abdi said : "I tell you to go on ; now I am going to leave you, and will tell the Bwana."

Kobe then got up a fight with some men who had nothing to do with it, and some of the other porters chipped in. Seeing this, a great number of Gallas turned out with sticks, and severely beat several of the porters, especially Majaliwa, whilst Kobe himself got off very lightly. The porters then retreated on their loads, and came after me.

When I heard this I was very angry, as it is a most dangerous thing when one's men get up quarrels with the inhabitants of a country one passes through. Moreover, I could not overlook Kobe's disobedience to the headman.

The discipline of the men was very good now, and they had implicit confidence in me. Yet, knowing the workings of their minds so well, I felt certain that it would do little good to punish Kobe at once, as they would not see the justice of it. A native has as a rule only room in his mind for one idea, and that uppermost in theirs at the present moment was that the man had been robbed, and they had been beaten by the natives. They could not then see why Kobe should be punished for this, and would think that he had been unjustly treated.

Nevertheless, I could not overlook the offence of disobedience to Abdi and Omari, so I had first to talk them over before any punishment would be of practicable value.

So I called them all together, and said : "Now listen to my words. Have I not told you every day that the people of this country have no equal as thieves ?"

They replied : "You have told us."

"Have I not told you never to trust them ?"

"Yes, you have."

"Yet you think that my words are those of a fool, and you do not listen to me, but throw away your money by giving it to these people. Now tell me, if a man throws his money into the sea, will he see it again ?"

They answered : "No, he will lose it."

"And should he throw himself in after it, what will happen ?"

They answered : "He will be drowned."

I said : "Exactly so. Now, men of greater wisdom than

yourselves, Abdi and Omari, said to this man, ' You have
thrown your money into the sea : you must leave it there,'
but he answered, ' No, I will throw myself in after it.'
Is he a fool or a wise man ?"

They said : " He is a fool."

" Again," I said, " is it customary in my caravan to
disobey the orders of the headman ?"

They answered : " No."

" When we fought with the Wahabashi at my order,
were we successful or unsuccessful ?"

They replied : " We defeated the Wahabashi."

" And to-day, have you defeated them or been defeated,
and beaten ?"

They answered : " We have been beaten."

" Now, do you think it is a disgrace to be beaten by
these Galla or not ?"

They replied : " It is a disgrace."

" Do you think that the news will travel forward or
remain just in this place ?"

They said : " It will go forward."

" Just so. By reason of this man's folly we are all
disgraced, and have become as women in the eyes of these
people, and the news will go on before us, and who has
brought this disgrace on us ?"

They said : " Kobe."

Then I said : " This Kobe, if he had only started a
successful fight it would have been better, but he has
started a fight in which we have all been disgraced. Has
he done well or ill ?"

They replied : " He has done ill."

" Yes, he has done ill, and he has, moreover, disobeyed
the order of my headman, so he must be punished."

At this the unfortunate Kobe immediately lay down

on the ground to receive his beating, and having got over this unpleasant little episode, everyone proceeded in the best of spirits. I asked Kobe : " Now, don't you think that you have been a fool ?" He said : " Yes, Bwana, I have." Then I told him that he must be careful of the people in future, or they would rob him of everything, even the clothes off his back. I asked him what sort of disgrace it would be for me if I arrived in Addis Ababa with a caravan of naked porters. What would my fellow white men say ? " Can't you afford to give your men clothes ?" I should say : " Yes, they all had clothes to start with, but they had them stolen on the way."

At this Kobe laughed good-humouredly, and shouldering his load, a buffalo head, he ran on, bearing me no ill-will for the punishment he had just received.

It was very pleasant being able to pick up plenty of firewood round our camp instead of having to buy with great difficulty a little at a time. However, many of the porters were much too lordly to pick up the firewood lying ready to hand, but used to walk off to a village several hundred yards away and there buy some. As they had been unable to spend anything in the low country they now had a lot of back pay due to them, which they did their best to get rid of. They enjoyed immensely posing as millionaires before the very poor inhabitants of the country. They were never so happy as when stalking back to camp followed by a woman staggering under a load of firewood, and a boy carrying chickens and flour which they had purchased.

A descent through rolling country covered with thorn-trees brought us to the River Hawash, over which is a well-made bridge of European construction. We crossed this, and camped a few miles from the other bank.

Now we were only two days' journey for the porters from Addis Ababa, so I decided to leave the men to come on slowly, and go ahead with Abdi.

For five months I had not seen a single white man, or heard a single word of English spoken, whilst all my stores, save tea and salt, were finished. Some might think that I was overjoyed at the prospect before me of meeting the comforts of civilization, having good food, and a comfortable bed, and a rest from the continual trek. It was not so, however, for I felt a strange diffidence in taking on all the responsibilities of civilization once again. I thought of the bills that might be awaiting me, and all the worries and trials of ordinary life. At that moment I would have given anything to be able to turn round and go back, without ever having reached the civilization so close.

It could not be, however, as my funds and my leave were both already overspent, so I had to make up my mind to throw myself into the whirl of civilized life once again.

Abdi and I started at 5 a.m. on mules, and, alternately walking and riding, proceeded on our way to the great city of Abyssinia.

We soon left the thorn country, and embarked on the cold, bare downs of Shoa. Here again firewood of any sort is unobtainable. Owing to the lack of wood, huts here and in Addis Ababa are made in the usual form of the circular thatched building, but with stone walls.

About one o'clock we came in sight of the town, and its many houses of European and Arab structures. Outside these were clustered thousands of stone-walled huts.

Behind the city rises up a low rocky hill, whilst on the other three sides were vast encampments, consisting of thousands and thousands of tents, stretching three or four miles from the town in each direction. We passed through this belt, consisting of tents of all sizes, from the little soldier's *tente d'abris* to great marquees for the more important men. Some were made of calico, and others of black material, like the wool of the Bernus cloak.

We passed through to the other side of the town, and at last reached the British Legation, a neatly constructed building, consisting of a number of well-made huts in the form of a square, connected with each other by passages.

I arrived here about four o'clock, and was most hospitably received by the Acting Minister. In spite of my modest disclaimers that I was not hungry, he immediately ordered his Goanese butler to prepare a meal. For this I was very thankful, as I had had nothing all day except a hurried snack at 4.30 that morning.

This was followed by a hot bath and a hair-cut, the latter an operation I badly needed, as my hair reached almost to my shoulders.

That night, after a good dinner, I turned in to sleep between sheets for the first time for three years, but the luxury was so unaccustomed that I failed to get any sleep the whole night.

As Addis Ababa is so well known, I will not attempt to describe it, nor will I dwell on the journey from there to Dirre Daua and the coast, as that has also been travelled over by many white men.

CHAPTER XXIII

THE END OF THE JOURNEY

THE two chief tribes in Abyssinia are, as is well known, the Tigre and the Amara (generally called Amhara). The Tigre were the old reigning dynasty, but on the death of King Johannes, Menelek made himself King, and now the Amaras of Shoa are the ruling class.

The Amara are generally very dark, much darker than the majority of tribes they govern, whilst the Tigre are much lighter. Amongst the Amara lighter-coloured women and children are often met with, and this usually means that the husband or father has married a woman of some other tribe, such as Wallamu or Garaugi.

A few Amara and also Tigre are Muhammadans, but the great majority are Christians. They have forced this religion on some of their subjects, such as part of the Garaugi and Galla tribes. A black cord is worn round the neck as a badge of their religion.

Many of the other tribes in Abyssinia, including the greater part of the Gallas and Garaugi, are Muhammadans, and also, of course, the countries on either side of Abyssinia, east and west, are purely Muhammadan.

Although the Muhammadan element have always outnumbered the Christian, the latter have always been able to hold their own, although bitter struggles have taken place in the past between the two religions. The chief difference between Christianity as practised by the Abyssinians and by us is in the killing of meat, for with them no meat is lawful that has not been prepared in the orthodox way by a Christian.

The method of killing resembles that practised by the Jews. It is not permissible to use for this purpose a knife that has been used to kill or carve meat by a Muhammadan.

On our way up to the capital we heard at different places that the Governors of all the provinces we had passed near had been called up to Addis Ababa. It was only when we reached this place that I heard the reason. Menelek had been ill for some time, and was now practically only a figure-head, while Queen Taitu was the virtual ruler. There had long been difficulties about arranging for a successor to Menelek, as he had no legitimate son, and his nominated successor, Ras Makunan, had died before him.

Queen Taitu, an ambitious woman, who is a sort of Dowager Empress of China, took advantage of Menelek's prostrate condition to advance the claims of her own candidates for succession. Now matters had been arranged between them, to the apparent satisfaction of both parties, and Menelek's nominee, a boy called Lij Iyasu, had been selected as successor. To make things straight with Taitu, he had been married to a six-year-old girl, a relation of the Queen. It was for the proclamation of this heir that all the Governors had been called in from the provinces, so that they might swear allegiance to him.

Although both parties have declared that they are satisfied with this arrangement, there is no guarantee that the young heir will come to the throne on Menelek's death. Queen Taitu is a thoroughly unscrupulous woman, who has her own followers, army, and provinces apart from those of her husband.

On, or perhaps even before, his death she can be counted upon to play for her own hand entirely, and a small boy will be no obstacle to her in attaining her ends.

No wonder, then, that she has agreed, and expressed herself satisfied with the arrangement in question, because she will be able either to act as regent for Lij Iyasu, or get rid of him, as suits her purpose best.

Succession is not considered of much account in Abyssinia, and any strong man in the kingdom has a greater chance of obtaining the throne on the death of a ruler than the heir himself, if the latter is a weak man. Menelek himself and most of his predecessors took the throne by the sword, and it is quite likely that the next ruler will not depart from the usual custom in this respect.

In Addis Ababa I parted with the new Abdi, who had joined us a few days before, and also with Alamu, who had come the whole way from Uba. I also hired some mules and mulemen to take some of our loads to Dirre Daua. There was little food to be obtained on the way, so we had to carry a certain amount for the porters, and also I wanted to reduce the porters' loads to thirty or forty pounds each, so as to make rapid marches.

As there were several final arrangements to make in Addis Ababa, such as obtaining passes and so on, I sent off the caravan in front, keeping Abdi to follow on with me. We did not get away until late in the afternoon. We were assured that it would be impossible to mistake the road, and that it was quite unnecessary to have a guide. However, I did not feel competent to find my way along an unknown path on a dark night to an unknown destination, so I insisted on having a guide.

Soon after starting it began to rain, and the roads were very bad and clayey, resembling ploughed fields.

Enormous clods of earth, weighing many pounds, collected on each foot, and made walking extremely unpleasant, whilst the clouds made the night pitch black.

With great difficulty we descended the steep-sided nullah in which the Akaki River flows, and crossed the bed, which was a mass of loose boulders.

After marching four hours in the dark it at last dawned on me that even with a guide we had mistaken the way. At last we heard voices, and, making our way towards them, found a kraal. It was with considerable difficulty that our guide could establish communication with its occupants, as natives mistrust voices coming out of the darkness at night, attributing them to devils.

After carefully explaining who we were, they told us that there was a white man's camp somewhere to the south, so we set off in that direction. We passed two more kraals, but the inhabitants would not answer, and then we saw a light in the distance.

We made for this, and when we came near saw that it was my lamp. As the country was open the way was easy, except for one large stream, which held us up for some time before we could find a crossing. When we arrived in camp I found a pile of loads covered over by the fly of my tent, on the top of which was my lamp.

When Omari came out of his tent I wanted to know why my tent had not been put up, and he said that Tumbo had been carrying one of the poles, and driving one of our mules which was not loaded. The mule had left the path and run away, and Tumbo had followed it, and had not been seen since. He also said that porters had been back as far as the Akaki with the lamp looking for me, and only returned shortly before midnight.

He had done his best, but anything out of the ordinary

:outine upsets the native, and it had never dawned on
aim that he might have put up my tent with the poles of
one of theirs.

I told him to put up the tent at once with his tent-poles,
and get the things out of the rain, whilst he could sleep
in one of the porter's tents. I then sat down in a wet
chair in the rain, and presently Sadi and the cook produced a cold leg of mutton and some tea.

As the light of the lamp was required to put up the
tent with, I had to feed in the dark, a circumstance that
made the joint present a very curious appearance next day.

Next morning Tumbo appeared rather late, and said
that the mule had run into a camp amongst a lot of other
mules, and that there he had been unable to recognize
it, and the Abyssinians had turned him away.

He had then gone back to the Legation, and fetched
the only man whom he could speak to there, the door-
keeper, who happened to be a Swahili, and taken him to
explain to the Abyssinians, but the latter had refused to
let them come into their camp.

I could not afford the time to go back and see about
it, so I had to leave it. Abdi said that it was written in a
book somewhere that some men were lucky with four-
legged animals, while others were unfortunate, but lucky
with other things.

One man might obtain one cow, and from that would
breed and fill a kraal, while another might have a kraal
full, and lose them all. I was evidently one of the
unlucky ones with four-legged beasts, so I ought never to
buy an animal. I asked him what I was lucky with
then—two-legged animals? which in Swahili means
slaves.

After two to three days' trek over the bare, cold and

wet Shoa Downs we commenced a series of descents, which eventually brought us to the low desert country of the Danakils.

After descending the second escarpment we left the rain and mud behind us, and reached a dry country called Balchi, where the Galla inhabitants store water in large reservoirs or ponds fenced round. They are connected by aqueducts with watercourses, and fill up quickly during a shower, as, owing to the rocky nature of the surface, the little water there is does not sink in.

A further descent brought us to Choba, at which place water is only to be had by purchase from a walled-in cistern on the side of the hill.

On the hill above this place lives a very fat Gerezmach, who sits like a spider in its web, fattening himself by bleeding all who pass by. Shortly after I arrived he came down to my camp, and we went through the lengthy formula of saying " How-do-you-do."

He asked where I had come from, and several other things ; then, having done the polite, he gave a sigh of relief, and thought about turning to more profitable things. He commenced by asking where my Abyssinian interpreter was. I said that I had none. " You must have an interpreter," he said. I replied : " I am the interpreter, and you can ask me anything you want to know."

This rather disconcerted him, as the usual practice is to get hold of the Abyssinian interpreter, and tell him how much his white man has to pay up before passing on. The interpreter breaks the news to the white man that it is customary to pay so much, and if he objects the Abyssinian mule-men are made to refuse to proceed. When the money has been extorted the interpreter gets a small share of the proceeds. In my case, however, the

BALCHI ESCARPMENT

Abyssinia is a mountainous country surrounded by waterless deserts. It can only be entered at certain places by such narrow, precipitous paths as the one here depicted. This path is a mule-track cut in the face of the mountain. A glance at it will be enough to explain how disaster has overtaken the various forces which, at different times, have tried to invade this country.

Gerezmach was at a loss how to proceed, and he stood first on on leg, then on the other, wondering what to do.

Then he tried several of my men, but was received with stony stares. I tried to carry on the conversation that we had started so well, but he now pretended not to understand me.

At this moment Abdi returned, so I told the Gerezmach that here was a man who could speak Galla. As the Gerezmach himself could not speak this language, he had to speak to Abdi through an interpreter, and as I could understand what he said to the interpreter, I could answer him before his remarks reached Abdi.

This was not much use to him, so he gave it up, and began talking to me again. Presently he asked me if I could give him a pencil and some paper. To this modest request I immediately acceded, and went off to my tent to fetch some.

Directly I had gone he called Abdi, and said to him: " We Abyssinians and you Somalis are friends, and these white men are our enemies. You must make your white man pay me so much before he can go on." He struck rather the wrong note here, as the Somalis hate the Abyssinians. Anyhow, Abdi said : " Well, the white man understands your language, and I do not ; you had better ask him yourself."

When I returned I found the Gerezmach looking rather discomforted. He then made his adieux, and asked me if I was not going to give him anything. I said, " Certainly not," as I had not received the slightest hospitality from him.

He said that most white men that passed gave him a rifle and a box of ammunition, so I said that even amongst white men there were unfortunately fools.

At this he went off, and in the evening he returned again with two bottles of milk and a very skinny chicken as a present. On receiving this I gave him the saddle and bridle of the horse, which were no longer any use to me. Abdi was very annoyed with me for giving him anything at all, and said that he deserved nothing.

After leaving Choba we descended a steep escarpment by a mule-track, some idea of which may be gathered from the photograph.

At the foot of this we came to the desert country of the people we call the Danakil.

This word is presumably derived from the Arabic Dankeli, but the people call themselves the O'da Ali. The route from Dirre Daua to Addis Ababa, passing through this corner of their country, is, of course, well known, but the rest of their country, between here and the Red Sea littoral, is some of the most unknown country in Africa.

They are a truculent people, and give the Abyssinians constant trouble. Even on the Addis Ababa route itself they occasionally waylay a solitary man and kill him, and for this reason the Abyssinians always go in parties. At the present moment many of them had gone off to fight with the Black Esa.

At the foot of the last of the Balchi escarpments we met with an arid and stony desert country, and were once again amidst camel-owning peoples. Nairobi, having trekked for several months with camels, was quite indifferent to them, but our Abyssinian mules were wild with fright at seeing these strange beasts.

As there was only one road, and no chance of the men losing the way, I rode on ahead some distance, and then sat under a thorn-tree to graze my mule, and await the advent of the caravan.

As I sat here some Danakils passed, cheery customers with broad-bladed spears, and *tobes* like the inland Somalis. I stopped them, and managed to hold quite a long, but rather laboured, conversation with them by means of a few words of Somali, Arabic, and Amharic mixed.

They asked me if I was not afraid to go alone in this country. I said : " Afraid of what ?" They replied in the most cheery fashion possible : " Why, don't you know that we Danakils kill people if we find them alone on the road ?" I have not the least idea if they were trying to get a rise out of me or not, but this is certainly what they said.

I did not quite know what the reply courteous was to this remark, so I asked if they did not prefer Abyssinians to white men. I then asked where they were going to. They replied that a camel had just died in a neighbouring kraal, and that they were going off to eat it. They then ran off in a hurry, lest they should be late for the feast.

On the arrival of the men we proceeded to a stream called Tadacha Malka, meaning " the drinking-place of the thorn-trees."

In this hot, low country it was necessary, for the sake of the men and animals, to do as much marching at night as the moon would permit of, and so we generally started at somewhere between two and four in the morning.

It was the duty of the night-watchman to wake me up in time to start. As the men could not tell the time from a watch, I used to resort to various stratagems to make them call us at the proper time. If the moon was suitable, I used to say, " Call us directly the moon rises." When the moon was small and waning, it would be necessary to pack and load up before it arose, so as to make the most of it after it rose and before dawn.

Sometimes I used to select a star, and tell them to call

22

us when it set, or when it reached a certain branch of a tree, but this was most unsatisfactory, as they would forget which star had been indicated.

Their most usual method was to wake up either Abdi or myself from time to time, and ask us the hour. Abdi had had the watch I gave him stolen in Addis Ababa, and so now it was necessary to wake me up to ascertain the hour. This I did not object to at all, as I think it is very dull just to sleep through a night till one is told that it is time to get up; moreover, one always feels tired and sleepy after a long sleep.

To be called from time to time, and think that it is time to get up, and then find that one can go to sleep again, is most pleasant, and when one finally does get up one feels as if one has had a lot of sleep.

However, even this arrangement did not always work smoothly. The porters generally went to bed about seven or eight o'clock, as our marches were long and trying. I used to sit up till about twelve as a rule, writing and working out observations. The day we came to Choba I sat writing till 10.30, and then went out and spoke to the sentry, and returned again, and after doing a little more work turned in, having put my watch and lamp ready beside me on a box.

I had only just got to sleep when I heard the sentry calling me, and asking if it was time to get up. Looking at my watch, I saw that it was only one o'clock, so I told him that it was seven o'clock (Swahili reckoning). Congratulating myself that it was not yet time to start, I turned over and went to sleep again.

Presently I was awakened by the hum of voices, and, looking at my watch, saw that it was 1.30. I called out to know what was the matter, and Sadi came to say that they had all been told to get up by the sentry. Telling them to go to sleep again, I turned over, but the men had been thoroughly roused, and the hum of voices persisted, so it was no good trying to sleep any more. I got up very cross, and we had to wait in the dark until the moon rose, and it was light enough to proceed.

Next morning the sentry called me at three o'clock, and as I had decided to get up at 3.30, and start trekking at four, I told him to wait for half an hour before waking up the men. Evidently he did not want to incur my displeasure, like the man of the day before, so he went away, and did not come back at all. When I next looked at my watch it was nearly five o'clock, and dawn was about to break, so we lost a valuable hour of the cool marching hours. The men, however, marched well, and we reached that day a shallow pool in a rocky watercourse near Fantali Hill.

The water was filthy, as it was only a few yards broad, and had been stirred up and fouled by hundreds of men, camels, and mules daily.

Dirty water is all right if one cannot possibly get any other, but many natives get so accustomed to it that they never trouble to look for anything better. This pool was on the track itself, and had a dirty camping-place on each side. I thought that as there was a pool here in the river-bed, there would possibly be another, and that it would probably be purer. I waited about half an hour by the water, watching the different natives pass wading into it with their animals, and filling up their water-bottles from its foul contents.

When I saw my caravan approaching I set out for a search for water, expecting to have to go a mile or two. Twenty or thirty yards from the first pool I found a little hole in the rock with much better water, and in the next hundred yards two or three more with beautiful clear rain-water.   These had been absolutely untouched by the many caravans that passed daily, just because every native follows those in front like sheep, and never tries to strike out a line of his own.   The same thing applies to camps, as they always want to pitch camp on a dirty old camping-ground because everybody else camps there, although anywhere else may be just as suitable, or more so.

We crossed the Hawash River by a well-made though narrow bridge, and after this crossed some clear-running streams which come from the Harrar highlands.   It was occasionally necessary to make rather a long march to reach water, but we never had to stop a night without water the whole way to Dirre Daua.

On June 3, 1909, I went to bed about nine o'clock. The sentry awoke me about midnight, and from then onwards every quarter of an hour or so till 2 a.m., when I gave the order to break up camp.   Finally, when we had got everything packed up, there was a total eclipse of the moon, so we had to proceed in the dark.

I had never had an opportunity of watching natives during an eclipse before, but, according to the usual story-book accounts, they should show the wildest fright and consternation.   My men were very indifferent to the phenomenon, merely remarking, " The moon has been caught to-day."

I asked them what was happening to the moon, and so they told me.   It appears that what we call an eclipse, and think is due to the penumbra of the earth, is in reality something very different.   A large snake that had been chasing the moon for a long while had at last caught it, and was now swallowing it, and as we looked we could see its jaws slowly but surely closing over it.

However, my men assured me that we should not lose that celestial body for ever, as this enormous pill in the end always proved too much for the snake, and it had eventually to disgorge it. This proved to be quite correct, for just before sunrise the moon began to reappear, and the next night it was in its accustomed place none the worse.

We camped that night by a zariba of Hawiya Somalis, and Abdi and I visited one old man in his *gurgi*, and he gave us milk, and told us the news. A *gurgi* is a dwelling of camel-mats supported by poles. In this case it was built in the form of a rectangle, and supported on the sticks called *hangol*, a description of which was given in the chapter on the Rendile.

These sticks were stuck upright in the ground, and supported the roof, which was flat, and made of camel-mats. The *gurgi* was divided in half by an interior wall, and one of these halves was again subdivided. The entrance-door led into the undivided part, which was a shelter for the recently born calves at night. From this outer apartment a doorway led into an inner apartment or sitting-room, and this again led into the sleeping-room. The whole structure was about six yards square and four feet high, a regular palace for a Somali.

We heard from our host that an Esa had killed one of the O'da Ali, which led to a small fight between two kraals, and then a bigger fight, in which more had joined in.

The O'da Ali (Danakils) had attacked the Black Esa near a place called Ôdol, some days to our north, and captured some stock. The Esa, reinforced, followed them, and killed a certain number. Now both sides had retired, and were waiting reinforcements before again opening hostilities. The O'da Ali had declared their intention of sitting and eating at a place called Den until the end of the month, when they were going to attack the Esa. The former had a good number of ponies and rifles, whilst the latter had only a few.

Two days later we arrived in country inhabited by Esa Somalis. Some of them came and asked Abdi to visit them in their kraal, saying that they would give him as much milk as he could drink, and kill an animal for him. Abdi told me that he knew them too well to accept their hospitable invitation, so he went later, with two armed men, to buy me some milk. As he told me : " Let alone the animal they were going to kill for me, it was only by paying an exorbitant price for it that I could even obtain a little milk for you."

The Esa are very treacherous people, and Abdi said that he would never go into one of their huts, as they would give a man some milk to drink, and then stab him in the back. At this spot four different tribes meet, and so it often happens that solitary or unprotected passers-by are robbed, as it is then difficult to tell which tribe was responsible.

I was told that in Abyssinia and also here robbers used to disguise themselves by plastering mud all over their faces and bodies. On hearing this, Omari said that in the Comoros robbers used to smear themselves all over with smoke-black, and stand near a path pretending to be charred trees. If any solitary man passed they would seize on him and rob him.

One evening on the way to Dirre Daua I heard my men playing a game that I had not seen before, called *karingi*. Omari said that it was a very bad game if people gambled at it, as he had heard of men losing as much as ten rupees over it.

It is played in this way. Ten little holes are scraped in the ground in a row. Stones are placed in these holes : in the first hole one stone, and in each successive hole one more than the last up to the tenth, which has ten stones.

One man sits in front of the holes, while another sits at a distance with his back to them. The first man takes a stone out of the first hole, and says, "Here?" The second sings, "One and again (I say) one ; we play the game of the *karingi* animals."

The first then takes a stone out of the second hole, and asks, "Here?" The player sings, "Two and again two," etc., and so on up to ten. After this the first man comes back to the first hole, and says, "Here?" to which the answer is, "Nothing," and then to the next nine the answer is one less than the first time. This goes on until all the holes are empty, when in the last round the answer will be, "Ten nothings." If the player successfully answers the right number each time, he has won.

On the fourteenth day from Addis Ababa we arrived at Errer, a small stream whose banks were irrigated and cultivated by a tribe called Koti. This is the only cultivation met with in the low country from Balchi to Dirre Daua.

Near Errer were some kraals of a small tribe of Somalis called Gurgurr. Abdi went off to look for some milk for me, and presently returned with a large *han* full, and accompanied by the chief of these kraals.

This chief refused to accept any payment for the milk, but asked for some medicine. He then told me to be sure and send again at night for some more milk when the cattle were driven in. He asked me if I was likely to be coming back here again, and when I replied in the negative, he said : " Why do you not live at Dirre Daua, and then I should come to see you, and bring you an ox or a sheep ? Write down my name, so that if you ever return you will be able to ask after me. I am Sheikh Yusuf, son of Sheikh Mumin. Write it down ; it may be useful. You may find that you have lost something, or a mule might run away, or anything might happen, and you will have someone to send to about it."

He told me that the Danakils had been badly defeated in their recent fight with the Esa, and, according to him, lost four hundred men on one day and three hundred on another. However, this is probably an exaggeration.

Sheikh Yusuf then took his departure, saying : " I don't know when I shall see you again." He was as good as his word, as in the evening he sent another *han* full of milk. He was a most kind and pleasant man, although a Somali, and I was very glad to meet him.

Thus, on the first day I arrived in Abyssinia, and almost the last day before I left it, I met two remarkably kind and generous natives, Azach Kalilo and Sheikh Yusuf, giving me a good impression to commence with and to finish with.

It was now only two days for the caravan to Dirre Daua, so I resolved to push on. Taking the sais with me, I left Errer just after midnight, and arrived in Dirre Daua about noon.

This is quite a big place, boasting of three or four hotels. A large party of French engineers were camped outside, and Dirre Daua itself was full of officials, as the works for the extension of the line to Addis Ababa had just commenced. The manager of the bank looked after me in the most kind manner, and arranged for my passes and baggage.

I left two old friends behind in Dirre Daua—Abdi, and Nairobi, the mule. Abdi, now the journey was at an end, wished to go to Harrar, and thence to Somaliland. I was very sorry to lose this faithful servant, but in any case I could not have taken him farther than Aden.

I have never met a native who has served me better, for he was intelligent, yet honest, good-tempered, tactful, and conscientious—a most unusual combination of qualities to be possessed by a native. He was also modest and unassuming. He had charge of all my trade goods during the whole journey, and I lost nothing from them except once when Abdi had been left behind. He acted as interpreter between myself and most of the numerous tribes whom we met with, with the result that we had practically no unpleasantness with any of them, but, on the contrary, were received exceptionally well everywhere. In fact, the success of the trip was almost entirely attributable to Abdi's zealous work.

With regard to Nairobi, he was the sole survivor amongst the animals, and had performed the whole trip from start to finish, and was little the worse. As Omari said, had he been a slave, he would by now have won his freedom.

I could not bear to think of his falling into the hands of the Abyssinians, to spend the rest of his days being beaten and galled with loads. The bank manager very kindly consented to take him and treat him kindly, and on changing stations, to pass him on to another white man, so that he would not fall into the hands of natives.

Abdi came to see me off at the station. A day's journey in the train brought us to Djibouti. Here I hired a house in which to deposit my strange-looking crew. Next day we crossed to Aden on the local boat, and arrived the following morning.

Here I was lucky enough to find a German liner bound for Mombasa calling in the same night. I paid off all my men the same afternoon, provided them with rice and dates for the journey, and train fares to Nairobi, and saw them on board.

In spite of all the hardships they had suffered, and the heat and thirst they had endured, they were not as boisterous over returning home as I expected them to be.

They did not express any regret at leaving me, for it is not in their nature to do so. All they said was: " Good-bye, *bwana*—good-bye till we see you in our country again."

I think, however, that in some strange way they felt sorry that our journey was over, or perhaps it was the large ship, the strangeness of all around them, and the prospect of seasickness, which made them so quiet and subdued.

I exhorted them to behave well on the return journey, and then, wishing them a good voyage, returned to shore to await the P. and O. for England.

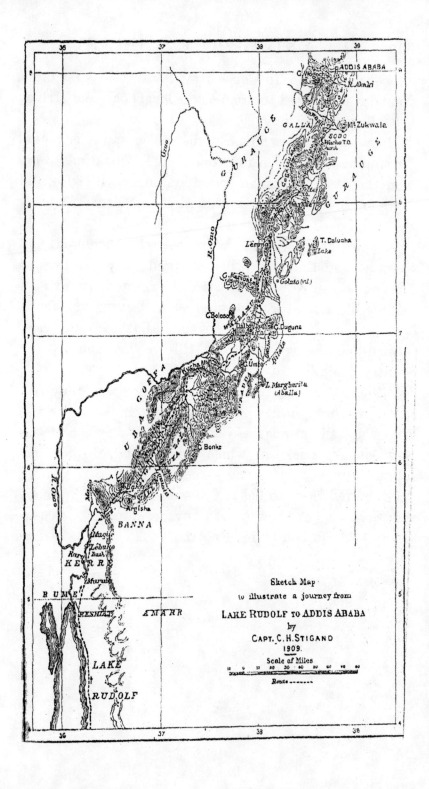

Sketch Map
to illustrate a journey from
LAKE RUDOLF TO ADDIS ABABA
by
CAPT. C. H. STIGAND
1909.
Scale of Miles

Route - - - - - - -

INDEX

Cross amount p 40

Printed in the United States
115280LV00003B/9/A